Making Multicultural Education Work

THE LANGUAGE AND EDUCATION LIBRARY

Series Editor: Professor David Corson, *The Ontario Institute for Studies in Education, 252 Bloor St. West, Toronto, Ontario, Canada M5S 1V6.*

Other Books in the Series

Critical Theory and Classroom Talk
  ROBERT YOUNG
Language Policy Across the Curriculum
  DAVID CORSON
Language, Minority Education and Gender
  DAVID CORSON
School to Work Transition in Japan
  KAORI OKANO
Reading Acquisition Processes
  G. B. THOMPSON, W. E. TUNMER and T. NICHOLSON (eds)
Worlds of Literacy
  D. BARTON, M. HAMILTON and R. IVANIC (eds)

Other Books of Interest

Education of Chinese Children in Britain and USA
  LORNITA YUEN-FAN WONG
European Models of Bilingual Education
  HUGO BAETENS BEARDSMORE (ed.)
Foundations of Bilingual Education and Bilingualism
  COLIN BAKER
World in a Classroom
  V. EDWARDS and A. REDFERN

The Open University Readers

Language and Literacy in Social Practice
  JANET MAYBIN (ed.)
Language, Literacy and Learning in Educational Practice
  BARRY STIERER and JANET MAYBIN (eds)
Media Texts: Authors and Readers
  DAVID GRADDOL and OLIVER BOYD-BARRETT (eds)
Researching Language and Literacy in Social Context
  DAVID GRADDOL, JANET MAYBIN and BARRY STIERER (eds)

Please contact us for the latest book information:
Multilingual Matters Ltd,
Frankfurt Lodge, Clevedon Hall Victoria Road,
Clevedon, Avon BS21 7SJ England

THE LANGUAGE AND EDUCATION LIBRARY 7
Series Editor: Professor David J. Corson
The Ontario Institute for Studies in Education

Making Multicultural Education Work

Stephen May

MULTILINGUAL MATTERS LTD
Clevedon • Philadelphia • Adelaide

ONTARIO INSTITUTE FOR STUDIES IN EDUCATION
Toronto

Library of Congress Cataloging in Publication Data

May, Stephen, 1962–
Making Multicultural Education Work/Stephen May
(The Language and Education Library: 7)
Includes bibliographical references and index.
1. Intercultural education–New Zealand–Case studies. 2. Intercultural
education. 3. Educational sociology. 4. Educational sociology–New Zealand–
Case studies. 5. Critical pedagogy. 6. Critical pedagogy–New Zealand–
Case studies.
I. Title. II. Series.
LC1099.5.N45M39   1994
370.19′6′0998–dc20   94-9690

Canadian Cataloguing in Publication Data
May, Stephen, 1962–
(The Language and Education Library: 7)
1. Intercultural education–New Zealand–Case studies. 2. Intercultural educa-
tion. 3. Educational sociology. 4. Educational sociology–New Zealand–Case
studies. 5. Critical pedagogy. 6. Critical pedagogy–New Zealand–Case studies.
I. Title. II. Series.
LC1099.5.N45M39 1994 370.19′6′0993 C94-931801-9

British Library Cataloguing in Publication Data

A CIP catalogue record for this book is available from the British Library.

ISBN 1-85359-237-4 (hbk)
ISBN 1-85359-236-6 (pbk)
ISBN 0-7744-0417-5 (pbk: Canada only)

Multilingual Matters Ltd

UK: Frankfurt Lodge, Clevedon Hall, Victoria Road, Clevedon, Avon BS21 7SJ.
USA: 1900 Frost Road, Suite 101, Bristol, PA 19007, USA.
Australia: P.O. Box 6025, 83 Gilles Street, Adelaide, SA 5000, Australia.

Printed and bound in Great Britain by the Longdunn Press, Bristol.

To Jim Laughton, whom I never met, but would have liked to:

He pōkeke uenuku i tū ai

Against a dark cloud the rainbow stands out brightly

Contents

Preface

This is the story of one unusually successful multicultural and multilingual school: Richmond Road Primary School in Auckland, New Zealand. As Stephen May shows, it is successful in ways that are each rare alone, and even rarer together. In the words of one of the school's own documents, the school combines 'cultural maintenance' with 'access to power'. It combines, in other words, pluralism with equality.

Richmond Road's life evolved from the vision of its Māori principal of 16 years, James Laughton. From a combination of personal experience and theoretical readings, he created a learning community for the staff, and together they embodied his vision in organisational structures and thereby in patterns of interaction among staff, children, and parents.

During 1983 and 1987, when I was regularly attending Tuesday staff meetings at the school, Jim often mentioned the book about the school that he and Wally Penetito (now at Victoria University) would write, based in part on the many workshops for school principals they were asked to give. That book was never written. So until now, knowledge about Richmond Road has been available only to participants in the school community and visitors from New Zealand and overseas; in documents — notably the principal's reports — in the school files; in several articles by Stephen May and from an article based on my interviews with the school staff in 1989, six month's after Jim's death. Now this book brings a fuller picture to those who cannot know the school at first hand.

Readers primarily interested in Richmond Road itself may want to start reading in Chapter 5 and then, with the school vividly in mind, go back to the more theoretical discussions in the first four chapters. These discussions help to explain why schools like Richmond Road are so rare, and why documentation of them is so important.

The lovely proverb that is the book's epigraph catches that importance and, because it is a *Māori* proverb, also invites awareness of the special meaning of multiculturalism in New Zealand — a meaning that may be missed by readers from other countries. Briefly, as May explains, the Treaty of Waitangi, signed in 1840 between Māori chiefs and the British Crown, promised a 'partnership' between the two peoples. Struggles continue for 'honouring the Treaty'. One goal of that struggle is that in all domains of social life, multiculturalism for all New Zealand peoples must be based first on the country's bicultural responsibility to the indigenous Māori.

In education, the Richmond Road experience thus shows us how the universally relevant goals of cultural maintenance and access to power have to be worked out with respect for the unique particularities of time and place in each community.

Courtney Cazden
Harvard Graduate School of Education

Acknowledgements

Writing a book, especially your first, is not the easiest of tasks. Nor, at least in my experience, is it a short one. For those who helped me see it through to its conclusion, I am most grateful — as, I'm sure, are they!

To David Corson, my thanks for encouraging me to write the book in the first place, and to Mike and Marjukka Grover at Multilingual Matters, for waiting longer than they should for its arrival. My thanks too to Courtney Cazden for writing the Preface.

I am also indebted to numerous friends and colleagues for their individual and collective input over the last few years. As I argue in the book, teaching and learning is most effective as a cooperative venture, and this view has been reinforced in the assistance given to me in my own writing endeavours. In Palmerston North, my thanks to: David Giles, Roy Shuker, Dick Harker, Jan McPherson, Colin Lankshear, Peter Lineham, Bill Anderson and Colin Gibbs. Also, to the Palmerston North College of Education (PNCE) Research Committee for agreeing to fund the reading analysis described in Chapter 8 and to the PNCE library staff for my numerous demands on their time and expertise. In Bristol, my thanks to Jackie West and Will Guy for making a New Zealander feel so quickly at home in Britain and to Steve Fenton for allowing me the time to complete the book when I should have been otherwise engaged. My thanks too to Sharon Priest and Amanda Dennis for educating me in the ways of SPSS and to Andy Luxford for making the resulting graphs presentable.

It is to Richmond Road School, however, that I owe perhaps the greatest debt, not only for the assistance given me throughout by the school, but for the opportunity to undertake this study in the first place. The school's willingness to trust their educational intentions and their history to the researcher who requested an interview with them in early 1990 is indicative of the school's openness. Also indicative, however, has been the close critical engagement with, and critique of, my subsequent work. Reciprocity and mutual responsibility for teaching and learning are hallmarks of the school's educational approach and, as a result, I have learnt more about education over these last four years than perhaps at any other time. Richmond Road staff meetings have to be experienced to fully understand the depth of educational thinking which goes on within the school. They were something I always looked forward to, as were the numerous informal discussions on educational theory and practice that I was invariably engaged in as soon as I entered the door.

In particular, my thanks to Lionel Pedersen, Shona Pepe, Pita Taouma, Jacqui Laughton, and Graeme Page at the school and to Wally Penetito in Wellington. My thanks also to current and past staff, parents, friends of the school, and past and present pupils. Firstly, for allowing me to use their thoughts and observations in the following pages and secondly, for their recollections of Jim Laughton. In talking with all those who knew Jim it became clear that they wanted his story (and their story) at Richmond Road to be told. I hope that this book might do justice to their wishes.

Finally, I would like to thank Janet, whose love and support throughout, helped this book eventually to see the light of day.

Stephen May
Sociology Department, University of Bristol,
March 1994

Glossary of Māori terms

hangi	traditional feast; literally, earth oven
hui	meeting
kaiārahi reo	Māori language assistant; literally, language leader
kaiwhakahaere	coordinator; director
karakia	prayer; chant [In Māori protocol, a karakia always opens a formal meeting]
kōhanga reo	Māori language pre-school; literally, language nest
mana	power; influence; esteem
Manatū Māori	Ministry of Māori Affairs
Māori	ordinary; indigenous people
mauri	life force; the beginning; life principle
Pākehā	not Māori; European
Ritimana	[a transliteration of] 'Richmond'
rōpū	group
taha Māori	things Māori; literally, the Māori side
tangata whenua	Māori; literally, the local people
tangi	funeral; literally, to cry; weep; mourn
taonga	treasures; property
tapu	sacred; forbidden
Tāwhirimatea	God of the winds and the storms
te ihi me te wehi	power and importance; literally, power and awe
tuakana-teina	older sibling - younger sibling; literally, older brother - younger brother
whakataukī	proverb
whānau	(extended) family

- Literal translations are taken from Ryan (1989).
- Unlike English, Māori nouns do not take the plural 's', although in popular New Zealand usage the 's' is sometimes added.
- Māori words are not differentiated in the following text.

Glossary of Māori terms

1 Introduction: Theory into Practice

> Freedom is not something given: it is something you conquer—
> collectively. (Bourdieu, 1990a: 15)

The gap between theory and practice in education is a worrying one. While various educational theories are regularly expounded, and regularly replaced in academic circles, they often bear little relevance to or have little impact on classroom life. No wonder then, that educational theories discussed in universities and colleges of education during their training come to be seen by many teachers as marginal; of academic interest perhaps, but of little 'practical' value. Recent developments internationally to deskill the teaching profession have further removed theory from the realms of educational practice (Apple, 1986). For many teachers, education is simply a matter of survival; teaching children as best they can, and with what limited time and resources they have at their disposal.

Explaining Differential Achievement in Schools

The problems of combining theory and practice within the context of the real life of the school are no more evident than in the critiques, over the last 30 years, of the reproductive nature of education. Since the emergence of the New Sociology of Education in the 1970s, reproduction theorists have—rightly in my view—outlined how education serves to advantage certain groups at the expense of others. The patterns of advantage and disadvantage are complex and, at times, contradictory (see below) but a broad trend can be detected. Put simply, white and/or middle-class students tend to do better academically at school than children from ethnic minority and working-class backgrounds. By drawing attention to these differential achievement patterns, reproduction theorists effectively dismantled the previous 'liberal democratic' view of education. This view had held that education was neutral—a 'level playing field'—and that any differences in educational attainment were thus the responsibility of particular individuals and groups. As we shall see in Chapter 2, the 'common sense' conception of education[1] on which this liberal-democratic view of education was based had led to a pattern of 'blaming the victim'.

1

The 'failure' of certain individuals and groups in schools was accounted for by focusing on their supposed deficiencies in family, class, and/or ethnic background. In the case of ethnic minorities, their persistent pattern of educational failure in western schools was attributed to a range of supposed individual and group 'characteristics'. These included, in the more extreme forms of analysis, different intellectual capacities (see, for example, Jensen, 1981) and 'different' (i.e. deficient) family backgrounds.[2] Even when analysis of these factors was well intentioned (and not all were) the framework was inevitably pathological. Minorities were seen as the 'problem', and discussions centring on their 'underachievement' in schools only served to highlight this.[3] The results in schools of this deficit perspective were 'compensatory' programmes which aimed to 'redress' the variables 'identified' in the research as hindering the academic achievement of disadvantaged groups.

To a large degree, reproduction theorists were able to successfully redirect this debate away from individual and group explanations (and the apportioning of blame this involved) by emphasising the role of the 'system' in perpetuating inequality. In this view, the school came to be seen as *complicit* in the reproduction of unequal educational outcomes; an institutional reflection of wider social and cultural processes of advantage and disadvantage at work within society. Education is not neutral and never has been. Rather, as a part of the social and cultural process itself, education reflects the interests and expectations of the dominant social and ethnic group(s) within society. Thus, those who come to school from a background of social and/or cultural advantage are more likely to find and have reinforced within school their previous social and cultural experiences. This is because the school's store of social and cultural knowledge tends to reflect and reinforce the knowledge and experiences of majority group children. In contrast, disadvantaged groups are faced with discontinuities between home and school. They may bring to school a range of social and cultural knowledge(s) but this is not recognised or valued by schooling. Bourdieu's notions of *habitus* and *cultural capital* (1974; 1990a; 1990b; see also Bourdieu & Passeron, 1977; 1990) are particularly useful in explaining this process,[4] and will be explored further in Chapter 2.

Admittedly, difficulties were also to emerge in reproduction theory (although, as I will argue in the following chapter, this is not necessarily true of Bourdieu's analysis). Reproduction theories of education have been subsequently criticised by radical or 'resistance' theorists for placing too much emphasis on structural constraints. Radical theorists (see, for example, Apple, 1986; Giroux, 1983a; 1983b; McCarthy, 1990) argue that reproduction accounts underestimate the processes of resistance and individual agency that can be mounted in schools, both by students and teachers, against reproductive processes. If reproduction theorists are to be believed, the radicals insist, there is no hope for institutional and social reform; no hope that schools might end up redressing, rather than just perpetuating, the social and cultural inequalities of the wider society. Radical theorists stress the dynamic and dialectical relationship between school structures and the particular constructions of school knowledge which result. They also emphasise the capacities of school participants to resist and transform these structural arrangements—both within schools and, hopefully, also within the wider society (McCarthy, 1990).

Clearly, theories in the sociology of education over the last 30 years have become increasingly sophisticated and critical in their attempts to account for the differential performance of disadvantaged groups within education. These theoretical developments have also come to include a recognition that the processes of reproduction and resistance within schools are complex, interwoven, and, at times, contradictory, and that they involve the dynamic interrelationship of class, gender, and ethnicity variables (see, for example, McCarthy, 1990; Corson 1993). Recognition has also been accorded to the limitations of a 'group-level' analysis which has in the past tended to overlook the many inter- and intra-group differences in educational achievement evident among disadvantaged groups.[5] In the area of minority education, the most notable of these is perhaps John Ogbu's distinction between *voluntary* (immigrant) minorities and *involuntary* (caste-like) minorities (Ogbu, 1987; Gibson & Ogbu, 1991). Ogbu argues that voluntary and involuntary minority groups can be distinguished by their differing positions within society and that this positioning in turn leads to somewhat different educational trajectories. While both groups are subject to racism and discrimination, voluntary minorities are more likely to succeed in schools because they see their position in the host society as better than the one from which they came and so are more likely to accommodate to the cultural norms that schooling requires. In contrast, involuntary minority groups are characterised by a history of exploitation and/or subjugation *within* a particular country. The attendant responses of involuntary minorities to this history of marginalisation, often in the form of a rejection of school culture, combine with the structural disadvantages they already face to militate against their educational success. Ogbu includes in this latter grouping Native Americans and African Americans in the USA, African-Caribbeans in the UK, and Māori in New Zealand.

However, what remains problematic—despite these theoretical advances—is the paucity of theories currently available which offer both a critical account of the difficulties faced by disadvantaged students in our schools *and* an emancipatory educational model that can be applied, in practice, to making a difference for these students. It is one thing, after all, to identify the problem, quite another to provide workable (and generalisable) solutions. Radical theorists are particularly remiss in this regard, for while they rightly highlight some of the inadequacies of previous theories of social and cultural reproduction, they have also been criticised for offering little of practical value to schools in return. As I will argue in the next two chapters, criticising 'common sense' approaches to the education of disadvantaged students is important— we need to situate the debate within a critically informed perspective of school and societal relations—but, if that is all we do, what are we left with in the end? Perhaps it is these difficulties of application which have contributed to the unease with which many teachers view educational theory. Perhaps, too, this is why 'common sense' solutions, no matter how inadequate, often win out in schools over more critically informed approaches to education.

The Multicultural Education Debate

Current debates in minority education on the merits or otherwise of 'multicultural education' demonstrate this pattern all too clearly. In the 1970s, and into the 1980s, multicultural education came to be seen by many liberal educationalists as the new panacea for redressing the educational difficulties faced by minority children; the 'common sense' solution of its time. Much was made of the contrast a 'multicultural' approach to education would provide to its unfortunate predecessors in minority educational policy—assimilation and integration. Targeting the inherent monoculturalism of these previous policies, advocates of multicultural education argued in their stead for the fostering of 'cultural pluralism' at the school level. By this, it was thought, the educational 'underachievement' of minority children would be redressed. This enthusiasm for multicultural education was also enhanced by the apparent ease with which multicultural programmes could be adopted in schools; not only was it seen as a theoretical advance but it was practical as well, or so it seemed.

Unfortunately, multicultural education, like its predecessors, has come to face increasing criticism of its own, particularly from radical theorists. The emphasis on cultural pluralism in multicultural education has come under fire from radical critics for its inability to move beyond the surface manifestations of culturalism, and its consequent inability to address the structural inequalities which limit the life chances of minority children. The multiethnic perspective of multicultural education is an advance at least on previous positions. However, too much importance has been placed on cultural and ethnic *identity*, and too little on what it is that determines successful negotiations for ethnic minority groups in their interactions with the dominant group(s) in society, and within education (Bullivant, 1981). The results in educational practice have tended to be a well intentioned and ineffective *ad hocism*. Educational programmes promoting cultural pluralism have been added to the existing (monocultural) curriculum but have done little to challenge or change the cultural transmission of the dominant group within schooling. As Olneck observes:

> multicultural education as ordinarily practiced tends to merely 'insert' minorities into the dominant cultural frame of reference...to be transmitted within dominant cultural forms...and to leave obscured and intact existing cultural hierarchies and criteria of stratification... (1990: 163)

While this critique of multicultural education is one with which I largely agree, the problem with combining critical educational theory and practice remains. Practical 'common sense' programmes like multicultural education initiatives—while well intentioned and easy to implement—are riven with theoretical inconsistencies and do little to change the position of minority groups within education. The radical critics have this right. However, more critically conceived educational approaches fare little better in being able to successfully put their emancipatory intentions into practice at the school level. This is clearly demonstrated in the debates in Britain where radical critics of multicultural education have advocated instead for antiracist education in schools (see, for example, Brandt, 1986; Carter & Williams, 1987; Sarup, 1986; Troyna & Williams, 1986). These theorists argue that antiracist education moves the debate away from the problematic emphasis on individual and group educational 'performance' to situate minority disadvantage in schools within the wider societal issue of racism. However, in turn, the antiracist lobby has been criticised for the difficulties in implementation that their pro- gramme(s) represent for schools. Carrington & Short, in their informative and lucid account of these debates in Britain, directly address this difficulty of implementation when they argue:

> In recent years, there has been a tremendous growth of literature on mul- ticultural and antiracist education ... Although the expanding literature has served to highlight some of the dilemmas faced by practitioners, it may also have led many of them to perceive the issue as unduly esoteric, politically contentious and divorced from classroom reality. Teachers' resistance to these innovations may also be due partly to the failure of those concerned with the formation and implementation of policies in this area to provide unambiguous and workable strategies for implementation. (1989: ix)

It is my contention here that these problems of implementation at the school level can be overcome by a more critically conceived approach to multicultural education. For this to occur, multicultural education would first need to address the inadequacies of its theoretical development, as currently formu- lated, in order to account for the criticisms of radical theorists. Second, it would need to provide a model of educational practice which actually makes a difference for minority children. This is no small task, but it can be achieved if the prominent advocacy of *cultural pluralism* associated with the field is complemented by a recognition of the additional need for *structural pluralism*—that is, structural or institutional change within the school. Such recognition takes cognisance of reproductive forces within education and the inequalities which ensue from them for minority students, and posits the multicultural education debate within an 'informing theory' (Mallea, 1989) of social and cultural reproduction. In so doing, it is able to locate, as Cummins observes:

> the pathology within the societal power relations between dominant and dominated groups, [the] reflection of these power relations between school and communities, and [the] mental and cultural disabling of minority students that takes place in classrooms. (1986: 30)

The critically informed approach to multicultural education advocated here is also supported by recent developments in the multicultural and antiracist education debate in Britain, and by more critical conceptions of multicultural education outlined recently in the United States. Both Carrington & Short (1989) and Figueroa (1991) have argued, in the British context, that the artificial divide between multicultural education and antiracist education needs to be dismantled and that a new approach which combines both multicultural and antiracist education elements should be developed. This need not result, however, in some inadequate 'middle' stance. Rather, as Figueroa argues, it should be 'a "radical", thorough-going, well thought out, coherent education that is through and through multicultural and antiracist' (1991: 50). Carrington & Short also suggest that advocates of multicultural and antiracist education, *at the level of practice*, are increasingly espousing similar—and, at times, identical—pedagogical and organisational strategies.

This growing convergence between multicultural and antiracist elements in Britain is echoed in recent commentaries on multicultural education in the United States (see Grant, 1992; Nieto, 1992). Sonia Nieto, for example, cogently argues for a 'comprehensively conceptualized approach' to multicultural education which is situated within a broad 'sociopolitical context'. She defines, as follows, what such a conception of multicultural education would mean for schools:

> Multicultural education is a process of comprehensive school reform and basic education for all students. It challenges and rejects racism and other forms of discrimination in schools and society and accepts and affirms the pluralism...that students, their communities, and teachers represent. Multicultural education permeates the curriculum and instructional strategies used in schools, as well as the interactions among teachers, students and parents, and the very way that schools conceptualize the nature of teaching and learning. Because it uses critical pedagogy as its underlying philosophy and focuses on knowledge, reflection, and action (praxis) as the basis for social change, multicultural education furthers the democratic principles of social justice. (1992: 208)

Nieto's account recognises that given the stratification and social inequities present in the wider society no school programme, no matter how broadly conceptualised, can change things completely. However, she asserts that multicultural education, conceptualised as broad-based school reform, can offer hope for change. Having said that, she also concedes, as do many contributors to the British debate, that while 'most [recent] research on multicultural education seems to suggest...that only by reforming the entire school environment can substantive changes in attitudes, behaviors, and achievement take place... [m]ost schools have not undergone these changes' (1992: 253). The reasons for this are clear enough since such an approach—requiring, as it does, significant structural reform at the school level—necessarily places enormous demands on schools (and those who teach and work within them). It may well explain why so few schools, as yet, have attempted it. Some might wonder if indeed any school could.

The position I take on multicultural education in this book is closely aligned with the preceding analysis. However, in contrast to much previous work in this area (including Nieto's excellent contribution) the following account actually examines a school—Richmond Road School in Auckland, New Zealand—which has successfully undertaken a process of whole-school reform in order to implement a theoretically informed and emancipatory approach to multicultural education. In so doing, the school has applied a critical macro-sociological and macro-sociolinguistic conception of schooling to its educational practice and stands as an example of what *can* be achieved when critical theory and practice are successfully combined. The example of Richmond Road may also provide teachers and educators (the two are not mutually exclusive) with a new hope concerning the relationship between educational theory and practice, and its relevance and effectiveness in changing the nature of schools.

Overview

In the next two chapters I explore in more detail the theories in the sociology of education, and the debates on multicultural education, which I have briefly alluded to here. In Chapter 2, various theories in the sociology of education are discussed. I begin with the earlier liberal-democratic conceptions of schooling—which emphasise the egalitarian nature of education—and move on to examine more recent conflict theories which view schools as sites of social and cultural reproduction. Critiques of conflict theory, notably from radical theorists like Giroux, are also examined. However, I argue that radical theorists have tended to overstate the determinism of certain conflict accounts, particularly, Bourdieu's. They have also failed to provide, as yet, a viable critical *and* practical alternative. This is admittedly a difficult chapter—dealing, as it does, with abstract sociological theories—but it is worth persevering with, particularly as my intention in this book is to break down the theory/practice divide. However, it does not have to be read at this point and can be returned to at a later stage if the reader so wishes.

In Chapter 3 the issues arising from the previous chapter are discussed in specific relation to the area of minority education and, in particular, the current debates surrounding the efficacy of multicultural education. Previous policies in minority education are briefly discussed. However, the principal focus of the chapter centres on exploring the limitations of multicultural education, as popularly conceived, and the possible avenues by which these limitations might be ameliorated. I argue that combining cultural pluralism with significant school reorganisation is the most effective means of making multicultural education an effective vehicle for educational reform. While this chapter relates to themes in Chapter 2 it can also be read as a stand-alone chapter.

Chapter 4 outlines the critical ethnographic nature of this study. Critical ethnography has been chosen as a methodology because of its concern to explore the relationship between institutional or structural constraints and the possibilities of resistance which might lead to a transformation of these structures. Its recognition of power relations and its exploration of the nature of the intersection between choice and constraint seem particularly suited to an examination of the critical and emancipatory approach to multicultural education practised at Richmond Road School.

Chapters 5–9 constitute the specific account of Richmond Road School. Chapter 5 provides the background to the school and, in line with critical ethnography, the theoretical framework within which the school is discussed. Chapters 6–8 are loosely demarcated along the lines of the school 'message systems'—curriculum, pedagogy and assessment—outlined by Bernstein (1971; 1990), and with the addition of school organisation. Chapter 8 also includes an assessment of educational outcomes. Jim Laughton, Richmond Road's previous principal, who was largely responsible for implementing the structural changes now apparent within the school, features prominently throughout these three chapters in the recollections of those who knew him. Chapter 9 discusses Richmond Road's development since Laughton's death in 1988 and the particular issues and changes which the school currently faces. Outlines of various school policies are also provided in this chapter as practical examples of the process of organisational reform within the school that might be usefully applied elsewhere.

Chapters 10 and 11 attempt to tie in the theoretical concerns and dilemmas, outlined in the initial chapters, with the subsequent account of the school. They suggest that Richmond Road provides us with a working model that, in large part, successfully addresses these concerns. Richmond Road has effectively combined critical educational theory and practice within the context of school organisational reform. It is my argument that such a model offers us a way by which multicultural education might proceed.

Notes to Chapter 1

1. I use the term 'common sense' here, and throughout this book, to highlight views of education which seem to us to be logical and unproblematic. (They are, of course, also widely held exactly because of this). However, as we shall see, 'common sense' explanations usually hide and/or distort much more than they reveal.
2. Research on 'family background' has included examination of the family environment, child-rearing practices, and linguistic repertoires used in working-class and ethnic minority homes. Particular interest was expressed in the supposedly poor language development of children from these family environments as explained by one, or a combination, of the above variables. The debates and counter-debates over these issues, particularly in sociolinguistics, are well documented (see Ginsburg, 1986, for a useful review of deficit theories). However, whatever variables were used, the starting premise was invariably one of deficiency in relation to white, middle-class 'norms'.
3. I am aware that any discussion on 'minority educational performance'—of which this book forms a part—can, by its very nature, lend itself to a pathological conception. This is not my intention here. Rather, as Figueroa (1991) has argued, the argument should be moved away from a focus on the 'underachievement' or 'failure' of minority groups to a recognition that they are *unequally placed* within the education system; thus addressing the cause rather than the symptom. This is what I aim to do in the remainder of this book.
4. Bourdieu's analysis, as with much of reproduction theory, is principally a class-based analysis. However, his ideas can be equally applied to the education of ethnic minority students. As Foster (1990) argues, definitions of knowledge and ability in schools make little reference to the cultural forms of minority groups and there is therefore little likelihood that minority students will be able to display the sort of 'cultural capital' required by schools to be successful. Ethnic minority students are also implicitly included in a class analysis since many also come from working-class backgrounds.
5. While I agree with the limitations inherent in such an approach, this should not deflect us from acknowledging *the general pattern* of underachievement apparent among minority groups. As Figueroa argues, in a British context, 'despite the tendency in the literature to use the constructs of "achievement", "underachievement" and even "overachievement", the crux of the matter is that the educational system has often not met the needs of the Black ethnic minority children—and indeed sometimes actually worked to the disadvantage of these children' (1991: 156).

2 Consensus, Conflict and Resistance Theories: Addressing the Structure–Agency Dilemma

Much of the debate on inequality in schooling has centred on a 'class' analysis. While this does present some difficulties of application in discussing issues specific to minority education (see McCarthy, 1990: 57–70 for a useful critique here[1]), it is nevertheless a good place to start. As I have already argued, class analyses highlight many of the same issues of structural disadvantage which affect ethnic minority students within schools. These accounts have also increasingly recognised the complex interaction of class, ethnicity and gender variables.

Outlining these debates is also useful because it highlights a key remaining difficulty in the sociology of education—the question of balancing structure and agency in sociological theory. This question continues to feature prominently in discussions on the role of education in perpetuating inequality. Reproduction theorists, for example, have emphasised the *structural* processes of inequality to refute the earlier liberal-democratic conception that academic success in education was based, unproblematically, on individual effort. Radical theorists have subsequently been critical, however, of reproduction theory for overemphasising structural constraints and have tried to reintroduce human agency, as *resistance*, into the equation. These debates within the sociology of education are widely known and ongoing. However, at the risk of covering already well rehearsed ground, it may be useful to explore further some of the particular theoretical positions involved, and to assess—and, in some cases, reassess—which might offer the clearest way to proceed in addressing the structure–agency dilemma. It needs to be recognised before starting that what follows is, necessarily, a somewhat simplified account. Attempting a global view inevitably hides and/or distorts nuances of position. Also, as I have already indicated, my focus concerns the question of structure and agency.

10

Consequently, other dimensions in the following discussion are somewhat attenuated. The aim of the analysis, however, is to provide the theoretical basis for an approach to educational practice that can address, and redress, the inequalities faced in schools by ethnic minority students.

Consensus Theories of Education

Initially the notions of consensus and individual agency dominated in sociological accounts of schooling. The 'liberal-democratic' view of education, for example, prominent until the 1970s, saw education as politically neutral; as a key to change. Education was seen as a liberating force, allowing all pupils equal opportunity to succeed irrespective of social or cultural background. If children didn't succeed then, onus for this was placed on the learner; the focus was on the individual. Likewise, the focus of school evaluation centred on determining the variables that 'affected' an individual's, or group's success or failure in school (Apple, 1979).

The liberal-democratic conception of schooling led, in the 1960s and 1970s, to the development of compensatory models of education. These compensatory programmes were established in an attempt to redress the educational inequalities faced by particular groups within education—particularly working-class and ethnic minority students—who were seen as 'underachieving' in relation to their majority group peers. If there was any agreement about this problem of the comparative educational 'failure' of such groups, it converged on two key sources of influence: the 'family background' of pupils; and the internal functioning of schools. It was these two factors, and the relationship between them, which became the focus of subsequent inquiry and concern, and the basis of compensatory programmes. Compensatory programmes attempted to redress the variables, such as social and/or cultural background, which were seen to hinder educational achievement. The standard implied in such programmes was middle-class and competitive (Bee, 1980). The result of such programmes, however well-meaning, was that those who were in social and/or cultural groups other than the middle-class were deemed to be 'deprived'. Moreover, these social and cultural groups were 'compared not with middle-class reality but with middle-class ideals' (Bee, 1980: 53), further accentuating perceived differences.

Within the sociology of education at that time then, as the Education Group at the Centre for Contemporary Cultural Studies (CCCS) outline:

> homes and schools rather than the society as a whole were seen as *the sites of problems and pathologies*. What was demanded of schools and of homes, what kind of society was in fact being produced, was not the subject of deep questioning. Direct social criticism was limited to a politics of 'status' and

to the search for a fairer, more open society *within existing social relations*. (1981: 138; my emphasis)

The results of this saw a sociology of education which 'recognized that working-class [and ethnic minority] children were systematically disadvantaged at school [and] also recognized that the wider society was deeply stratified. Yet the fuller connections between these two sets of observations were not made'. Consequently, a stress on 'family background'—or for that matter, the practices of teachers—simply 'displaced attention and blame away from an unequal society and on to the principal sufferers'. (CCCS, 1981: 138)

Perhaps the principal reason why the sociology of education was constrained to an individualised account of school failure up until the 1970s was because it rested primarily on a structural-functionalist view of society.

Durkheim

Structural-functionalism has originated largely from the work of the French sociologist, Emile Durkheim, in the last century. Central to Durkheim's philosophy is the notion of the primacy of society over the individual; that is, the need to maintain the moral order (or what he terms the '*conscience collective*', or social 'mind') through society's various agencies. In Durkheim's view, the education system, as one of these agencies, should ensure that the basic principles of the common moral order (whatever these might be) are put into practice and obeyed. Education should also allow for behaviour which fails to conform to these principles to be defined, explained and controlled (Meighan, 1981). For Durkheim, education, as a pivotal agency in the inculcation of the *conscience collective*, is essential—both for meeting societal needs and for reinforcing societal structures. As he argues:

Society can survive only if there exists among its members a sufficient degree of *homogeneity*; education perpetuates and reinforces this homogeneity by fixing in the child, from the beginning, *the essential similarities* that collective life demands. (1956: 70; my emphasis)

Such a view of education presupposes that the primary function of education is the socialisation of the individual into the collective mores of society; the specific aspects of that socialisation being determined by each particular social milieu. Durkheim concludes:

Education is the influence exercised by adult generations on those who are not ready for social life. Its object is to arouse and to develop in the child a certain number of physical, intellectual and moral states which are demanded of him [sic] by both the political society as a whole and the special milieu for which he is specifically destined. (1956: 71)

At no point, however, does Durkheim ask to what extent the 'physical, intellectual and moral states' required by 'the political society as a whole' are determined by, or serve the purposes of, particular groups within that society (Lukes, 1973); advantaging some groups over others. Neither does he recognise the possibilities of determinism inherent in his comment 'the special milieu for which [the individual] is specifically destined'—that education may in fact *determine* social destination. As Lukes observes, 'Durkheim saw education purely as *adaptation* (in modern societies to national and occupational demands); he was blind to its role in pre-determining and restricting life-chances' (1973: 133). Other commentators have argued that Durkheim was aware of the deficiencies in modern societies and realised that the school system would inevitably reflect these (see, for example, Fenton, 1984; Pearce, 1989). However, education still comes to be seen in Durkheim's conception as essentially a conservative or integrating force. The emphasis is on the transmission of culture, or more specifically, the transmission and perpetuation of an *accepted* (or *acceptable*) culture. Who determines what is acceptable—'the essential similarities' of the culture—and who benefits from and is disadvantaged by this determination, are not questioned.

Parsons

Talcott Parsons is, arguably, the most notable proponent this century of this particular view of education and society. For Parsons, culture is the motivational input behind society and education is the process by which 'individual members of society are brought to "know", "command", and/or become "committed to" important elements of the cultural tradition of the society' (Parsons, 1970: 201). Parsons views society as an integrated, interdependent whole, which normally exists in a state of equilibrium—hence, the notion of 'consensus'. Accordingly, educational institutions and structures are seen to have two major functions within that society: student internalisation of basic societal values, as in Durkheim's conception; and the allocation of young people to adult roles. Schools are seen by Parsons, then, as agencies of both socialisation and allocation (Parsons, 1961). Parsons argues that the socialisation functions of the school

> may be summed up as the development in individuals of the commitments and capacities which are essential prerequisites of their future role-performance. Commitments may be broken down in turn into two components: commitment to the implementation of the broad values of society, and commitment to the performance of a specific type of role within the *structure* of society. (1961: 435)

Because society is seen as a system of roles, schools are seen as agencies which require that pupils become committed to, and be capable of, successful performance of future roles as adults. On this view, the curriculum is seen, unproblematically, as a selection of culturally universal features. These features include a common value orientation and also more specialised aspects of culture concerned with training for specific roles. Parsons also argues that the allocation of designated roles in society requires that schools establish differences between individuals:

> it is fair to give differential rewards for different levels of achievement, so long as there has been fair access to opportunity, and [it is] fair that these rewards lead on to higher-order opportunities for the successful. *There is thus a basic sense in which the elementary school class is an embodiment of the fundamental...value of equality of opportunity*, in that it places value *both* on initial equality and on differential achievement. (1961, 445; my emphasis)

It is clear that the Parsonian view of schooling regards the school as a neutral institution designed to provide students with the knowledge and skills that they will need to do well in the wider society. Some students will be more successful in this endeavour than others. However, it is assumed that because everyone has the same opportunities to begin with, the more successful must be so because of differences in their individual abilities and/or effort. What resulted from such a view was

> the promotion of a competitive, individualistic philosophy in the schools, which were themselves organized to reinforce these values... As differences among students emerged, the schools legitimated them on the grounds of equality of educational opportunity and open, meritocratic competition. Students frequently internalized these values and accepted the differences without complaint... As a result, stability, equilibrium and consensus were reinforced. (Mallea, 1989: 17)

And this is where the structural-functionalist account runs into difficulties. Functionalism, in effect, places too much emphasis on consensus and equilibrium in society. In so doing, it fails, or refuses, to interrogate the relationship between schools and the wider social order (Giroux, 1983a). Thus, while functionalists like Durkheim and Parsons may have provided a *description* of the relations between the education system and other social institutions, they failed to provide an *explanation* as to why these relations exist as they do and how they change over time. Moreover, functionalists have tended to look at the socialisation process as one of those common *values* that hold a society together. However, they have not examined the interests that underlie these values, and how these interests are related to social class—and, as we shall also see, ethnic minority relations—as an intervening variable in educational achievement. Finally, and relatedly, functionalists have often viewed the educational system as offering opportunities for *social mobility*, given that equality of access and opportunity is assumed. They have been unable, as such, to conceive the role of education as a means by which *structured social inequality* in the wider society is reflected and maintained (Karabel & Halsey, 1977). As a result, functionalist analysis has fallen into wide disrepute. It has been criticised for underestimating the importance of conflict and ideology, and has been charged with a neglect of the *content* of the educational process (Karabel & Halsey, 1977; Young, 1971).

Conflict Theories of Education

Much of the reason for functionalism's demise rests with the emergence of the New Sociology of Education in the 1970s (see, in particular, Young, 1971). These theorists have argued that emphasising personal rather than structural constraints renders the location of power as unproblematic. Schools are not neutral and never have been. They are rather a key form of social and cultural reproduction and are linked to the more general reproduction of existing social relations (Williams, 1981). By concentrating on family–school relations the liberal-democratic view of schooling had largely neglected the relationship between school and adult society, and the processes of political and cultural domination this involved. No wonder then that the results of compensatory programmes, founded on this view, seemed to regularly produce—despite their best intentions—the same or similar educational outcomes for those they were designed to help. The concern of such programmes with family and individual pathologies, however well intentioned, also inevitably ended up simply 'blaming the victim'.

Unlike liberal and structural-functionalist accounts, the assumption that schools are democratic institutions which promote cultural excellence, value-free knowledge, and objective modes of instruction is rejected by conflict accounts of education. The focus in conflict accounts is instead directed to the use of power and its role in mediating between schools and the interests of a capitalist society (Giroux, 1983a). In this light, schooling is seen not as a process which serves to socialise its pupils into the *conscience collective* but rather as a process which is significantly related to the *uneven* distribution of resources and opportunities in the wider society. Conflict theory is based on the assumption of opposed group interests in society rather than some notion of consensual integration. It stresses the importance of competition, recognises the existence of differential power relations, and argues that contest and struggle rather than consensus and accommodation are the key elements in establishing, maintaining and reproducing the dominant social order in society. As Giroux states, this change in the conception of schooling has meant that schools were stripped of their political innocence and connected to the social and cultural matrix of capitalist rationality. In effect, schools were portrayed as reproductive in three senses. First, schools provided different classes and social groups with the knowledge and skills they needed to occupy their respective places in a labour force stratified by class, race, and gender. Second, schools were seen as reproductive in the cultural sense, functioning in part to distribute and legitimate forms of knowledge, values, language, and modes of style that constitute the dominant culture and its interests. Third, schools were viewed as a part of a state apparatus that produced and legitimated the economic and ideological imperatives that underlie the state's political power. (1983b: 258)

In short, the main functions of schooling are the reproduction of the dominant ideology of a society, its forms of knowledge, and the distribution of skills needed to reproduce the existing division of labour. Following Giroux, the proponents of conflict theory can be broadly divided into two camps: those who have been principally concerned with the *economic* and *political* processes of reproduction; and those who have explored the notion of *cultural* reproduction.

Theories of Social Reproduction: Base and Superstructure

Conflict theory draws heavily on a Marxian analysis of society, with Weber (1978) and Gramsci (1971) also being seminal influences. The broad division between the two groups of conflict theorists arises, principally, out of the different emphases which have been taken from their various works. The association of schooling with economic and political reproduction, for example, has been drawn from Marx's conception of the base–superstructure model. Marx argues here that the economic base (or mode of production) underpins and directs the cultural superstructure; that is, the demands of a capitalist economy influence and shape social structure(s). This perspective came to influence the sociology of education largely through the work of Althusser (1971) and Bowles & Gintis (1976) and has been termed the 'political-economy model of reproduction'.

Althusser

In his essay *Ideology and Ideological State Apparatuses*, Althusser argues that 'Ideological State Apparatuses' (trade unions, churches, schools etc.) are crucial sites of class struggle and working-class subjugation. Moreover, he suggests that of these ISA's it is the school which is the most important institution in advanced capitalist societies:

it is by an apprenticeship in a variety of know-how wrapped up in the massive inculcation of the ideology of the ruling class that the *relations of production* in a capitalist social formation, i.e. the relations of exploited to exploiters and exploiters to exploited, are largely reproduced. The mechanisms which produce this vital result for the capitalist regime are naturally covered up and concealed by a universally reigning ideology of the School, universally reigning because it is one of the essential forms of the ruling bourgeois ideology: an ideology which represents the School as a neutral environment purged of ideology. (1971: 156)

The notion of ideology forms a crucial part in Althusser's conception of schooling and its relationship to the economic imperatives of a capitalist economy. Ideology is defined by Althusser in two ways. First, as a set of material practices through which teachers and pupils live out their daily experiences. Second, as systems of meanings, representations, and values which are embedded in the concrete practices that structure the unconsciousness of pupils; that is, the unconscious operation and influence of ideology (Giroux, 1983a; 1983b). Althusser argues that through the workings of ideology, schools carry out two fundamental forms of reproduction: the reproduction of the skills and rules of labour power; and the reproduction of the relations of production (Giroux, 1983b). By this, schools serve the political function of providing not only the 'know how' deemed appropriate for the relations of production but also the appropriate attitudes for work and citizenship.

The problem with this view of schools, however, is that it is largely determinist; the labour demands of the capitalist economy simply end up *directing* the processes of schooling. While Althusser does allow some autonomy for schools,[2] his account remains too abstract to be usefully applied in this regard to concrete school practices. Consequently, his notion of ideology ends up being largely reductionist. There is little or no room in his description of the processes of schooling for viable human agency. Indeed, as Giddens observes, Althusser concedes that the 'true subjects' of his *mise en scene* are not the agents themselves but the 'places and functions' they occupy (1970: 180; cited in Giddens, 1979: 52). Given this, Giddens further suggests that Althusser's conception of human agency ends up being little different from the functionalism of Parsons. In both accounts, there is

a blindness to the everyday fact that all social agents have an understanding, practical and discursive, of the conditions of their action. In both Althusserian Marxism and Parsonian sociology the reproduction of society occurs 'behind the backs' of the agents whose conduct constitutes that society. The involvement of actors' own purposive conduct with the rationalisation of action is lacking in each case: in Parsons's sociology as a result of the value consensus-norm-internalised need-disposition theorem, and in Althusser's writings as a consequence of his deterministic account of agency; hence the teleology of the system either governs (in the first) or supplants (in the second) that of actors themselves. (Giddens, 1979: 112)

Human agents in both Parsons's and Althusser's accounts end up merely as 'cultural dopes'. Moreover, to the degree that individuals are reduced to being 'automatic parts' of a pre-given process, they may cease to be agents at all (Giddens, 1981: 18, 224).

Bowles & Gintis

Whatever objections may be raised against Althusser's conception of ideology, Giddens does concede that 'one of his most important contributions [has been] to stress that "ideology" should refer to the whole content of day-to-day "lived experience"' (1981: 67)—even if Althusser himself was unable to achieve this! In this regard, his work can be contrasted with Bowles & Gintis (1976). Bowles & Gintis share similar conceptions to Althusser about the relationship of schooling to the capitalist economy. However, they actually attempt to show how the social relations of the workplace are reproduced in the social relations of the classroom. Instead of using ideology to explore this connection they posit in its place the notion of the *correspondence principle*. Their argument is that, in most schools, pupils from different classes are taught the kinds of qualities, skills, values, and personality characteristics that they will need to occupy the highly stratified and class- and gender-specific positions they will subsequently move into in the labour force. As they state:

> The educational system helps integrate youth into the economic system, we believe, through a *structural correspondence* between its social relations and those of production. The structure of social relations in education not only inures the student to the discipline of the workplace, but develops the type of personal demeanour, modes of self-preservation, self-image, and social identifications which are crucial ingredients of job adequacy... By attuning young people to a set of social relations similar to those of the workplace, schooling attempts to gear the development of personal needs to its requirements. (1976: 131; my emphasis)

In other words, schooling tailors pupils' attitudes. Working-class pupils learn how to be punctual, how to follow the rules, and how to cope with the alienating demands of menial work. Pupils of the upper classes learn how to lead, think creatively, and work with a high degree of autonomy (Giroux, 1984). These attitudes are inculcated through both the overt curriculum which is taught in schools and, particularly, the 'hidden curriculum'. Parsons had previously seen the hidden curriculum (those 'unwritten rules' of the school) as a relatively benign means of socialising pupils into the shared norms of 'society' and the dispositions and rules required of it (Apple & Taxel, 1982). In Bowles & Gintis's account, however, the hidden curriculum is reconceptualised to account for the underlying logic which determines why certain values—i.e. the values of the capitalist economy—become the dominant values in society and, thus, also in schools. As Bowles & Gintis suggest, the correspondence between schools and the workplace is able to be accomplished because the power of the capitalist class determines what is to be taught—both overtly and implicitly—in schools. This correspondence of social relations is further reinforced by the class differentiated expectations of parents, with these expectations being in themselves a 'reflection' of class experiences in general (Liston, 1988).

However, like Althusser's account, correspondence theory was not to survive for long. Even Bowles & Gintis were subsequently (1980) to admit to reservations. The correspondence principle was certainly more accessible than Althusser's notion of ideology in examining the relationship between schooling and the capitalist economy, but the base–superstructure framework within which it was situated continued to function as a deterministic straitjacket. Critics have argued that the interlocking nature of social relations in the schools and the workplace is not as constant as the correspondence principle would suggest. Consequently, the social organisation of the classroom cannot exactly mirror that found in economic life. Like Althusser, Bowles & Gintis are criticised for their inability to recognise the possibility of human agency in their account. They fail to recognise that classroom relations are never static and that the presence of agents—in both teachers and pupils—always allows for the possibility of opposition and resistance. Even if this resistance is limited and/or ineffective it at least needs to be recognised and acknowledged in sociological accounts of schooling:

> [Bowles & Gintis] grossly ignore what is taught in schools as well as how classroom knowledge is either mediated through school culture or given meaning by the teachers and students under study. The authors provide no conceptual tools to unravel the problem of how knowledge is both consumed and produced in the school setting. What we are left with is a theoretical position that reinforces the idea that there is little that educators can do to change their circumstances or plight. In short, not only do contradictions and tensions disappear in this account, but also *the promise of critical pedagogy and social change.* (Giroux, 1983a: 85; my emphasis)

Theories of Cultural Reproduction: The Social Construction of Knowledge

Tying the processes of schooling to the nature of the economy had proved debilitating for conflict theorists like Althusser and Bowles & Gintis. As Giroux's previous comment indicates, this is because what is often left out is an explanation and explication of how *knowledge* is constructed, inculcated and, at times, resisted in the classroom. In order to redress this, conflict theory has had to turn to the work of Weber, and particularly Gramsci.

Weber

Weber provides significant insight into the impasse at which conflict theory seems to have arrived in adopting a base–superstructure model by arguing that individuals are both actively involved in constructing and maintaining meaning yet, at the same time, are constrained in these actions (Burtonwood, 1986). As King comments of this, 'to regard teachers and pupils as both bound and free does not make for simple explanations, but it is honest to the experience of what it is to be social' (1980: 20). Collins, in possibly the most well known application of Weber in conflict theory, has also employed Weber's (1978) notion of 'status group' to argue that 'the main activity of schools is to teach particular status cultures, both in and outside the classroom' (Collins, 1977: 126). Status groups struggle with each other for dominance in society, and 'insofar as a particular status group controls education, it may use it to *foster* control within work organisations' (1977: 127; my emphasis). On this basis, schools will be used by employers to select people with 'appropriate' cultural attributes. Thus, while still advocating the reproductive nature of schooling, the notion of 'status group' allows Collins to recognise the possibilities of contest and conflict that inhere in the term. For Collins, cultural dominance is *fostered* rather than *determined* by elite groups in society. The advantage of such a conception is its recognition that individuals are actively engaged in the process of education, even if the social and cultural forces arraigned against them may significantly constrain these activities.

Gramsci

Similarly, Gramsci, a major influence on the Marxists of the culturalist school, has argued against structural determinism. For Gramsci, control by the dominant class is never total, it is always open to contestation. Gramsci's explication of this process is encapsulated in his use of the term *hegemony*. Hegemony, stated simply, is the organisation of consent (Simon, 1982). It involves political and ideological leadership by a particular group in society through the diffusion and popularisation of their world view. Gramsci's crucial idea is that hegemony acts to 'saturate' our consciousness so that the educational, social and economic world we see and interact with, and the way we interpret it, becomes the only world; the 'common sense' or 'natural' way of seeing things.

The concept of hegemony, and its subsequent development by Gramsci, has allowed conflict theorists to develop a theory of schooling which moves beyond a simple economic determinism. The focus is redirected instead to the selection, organisation and interpretation of our 'common sense' experience in education within an effective dominant culture; what Williams (1976) has termed the process of 'selective tradition'. As Young (1971) argues, schools not only process pupils, they process knowledge as well. Within such a conception, knowledge comes to be viewed as a *social construction* which is deeply implicated in specific power relations. Likewise, the school curriculum comes to be recognised as a particular 'ordering of school knowledge' (Giroux, 1984) that recognises and values the knowledge of some groups but not others. This recognition allows linkages to be made between economic and political power and the knowledge made available, and not made available, to pupils in schools (Apple, 1979). Accordingly, schools come to be viewed as sites of cultural as well as economic reproduction. Agency is still possible here because hegemony always has to be maintained by the dominant group; it is never just given. Concentrating on the construction of knowledge within schools has also led to a combining of macro-sociological explanations of education with micro-sociological examinations of what actually goes on in classrooms. This is a significant advance on both base–superstructure conflict theory and structural-functionalism. These positions may have been antagonistic to each other, but both had shared an inability to move beyond a macro-sociological account of schooling.

Bernstein

Exploring the construction of knowledge in schools, and trying to link micro and macro analyses, have characterised the work of another notable conflict theorist, Basil Bernstein. In fact, one could argue that his long and distinguished academic career has been dominated by these two aims. In a recent publication, Bernstein argues:

> Behind the research is an attempt to create a language which will permit the integration of macro and micro levels of analysis; the recovery of the macro from the micro in a context of potential change. The project could be said to be a continuous attempt to understand something about the rules, practices, and agencies regulating the legitimate creation, distribution, reproduction and change of consciousness by principles of communication through which a given distribution of power and dominant cultural categories are

legitimated and reproduced. In short, an attempt to understand the nature of symbolic control. (1990: 112–113)

Bernstein's early notoriety as a deficit theorist for his advocacy of 'elaborated' and 'restricted' codes—particularly among linguists—obscured for many years the broader structuralist intent of his work. It has only been recently that Bernstein's structuralist agenda has come to be fully recognised, and the conceptual confusions surrounding his use of codes put to rest. Bernstein has always been interested in the forms of social control exerted in education and in the class cultures which differentially structure pupils' educational experience (Fenton, 1984). He has attempted to explore this process of what he terms *symbolic control* through the notion of *code*, and his related concepts of *classification, framing*, and *visible* and *invisible pedagogies*.

For Bernstein, the pedagogic practices of schools can be examined via the various *message systems* which he sees as underlying schooling. These 'message systems' of curriculum, pedagogy and evaluation are considered by Bernstein to constitute the structure and processes of school knowledge:

> Curriculum defines what counts as valid knowledge, pedagogy defines what counts as a valid transmission of knowledge, and evaluation defines what counts as a valid realization of this knowledge on the part of the taught. (1971: 47)

Bernstein uses the concept of 'code' to explain the regulative principles underlying these message systems and the differential access various social and cultural groups have to them. The code theory articulated by Bernstein posits that:

> there is a social class-regulated unequal distribution of privileging principles of communication, their generative interactional practices, and material base with respect to primary agencies of socialization (e.g. the family) and that social class, indirectly, affects the classification and framing of the elaborated code transmitted by the school so as to facilitate and perpetuate its unequal acquisition. Thus the code theory…draws attention to the relations between macro power relations and micro practices of transmission, acquisition and evaluation and the positioning and oppositioning to which these practices give rise. (1990: 118–119)

The code theory aims, as Atkinson observes, 'to account for the differential positioning of persons (subjects) within the division of labour. Such positioning is a function of power, and the coding of power is implicated in language' (1985: 101). Codes in this sense are not to be misunderstood as sets of performance rules, nor as descriptions of particular language varieties, as has often occurred with the criticism of 'elaborated' and 'restricted' codes. Rather, they should be seen as 'principles of structuration' which regulate which cultural elements it is appropriate to select in any given circumstance and how these may be combined into 'permitted arrangements' (Edwards, 1987). The selection of the curriculum into such arrangements is determined by the construction and maintenance of its boundaries. This process is similar to William's notion of 'selective tradition' and Bernstein refers to it as the *classification* of school knowledge. The combination of educational content, or the context of the pedagogic encounter, arise from the curriculum's internal differentiation and this is described by Bernstein via the notion of *framing*.

From these principles of classification and framing, Bernstein identifies two curricular types. A *collection* code consists of a strongly classified and framed curriculum (where subjects, for example, are clearly demarcated), and implies didactic teaching. An *integrated* code, in contrast, sees a more relational curriculum where the locus for teaching and learning rests with the expectation of self-regulation by pupils. Bernstein outlines three rules as constitutive to these two pedagogic practices. Rules of *hierarchy*, which he suggests are dominant or *regulative*, establish the relationship between the transmitter (teacher) and the acquirer (pupil) in any pedagogic relationship. They are essentially rules of conduct—determining the conditions for order, character, and manner and delineating the space available for negotiation between the teacher and pupil. Rules of *sequencing* determine the progression of what is to be acquired and are tied to rules of pacing which determine the timing. *Criterial* rules delimit what is to be regarded as legitimate or illegitimate within the process of acquisition. These latter rules are seen by Bernstein as instructional or *discursive* rather than regulative. On the basis of these rules, and whether they are explicitly or implicitly constructed in relation to the acquirer—that is, whether they are explicitly made available to the pupil, or implicitly required from the pupil—Bernstein is able to develop his distinction between *visible* and *invisible pedagogies*. Visible and invisible pedagogies are distinguished by 'the methods by which explicit or implicit systems and modes of control are regulated in the pedagogic encounter' (Atkinson, 1985: 157).

Bourdieu

The development of code theory in Bernstein's work has often been seen as paralleling the work of Pierre Bourdieu, and particularly his notion of *habitus*. Bourdieu is also concerned to link macro and micro analyses and has been particularly interested in exploring the notion of *symbolic violence*—commensurate with Bernstein's notion of symbolic control—in and through education as well as (and unlike Bernstein) in many other aspects of social life (see Bourdieu, 1974; 1984; 1990a; 1990b; Bourdieu & Passeron, 1977;

1990; Bourdieu & Wacquant, 1992). However, it is my argument here that while Bernstein's notion of 'message systems' provides us with a useful heuristic device with which to examine schooling, Bourdieu's concepts of *'habitus'* and 'cultural capital' are much more useful than Bernstein's idea of 'code' for examining the processes of inequality at work in schools. In linking various pedagogic practices to social class, Bernstein's discussion is certainly similar in some respects to that of Bourdieu (see Apple, 1992 for a recent discussion of Bernstein's contribution here). But, as a general social theory, Bernstein's formulation is limited by the inflexibility of the concept of code and the difficulty of generalising it.[3]

For Bourdieu, *habitus* is the way a culture is embodied in the individual. *Habitus* comprises, in effect, all the social and cultural experiences that shape us as a person; Bourdieu uses the term 'dispositions' to capture its meaning. Bourdieu relates this concept directly to schooling by suggesting that some *habitus* are recognised as cultural capital by the school, and are reinforced with success, while others are not. He argues that schools have a certain cultural capital—the *habitus* of the middle class—which they employ as if all children had equal access to it. This cultural capital is not explicitly made available to all pupils but is nevertheless implicitly demanded by the school via its definition of success; a definition which includes competence in the language and culture of the dominant group (Harker, 1984). Bourdieu argues that by taking all children as equal, while implicitly favouring those who have already acquired the linguistic and social competencies to handle middle-class culture, schools take as natural what is essentially a social (and cultural) gift. It is inevitable, he argues, that such a system becomes the preserve of those classes (and ethnic groups) capable of transmitting the family *habitus* necessary for the reception of the school's messages. Such a situation immediately places at a disadvantage all those children from groups other than that whose *habitus* is embodied in the school. The possession of the dominant *habitus* then, in Bourdieu's terminology, becomes a form of *symbolic capital* and its legitimation as a natural rather than a social gift becomes an exercise in *symbolic violence* by the school in its power to dominate disadvantaged groups.

Bourdieu's conception of cultural capital is also particularly pertinent to the role of language as a legitimising agent of the dominant group within and via the curriculum. Language—particularly, language on display—is, after all, often central to the judgements made about children's educational ability and potential ability.[4] Teachers assume 'that they already share a common language and set of values with their pupils, but this is only so when the system is dealing with its own heirs' (Bourdieu, 1974: 39). By acting as if the language of teaching is based on shared understandings which any 'intelligent' pupil should perceive, teachers make academic judgements that they see as strictly fair but which actually perpetuate cultural privilege. Bourdieu argues that such judgements occur, and serve to reinforce social and cultural inequalities, because the notion of linguistic competence is divorced from the social and political conditions which legitimate its use and reproduce it as the dominant form of language (Thompson, 1984). Power relations implicit in all communicative situations are simply ignored because language is analysed in isolation from the social conditions in which it is used. This allows the imposition of, in Bourdieu's terms, a *cultural arbitrary* in schools that only recognises the knowledge of the dominant group as expressed in language 'appropriate' to that group. As a result, the cultural arbitrary—reflecting the dominant social class and ethnic culture within which the school is located—is confounded with what might be called the *cultural necessary*—the 'essential' or 'necessary' knowledge that schools believe they are in the business of passing on to pupils (Nash & Harker, 1988; see also, Nash, 1990a; 1990b). When this social construction of knowledge, and its form of expression, is tacitly accepted—even by those who do not have access to it—it allows for the exercise of symbolic violence through implicit consent. Ethnic minority and working-class children are, most often, victims of such violence.

Bourdieu offers a compelling account of how school knowledge and practice (including the requirements of school language use) operate to reproduce social and cultural inequality. However, he is not without his critics. He has, for example, been criticised for the apparent social and cultural determinism implicit in his conception of schooling. Radical critics, in particular, often cite his failure to acknowledge the importance of resistance, incorporation and accommodation in his analysis of cultural production and reproduction (Giroux 1983a; 1983b; Willis, 1983; see also Apple, 1986; Burtonwood, 1986; Mallea, 1989; Mehan, 1992). Giroux, for example, argues that 'the notion of *habitus* is based on a theory of social control and depth psychology that appears to be fashioned almost exclusively in the logic of domination' (1983b: 271). Similarly, he argues elsewhere that Bourdieu's theory 'is a theory of reproduction that displays no faith in subordinate classes and groups, no hope in their willingness to reinvent and reconstruct the conditions under which they live, work and learn' (1982; cited in Harker, 1990b: 102).

There is, undeniably, a degree of pessimism in Bourdieu's account of schooling, particularly with regard to the elusiveness of cultural capital for the disenfranchised. Notwithstanding this, however, the criticisms of Bourdieu's determinism may be misconceived. Bourdieu does, after all, offer some solutions for the unmasking of the hegemonic process in schools. For example, he advocates the need 'to relate structured systems of sociologically pertinent linguistic differences to equally structured systems of social differences' (Bourdieu & Boltanski, 1975; cited in Thompson, 1984: 51). Such an approach would be able to place the social positions of speakers and reflect the quantities of linguistic capital they possess, or do not possess—thus exposing the language hierarchies in operation within the school. Corson (1990; 1993), for example, specifically develops this theme in his discussions of school language policies. More pertinently, however, Bourdieu is openly critical of structural determinism—a position often missed by his critics—and this is where he can be distinguished from Bernstein and other conflict accounts (see Harker & May, 1993). In *The Logic of Practice*, he clearly states:

> If the dialectic of objective structures and incorporated structures which operates in every practical action is ignored, then one necessarily falls into the canonical dilemma...which condemns those who seek to reject subjectivism, like the present-day structuralist readers of Marx, to fall into the fetishism of social laws... [this] reduces historical agents to the role of 'supports' (*Träger*) of the structure and reduces their actions to mere epiphenomenal manifestations of the structure's own power to develop itself and to determine and overdetermine other structures. (1990b: 41)

If Bourdieu specifically rejects structural determinism, why is it then that his work is so often criticised for being deterministic?! The answer lies in the inability of many English-speaking academics to keep up with the development of his thought. Bourdieu's arguments are well known—a result of both a high level of interest in his work in the English-speaking world over the last twenty years and his own prolific publishing output. However, because Bourdieu writes predominantly in French, and is also constantly revising his work, there is often a time lag between the current development of his ideas and their publication in English. Consequently, what has tended to happen in the past is that Bourdieu has been criticised for holding ideas which he has, in fact, long since discarded.[5] It has only been recently that the English-speaking academic world has begun to appreciate the development of Bourdieu's later thought, and his extensive ethnographic research, with commentaries which more effectively summarise his overall work (see, for example, Calhoun *et al.*, 1993; Harker *et al.*, 1990; Jenkins, 1992; Robbins, 1991).

The criticisms of radical critics like Giroux, then, are somewhat premature. Bourdieu's work is simply not as reductionist as Giroux would have us believe. As Bourdieu clearly states:

> How could a philosophy of consensus be attributed to me? I know full well that those who are dominated, even in the education system, oppose and resist this domination (I introduced the work of Willis into France)... [Rather] the model I am putting forward...supplies us with the only rigorous way of reintroducing individual agents and their individual actions without falling back into the amorphous anecdotes of factual history... Notions like that of *habitus* (or systems of dispositions)...are

linked to my effort to escape from structuralist objectivism without relapsing into subjectivism. (1990a: 41, 46, 61)

Bourdieu rejects the often posited dichotomy between agency and structure as absurd and sees the notion of *habitus*, in particular—'as social life incorporated, and thus individuated' (1990a: 31)—as a means of transcending it. Harker reiterates this often missed complexity in Bourdieu's formulations when he argues that 'a careful reading of Bourdieu's ethnographic work adds a dimension not readily discernible from the educational writing. It provides for *a theory of practice* which incorporates social change...and human agency...as well as an examination of the structural limits within which they must work' (1990b: 102; my emphasis). It is clear from Bourdieu's analysis that schools do function to reproduce social and cultural inequalities but not in the mechanistic way so often ascribed to him:

> Bourdieu does not...argue that the school is merely a passive instrument for the reproduction of family acquired *habitus* which 'objectively' certifies the dominant cultural code of society... [In contrast,] it is clear that the role of the school is acknowledged as active, and not merely passive in its 'legitimation' of family acquired *habitus*... Bourdieu's theory does, therefore, and contrary to the views of certain critics, recognise the school as the productive locus of a particular *habitus*. (Nash, 1990a: 435; see also 1986: 123)

Bourdieu argues that schools operate *within the constraints* of a particular *habitus*, but also that they react to changing external conditions; economic, technological and political (Harker, 1990b). Bourdieu seeks to explain, by this, social practices in terms of objective structures (Nash, 1990a), but without excluding the possibilities of agency. Also, as his ethnographic work in many other areas of social life attests, this project is by no means confined to an analysis of education. There remain, admittedly, some ambiguities surrounding the nature of agency in Bourdieu's account (see, for example, Jenkins, 1992). It may be a 'dynamic functionalism' (Harker *et al.*, 1990) but the needs of the system continue to dominate, and this, along with a certain political agnosticism, militate against a socially transformative conception of education. However, as Nash (1990a) points out, the real value of Bourdieu's work is likely to be seen in both its thematic concerns and the breadth of attention paid to the processes of social and cultural reproduction which operate, not only in and through education, but in all facets of social life.

Resistance Theories

The strength of reproduction accounts of schooling has been its effect in moving educational theory away from the notion of consensus—the idea that education is neutral and simply transmits commonly held social values. In the place of consensus has arisen an emphasis on conflict and education's role as an agent of social and cultural reproduction. Where conflict theory has been criticised, however, is in its supposed structural determinism. Radical theorists, most notably the likes of Giroux, have argued that the structure-agency pendulum has now swung too far in favour of the former; reducing individuals to bit parts, or no part at all, in the face of structuralism's all pervading influence. Fiercely critical of this apparent determinism in conflict accounts, resistance theory argues for the reinstatement of the individual as an active participant who has the opportunity to resist as well as to accede to structural constraints. However, as I have already suggested, while radical criticisms of reproduction accounts are certainly true of the likes of Althusser, Bowles & Gintis, and even Bernstein, they are less convincing when applied to Bourdieu. Moreover, resistance theory has particular problems of its own.

Willis's (1977) *Learning to Labour*, which examined the social practices of a group of working-class 'lads' towards schooling, is recognised as the first significant attempt to introduce the concept of resistance into the new sociology of education. In his study, 'the lads' recognised (at least to some extent) the reproductive processes involved in schooling and resisted them through a variety of oppositional practices; having 'a laff' being perhaps the most notable. However, the *informality* of their opposition and its susceptibility to appropriation meant that in the end they were unable to change their educational positions or their consequent work destinations. In fact, as Willis concludes, their opposition was to consign them to the inevitability of the 'shop floor' on leaving school. Individual resistance and even collective resistance to the dominant practices of schooling are not necessarily sufficient, it seems, to alter such practices. While resistance theory has subsequently emerged and been promoted as just such an emancipatory vehicle—particularly in the writings of its most consistent advocate, Giroux (see 1981; 1983a; 1983b; 1984)—this caveat needs to be borne in mind.

Giroux

As we have seen, Giroux has been particularly critical of the apparent absence, in both functionalist and conflict accounts of schooling, of the forms of resistance that can be adopted by disadvantaged groups to contest the processes of social and cultural reproduction. In discussing conflict theories, he suggests that these need to be combined with ethnographic accounts which explore the notion of resistance 'in order to illuminate the dynamics of accommodation and resistance as they work through oppositional youth cultures both inside and outside of schools' (1983a: 98). What can result is a theory of resistance which clarifies its theoretical basis from the point of view of all the actors involved. As Giroux argues, it celebrates a dialectical notion of human agency that rightly portrays domination as neither a static process nor one that is ever complete. Concomitantly, the oppressed are not viewed as being simply passive in the face of domination. The notion of resistance points to the need to understand more thoroughly the complex ways in which people mediate and respond to the interface between their own lived experiences and structures of domination and constraint...inherent in a radical notion of resistance is an expressed hope, an element of transcendence, for radical transformation... (1983a: 108)

However, Giroux's attempts to elevate the primacy of the 'lived experiences' of students (1981) are problematic. Wexler (1983), for example, while somewhat overstating the case, is critical of this 'individualistic idealism'. And Senese (1991), drawing on Gramsci, argues that promoting alternative individual 'discourses' as a means to student empowerment may, in fact, have the reverse effect of further marginalising such students from the educational process. As he states: '"dialectal" radical pedagogies threaten to retreat from knowledge structures that are the basis of requirements for intellectual power' (1991: 15); that is, the *cultural necessary*, or necessary school knowledge, to which I referred earlier. In relation to working-class children (and we can also include ethnic minorities here), Senese goes on to argue:

the terrain of working-class possibility may be argued to center squarely on the effort to equip working-class children with the linguistic and cultural power contained in the power codes of traditional academic studies...to win for the marginalized and working-class children the right to the class codes and skills which the privileged pass on to their own. A lack of commitment to this goal leaves any theorist of possibility [i.e. resistance theorists] open to a more insidious possibility—development of anti-intellectuals who know not enough, nor how to, demand more of the world... [These theorists] have perhaps rightly indicted the Reproduction theorists for using theory to explain away the schools' failure to alleviate suffering. Yet, as it stands, their theory fails too, if for different reasons. It abandons traditional education wholesale, replacing this with sketchy references to varieties of 'discourse'. As such it becomes something like Esperanto, inclusive, well intentioned, yet with the potential to misequip any student who might otherwise gain the only tools for which public schools are ever likely to be held accountable. (1991: 16, 21)

Strategies of individual resistance, advocated by radical theorists like Giroux, may be overstated in their ability to provide an effective critical response to the ideologies being resisted. In fact, as Senese suggests, such resistance could conceivably have a reverse effect; exacerbating rather than ameliorating their influence. Giroux's attempts, through the formulation of resistance theory, to return 'an expressed hope, an element of transcendence' into the analysis of schooling are commendable. However, they seem unable to offer a guide to *concrete action* that might confront the processes of reproduction operating within schools.

The Possibilities of Critical Practice

If nothing else, then, it should be clear by now that defining the relationship between structure and agency remains a formidable task for the sociology of education. It is my contention, however, that the work of Bourdieu comes closest to accomplishing this. Bourdieu's theory of practice offers us the possibility of incorporating agency into a reproductive account of schooling, as a potential catalyst for change. As Gilbert summarises it:

> Bourdieu's theory suggests an explanation of the regularities of social practice as structured by the relations between, on the one hand, an objective set of historically produced material conditions, and on the other, histori- cally produced definitions of those conditions and predispositions to act in certain ways in any historical conjuncture. The notion of *habitus*, while recognising conscious intention, need not inflate it in explaining action, nor relegate the dynamic of social action to an ineffable consciousness. Further, the theory offers an explanation of human understanding and action which goes beyond individualism, but does not resort to abstract social forces, functionalist mechanisms or reified institutions as agents of social practice. Finally it allows us to see how ideologies through their symbols and representations are part of the objective presentation of the contexts of practice, the means for defining a situation, and the medium in which past and present practices are installed in the interpretive and generative opera- tions of the *habitus*. (1987: 40–41)

On the basis of Bourdieu's notion of social practice, and drawing also from Willis's (1977) conclusions on the limits of informal strategies of resistance (see above), Gilbert goes on to argue that:

> the need is *to develop a critical practice in a formal mode* to articulate and carry forward the informal practices by which the less powerful express their discontents. What does the concept of practice lend to the task? Initially it requires a commitment... An emancipatory practice must be constantly and centrally aimed at enhancing the material welfare and expressive capacities of all human beings. Further, practices are conducted by groups, and *a formal anti-hegemonic practice in education must be a group activity*, where the interests of the group...are sought, defined and promoted, both hypo- thetically, in critique and reflection, and actually, in classroom and school social relations. (1987: 52; my emphasis)

In other words, if resistance in schools is to make a difference it needs to be collective, coordinated, and formalised in a critical practice. The specific emancipatory possibilities such an approach holds for multicultural education, and the difficulties involved in achieving them, are the subjects of the next chapter.

Notes to Chapter 2

1. McCarthy argues that these accounts tend to undertheorise the racial dynamics operating at the level of institutions like schools (1990: 69).
2. Giroux argues, along these lines, that: 'schools, in Althusser's view, are relatively autonomous institutions that exist in a particular relation with the economic base, but that at the same time have their own specific constraints and practices. For him, schools operate within a social structure defined by capitalist social relations and ideology; but the social relations and ideologies that mediate between schools and the economic base—not to mention the state—represent constraints that are modified, altered, and in some cases contradicted by a variety of political and social forces' (1983a: 80).
3. I have argued this at length elsewhere in Harker & May (1993) by comparing Bernstein's reliance on 'rules' in his formulation of code theory with Bourdieu's more flexible use of 'strategies', 'fields', and the 'feel for the game', all of which are linked with *habitus*, and of which *habitus* forms a part.
4. The legitimising role of language in classrooms is also specifically explored by Corson (1990; 1993) and Young (1992) in the Language and Education Library series.
5. A clear example of this is Bourdieu & Passeron's much quoted *Reproduction in Education, Society and Culture*. This was actually written in the late 1960s and published in French in 1970 but was not published in English until 1977. Consequently, critics (as recent as Mehan, 1992) were ascribing ideas to Bourdieu as current which were actually a product of the 1960s! Bourdieu's reply to these criticisms in his preface to the 1990 reprint of *Reproduction in Education, Society and Culture* directly addresses this misconception. A further complicating factor here is that the translation of Bourdieu's work into English has not always been chronological.

3 Multicultural Education and the Rhetoric of Pluralism

The debate in the sociology of education on the nature of schooling has come down firmly, it seems, in favour of reproduction theory. Agency is not ruled out but structural constraints are clearly recognised as significant and not easily overcome. Radical theorists, who have been critical of this structuralist emphasis and have advocated instead for the rehabilitation of human agency via resistance, have themselves been criticised for their inability to offer *practical* solutions at the level of school practices. Achieving an educational approach at the school level which recognises the power relations in education *and* provides an agenda for social change remains an enormously difficult task. This difficulty is no more clearly demonstrated than in the area of minority education.

From Assimilation to Multicultural Education: Solutions to the Ethnic Minority 'Crisis' in Education[1]

The changing conceptions outlined in Chapter 2 on the role of schooling in society are clearly reflected in the various practices which have been advocated over time towards ethnic minority groups within education. Along with working-class children, ethnic minority students have been singled out as a 'cause for concern' in many western countries because of their relative (and continuing) underachievement in relation to majority group children. Initially it was thought that the language(s) and culture(s) of minority children were the cause of their educational difficulties. The policy of *assimilation*—with its emphasis on incorporation into the dominant culture and language—was championed as a means of redressing this. In this approach, minority cultures and languages were seen as impediments which, if they could not be stamped out in the wider society (although some might have wished it), could at least be removed from the realms of the school. Accordingly, the teaching of English was emphasised, and children were encouraged to and, in some cases, coerced into leaving their own culture(s) and language(s) 'at the school gate'.

As John Porter, one of the great advocates of assimilation in Canada has argued, the benefits of such an approach were that it placed

> emphasis on *individualistic* achievement in the context of a new nation with *universalistic* standards of judgement...it meant forgetting ancestry and attempting to establish a society of equality where ethnic origin did not matter. (1975: 293; my emphasis)

Porter's unquestioned endorsement of individualism (a specifically western cultural conception), and his assumption of universalism betray the ethnocentricity of the assimilationist account.[2] The rhetoric of nationhood also clearly situates assimilation within a structural-functionalist conception of society (see Chapter 2). It is the needs of 'the nation'—which is seen as a unitary whole, politically and culturally indivisible—for which education is preparing students. Accordingly, minority groups should be absorbed into that nation's 'culture' (i.e. the culture of the dominant group) as quickly as possible in order to be able to contribute fully to the creation and maintenance of society (Mullard, 1982). Conversely, maintaining ethnic minority language(s) and culture(s) is seen as a direct threat to the stability of society. As Mullard argues, in a British context:

> the assimilationist perspective was seen as one which embodied a set of beliefs about stability. The teaching of English along with a programme of cultural indoctrination and subordination...would help in short to neutralize sub-cultural affinities and influences within the school. A command of the dominant group's language would not only mean blacks could 'benefit' from the 'education' provided in school, but, more significantly, it would help counter the threat an alien group apparently poses to the stability of the school system and, on leaving, to society at large. Closely related to this viewpoint, as both a political and educational strategy for implementation and as a further base assumption of the assimilationist model, rested a notion of coercion and control. (1982: 123–124)[3]

Assimilation, however, did little to ameliorate the pattern of ethnic minority disadvantage in schools. The results of assimilation, in fact, seemed simply to entrench this structural disadvantage. As McCarthy observes, of the United States, 'the ideology of assimilation clearly benefited white Americans. Over time, white "ethnics" were able to share in the rewards of the society from which black Americans were systematically excluded' (1990: 40). In retrospect, many now think this was exactly because assimilation specifically demeaned and excluded minority languages and cultures.

The increasing disenchantment with assimilationist policies, particularly among minority groups, led in the 1960s to an advocacy for an *integrationist* model of education. Integration was influenced by the liberal-democratic ideology and the associated notion of *equality of educational opportunity* and attempted to recognise rather than exclude aspects of minority cultures in the curriculum. It was less crude than assimilation in its conceptions of culture but a clear cultural hierarchy continued to underpin the model. While well intentioned, minority cultures were still assumed to be somehow deficient, or at least inferior to the dominant culture. This 'deficit' view also resulted in the continued perception of minority groups as educational 'problems'. As Mullard again comments:

> The assumptions, then, of cultural superiority, social stability, and shared values and beliefs still figure prominently in [integration]... All the integrationist model affords, as possibly distinct from its predecessor, is that, while immutable, these dominant values and beliefs can in effect be reinforced through following a policy of mutual tolerance and reserved respect for other cultural values and beliefs. (1982: 127)

The overt ethnocentrism of assimilation simply became a covert aspect of integration, thus making the latter policy's associated advocacy of equality of educational opportunity for minority groups somewhat ironic. Equal opportunity, in practice, meant equal opportunity only for those whose ideas and values conformed to the dominant group's white, middle-class culture (see Chapter 2) and integration's short lived educational tenure suggests that minority groups were quick to see the inconsistency.[4] More durable, however, has been the subsequent promotion of cultural pluralism, and particularly its most popular form of expression, multicultural education.[5]

The Multicultural Panacea: Claims and Counter Claims

Both assimilation and integration—despite their best intentions—did little, if anything, to change the educational position of minority children. Ethnic minority pupils remained educationally disadvantaged in relation to their majority peers. Their singular lack of success has consequently seen many turn to a 'multicultural' approach to education as the means to improving the educational performance of minority children.[6] Targeting the monoculturalism of previous assimilationist and integrationist policies as the real cause of minority children's educational underachievement, advocates of multicultural education have argued instead for the fostering of cultural pluralism at the school level. As Modgil *et al.* argue, 'multiculturalists have sought to establish a new educational consensus. Rejecting assimilationist and ethnocentric philosophies of the 1960s, many have argued for a form of education that is pluralist in orientation and positively embraces a multiethnic perspective' (1986: 1). The British School Council's position on multicultural education, as outlined by Craft, is typical of such a view:

In a society which believes in cultural pluralism, the challenge for teachers is to meet the particular needs of pupils from different religions, linguistic and ethnic sub-cultures... All pupils need to acquire knowledge and sensitivity to other cultural groups through a curriculum which offers opportunities to study other religions, languages and cultures... At all stages this may enhance pupils' attitudes and performance at school through development of a sense of identity and self-esteem. (1982; cited in Crozier, 1989: 67–68)[7]

Banks, in discussing the North American scene, makes even bolder claims for multicultural education when he argues:

As long as the achievement gap between Blacks and Whites and Anglos and Hispanics is wide, ethnic conflicts and tensions in schools will continue. Improving the academic achievement of ethnic minority students and developing and implementing a multicultural curriculum that reflects the cultures, experiences, and perspectives of diverse ethnic groups will help reduce the racial conflict and tension in US schools. (1988: 12)

It seems that, as Bullivant—a leading Australian writer in the field—observes, 'for the time being educationists in...pluralist societies have adopted, or are moving into, multicultural education as the claimed panacea to cure the ills that beset their educational systems' (1986: 33). Olneck, another North American commentator, argues along similar lines that 'multicultural education is characterized by ringing proclamations celebrating differences and endorsing the cultivation and maintenance of distinctive cultural identities' (1990: 158); a promotion of a 'new and better way' of achieving educational change for minority students.

The increasing popularity of multicultural education has drawn criticisms from conservatives and radicals alike. Conservative opponents worry that a multicultural approach to education is too 'political' and simply panders to minorities, while also detracting from the 'basics' of education. Radical critics, on the other hand, think it is not political enough, and see it as merely an attempt to placate minorities while leaving unchanged the wider social issues (like racism) which continue to disadvantage them, both in schools and in society (Parekh, 1986). Like assimilation and integration, they suggest that multicultural education has done little to change the position of minority groups within education (see, for example, Modgil et al., 1986; Olneck, 1990; Troyna, 1987; 1993; McCarthy, 1990).

As I have already indicated, I believe that the radical analysis has it right. The field of multicultural education—as it is popularly conceived and practised—is, like its predecessors, riven with theoretical inconsistencies and a seemingly terminal inability to translate its emancipatory intentions into actual practice. Multicultural education may be, arguably, more benign than its assimilationist and integrationist predecessors but, beyond its well meaning rhetoric, it is no more effective. It simply continues to perpetuate, in another guise, a system of education which disadvantages minority children. Before discussing if and how these difficulties can be overcome, it is useful to briefly outline how the theory and practice of multicultural education has arrived at this apparent impasse.

The Problem of Definition

The theoretical difficulties apparent within the area are best illustrated by the enormous amount of conceptual confusion over the actual terms 'multiculturalism' and 'multicultural education'. Gibson, an early commentator on the multicultural debate in North America, comments to this end that, 'in reviewing the literature on multicultural education, we find that program proponents have provided no systematic delineation of their views, and that all too frequently program statements are riddled with vague and emotional rhetoric' (1976: 16). The populist rhetoric associated with multicultural education, it would seem, obscures definitions. As Sleeter & Grant state, in their more recent review of multicultural education in North America, 'over the years it has become clear that it means different things to different people' (1987: 421–422). Similarly, conceptual confusion, ambivalence and, at times, outright antagonism have characterised the debates in Britain between multicultural education and antiracist education (see below). Distinctions of terminology have, consequently, featured prominently in the British debates (see, for example, Cole, 1986; Fenton, 1982; Jeffcoate, 1984; Mullard, 1982; Nixon, 1984). Likewise, in New Zealand education, discussions on multicultural education throughout the 1980s, particularly with regard to the much vaunted initiative of taha Māori (see glossary), have proved to be disparate and inconclusive (see Hingangaroa Smith, 1986, 1990; Irwin, 1988; 1989; Simon, 1986; Tait, 1988).[8] As the New Zealand Department of Education noted, somewhat prophetically it would seem, in a report written at the beginning of the 1980s:

> in identifying research in multicultural education as one of the priorities for educational research, the Department is conscious that it is seeking to plant something in ground whose potential is by no means fully understood or appreciated. (1981; cited in Irwin, 1989: 6)

And such would still seem to be the case, both in New Zealand and elsewhere. Banks has summarised these concerns in his observation that multicultural education remains 'an inconclusive concept used to describe a wide variety of school practices, programs and materials designed to help children from diverse groups to experience educational equality' (1986a: 222). Bullivant (1981) has taken this further by going so far as to suggest that the proliferation of definitions ascribed to the terms 'multiculturalism' and 'multicultural education' has led, not only to confusion about what the terms mean, but to a questioning of whether they retain any generalisable meaning at all. Put simply, the problem is that no-one knows exactly what 'multicultural education' is.

'Benevolent Multiculturalism'

If a consensus can be reached on what constitutes the *raison d'être* of multicultural education—and, in light of the above discussion, this would seem to be no easy task—it would appear to centre around the rhetoric of cultural pluralism. Three somewhat dubious claims emerge from this rhetoric:

> That learning about 'their' own cultures will enhance the self-esteem of ethnic minority children and will consequently improve their educational achievement.

> That ethnic recognition in the curriculum will lead to greater equality of educational opportunity for ethnic minority children; and

> That learning about other cultures and traditions will reduce discrimination within, and eventually outside of the classroom (see Bullivant, 1981).

Crozier has argued for a similar 'common code' in her discussion of multicultural education in Britain. She suggests that four common aims can be identified in the British literature:

(1) to promote and develop tolerance;

(2) to improve black children's self-identity, to develop 'cultural pride';

(3) to break down the ignorance of white children and through this to put an end to 'racism' which is (sometimes) fostered by ignorance; and

(4) to give value and respect to 'their' [minority] cultures. (1989: 67)

And Metge (1990), summarising the debates which have occurred in New Zealand, identifies three broad principles of: a promotion of a positive view of cultural diversity; encouragement of cross-cultural communication and understanding; and acceptance by majority as well as minority group members of the responsibility for change.

Admirable as these aims might appear, they have led to the dominance of 'benevolent' or 'naïve' multiculturalism (Gibson, 1976).[9] Benevolent multiculturalism emphasises the *lifestyles* of minority children rather than their *life chances*; what some have termed the 'spaghetti' or 'basket weaving' approach to multicultural education. In such an approach, an 'ethnic' component simply gets tacked on to the existing (and, invariably, monocultural) curriculum. This does little to challenge or change the cultural transmission of the dominant group within schooling. As Bullivant argues, 'selections for the curriculum that encourage children from ethnic backgrounds to learn about their cultural heritage, languages, histories, customs and other aspects of their life-styles have little bearing on their equality of educational opportunity and life-chances' (1986: 42).[10]

Benevolent multiculturalism places too much importance on cultural and ethnic *identity* and too little on what it is that determines successful negotiations for ethnic minority groups in their interactions with the dominant group(s) in society, and within education (Bullivant, 1981). In so doing, pluralism is confused with diversity. What results, as Olneck observes, is that 'multicultural education as ordinarily practised tends to merely "insert" minorities into the dominant cultural frame of reference...to be transmitted within dominant cultural forms...and to leave obscured and intact existing cultural hierarchies and criteria of stratification...' (1990: 163). Hulmes, a British commentator, argues along similar lines:

> pluralism [construed as simply diversity] does not extend the right to choose in matters of most serious consequence, and multi-cultural education (however well-intentioned) tends to conceal this limitation. *In important issues such as the content of the curriculum, teaching methods, assessment, the transmission of values from one generation to the next and the induction of the young into the adult community, the educational questions have already been answered.* The comprehensiveness of constituent cultures is subordinated at critical points to the practical judgement of an established educational philosophy which is assumed to be logically prior to all others. The voices of minority cultures are effectively ignored, except when they speak at other levels of cultural activity such as music, dance, cuisine and social customs. (1989: 13; my emphasis)

It seems that when questions of power come into the analysis the equation of diversity with equality begins to look doubtful. Furthermore, when attention turns from lifestyles to life chances the rhetoric of cultural pluralism loses its veneer of liberalism and is exposed as ethnic hegemony (Burtonwood, 1986). The assertions—that raising the self-esteem of minority children will result in their educational emancipation, and that programmes highlighting cultural difference will ameliorate the structural disadvantages that minority children face—prove to be hollow in a benevolent multicultural education. The net result may actually work against the life chances of children from minority backgrounds. The valuing of cultural differences, while appearing to act solely for the best interests of ethnic groups, simply masks the unchanged nature of power relations.[11]

Multicultural versus Antiracist Education

The most consistent critics of multicultural education along these lines have been radical theorists associated with the antiracist education movement. These theorists are primarily British since much of the debate between antiracist and multicultural education has been conducted there (see, in particular, Carrington & Short, 1989; Figueroa, 1991; Sarup, 1986; Troyna, 1987; 1993). However, a number of North American commentators, notably Cameron McCarthy (1990), have also made a significant contribution to the antiracist position.

Advocates of antiracist education are particularly concerned with the inadequate conception of 'culture' identified in much of the multicultural education literature. Richard Hatcher, for example, argues that while 'culture is the central concept around which the new multiculturalism is constructed, the concept is given only a taken-for-granted common sense meaning, impoverished both theoretically and in terms of concrete lived experience. It is a concept of culture innocent of class' (1987: 188). The consequent emphasis on changing individual attitudes, fostering cultural understanding and awareness, and raising the self-esteem of minority students in benevolent multicultural education reflects this ingenuousness because it fails to address the wider societal issue of racism. Even approaches which move beyond the incremontalism of benevolent multiculturalism to advocate wholesale changes to the curriculum are not enough. As McCarthy summarises it:

> radical school theorists have, with good reason, criticized the tendency of... multicultural proponents to lean towards an unwarranted optimism about the impact of the multicultural curriculum on the social and economic futures of minority students... For these reformist educators, educational change hinges almost exclusively on the reorganization of the school curriculum. But as Troyna & Williams (1986) have pointed out, attempts at the reorganization of the curriculum to include more historically and culturally sensitive materials on minorities have not affected the unequal relations that exist between blacks and whites in school and in society. (1990: 53, 54)

As I have already made clear, this is a position with which I entirely agree. However, in McCarthy's analysis, and in other antiracist accounts (see, in particular, Brandt, 1986; Troyna, 1987; Troyna & Williams, 1986), the next step is to assume that antiracist and multicultural approaches to education are, by definition, irreconcilable. McCarthy concludes, for example, that

> schools [in multicultural education accounts] are not conceptualized as sites of power or contestation in which differential interests, resources and capacities determine the manoeuvrability of competing racial groups and the possibility and pace of change. In significant ways too, proponents of

multiculturalism fail to take into account the differential structure of opportunities that help to define minority relations to dominant white groups and institutions... (1990: 56)

While I believe this to be so for multicultural education as it has been popularly conceived and practised, I do not share the necessary corollary of antiracist education literature that multicultural education is completely irredeemable. As Figueroa argues, in the British context: 'It is true that education... even when it was meant to be "multicultural" or "multiracial" has not done very well by many minority ethnic peoples... But this does not necessarily mean that "multicultural" education as such is at fault. It may rather be that it has either not been thought through with sufficient care and thoroughness, and/or has not been adequately put into practice' (1991: 48).

Beyond Benevolent Multiculturalism

It is clear from radical critiques that multicultural education, as popularly conceived and practised, has definite limitations. Radical theorists have argued that there would appear to be an irreducible gap between the emancipatory conception of multicultural education as cultural pluralism, and the realities of school practice(s). As Bullivant candidly observes, 'the optimism of continued reduction of inequality [for ethnic minority groups] is tempered by the realization that the cultural reproduction thesis and its variants...still holds' (1986: 36). If the theory and practice of multicultural education is to address these concerns it must situate the notion of cultural pluralism within a more critical conception of societal relations that takes account of the processes of social and cultural reproduction. As Olneck argues:

If pluralism is to have any distinctive meaning or to be authentically realized, it must enhance the communal or collective lives of the groups that constitute a society and must not be limited to the expression of differences among individuals in heritage, values, and styles. Pluralism must recognize in some serious manner, the identities and claims of groups *as groups* and must facilitate, or at least symbolically represent and legitimate, collective identity. It must enhance the salience of group membership as a basis for participation in society and ensure that pedagogy, curriculum, and modes of assessment are congruent with valued cultural differences. (1990: 148)

Olneck's observation, while specifically related to multicultural education, bears a remarkable resemblance to Gilbert's (1987) advocacy for a critical school practice which moves beyond individualism to achieve social change (see Chapter 2). Sharp & Green, in discussing the related context of progressive education, underline a similar need to move beyond the individual and situate attempts at educational reform within wider social and cultural processes. In a telling comparison with Matthew Arnold's efforts in last century's Britain, they argue:

> Without some clearer conception of the character of industrial societies and the limits on effective intervention that are imposed one can only depict progressive educators as utopian. The failure to consider the social preconditions for the effective institutionalization of their moral ideals which would involve a trenchant analysis of the social parameters of the educational system, reduces the progressive educator to little more than an unwilling apologist of the system and his [sic] utopian solutions ineffective. He is in the same dilemma as Matthew Arnold... [who] sought the solutions to the social crisis, brought about by industrialization, through the transformation of the individual through culture, an idealist solution which failed to provide an adequate account of the causes of the crisis... If the lack of culture is the cause of our social crisis, then merely to advocate culture to cure the crisis ignores the reasons why culture was absent or had become so degraded in the first place...*it is not enough merely to assert that the individual matters but to attempt to transform the character of the institutional framework.* (1975: 226; my emphasis)

Multicultural education's difficulty until now (like Arnold's) has been its inadequate conception of culture and its idealist conception of social and cultural relations. However, by adopting a critical perspective which recognises the power relations at work both within the school and the wider society, the multicultural education debate can be posited within an 'informing theory' (Mallea, 1989) of social and cultural reproduction. In so doing, it also needs to incorporate—as Sharp & Green suggest—institutional or structural change. The prominent advocacy for *cultural pluralism* associated with the field needs to be complemented by an advocacy for *structural pluralism*—that is, structural or institutional change within the school. Only then is multicultural education likely to achieve some commensurability for ethnic minority children.

What might this involve? Returning to Bourdieu (who, arguably, offers us the most powerful 'informing theory' to date; see Chapter 2), and his conception of cultural capital, the populist rhetoric surrounding the multicultural education debate can be effectively unmasked. If 'cultural pluralism' simply means the practising of a benevolent multiculturalism, the threat to the dominant group's monopoly of cultural capital is not a great one. While we have a curriculum organised around the knowledge code of the dominant group, there will always be educational inequalities attributed to social and ethnic origin in a mixed society (Harker, 1990a). As Hulmes argues, 'this is partly because, in practice, it turns out that [multicultural] education does not reflect the variety of approaches to knowledge and to the acquisition of knowledge. It continues to be an instrument of a particular (and, presumably, dominant) *western* culture' (1989: 15).

When cultural pluralism is tied to structural pluralism, however, resistance to the processes of social and cultural reproduction can be effectively mounted in schools. The result could be a genuine multicultural system which, as Harker defines it in his discussion of New Zealand education, would be one 'in which different value systems and lifestyles are accorded equal status and prestige, and with full institutional alternatives' (1990a: 42). Such a system would not only have various knowledge codes in operation but would have 'a variety of ways of transmitting these knowledge codes using culturally appropriate pedagogical methods, and with a variety of options available to evaluate when successful transmission has taken place. It goes without saying that [this] system would be bilingual (or multilingual)' (Harker, 1990a: 39–40). This stands in sharp contrast to the European-type *collection* code (Bernstein, 1971; 1990)[12] which dominates in most schools. Harker outlines what views of knowledge and practice result from such a code:

(1) Knowledge is seen as private property with its own power structure and market situation ...

(2) Subject loyalty is developed in students ...

(3) Students learn within a given frame ... they accept the authority of the teachers.

(4) The evaluative system places emphasis upon attaining states of knowledge rather than ways of knowing—how much do you know rather than how do you know it and how does it relate to other things that you know.

(5) The pedagogical relationship tends to be hierarchical and ritualised.

(6) The pupil is seen as ignorant with little status and few rights—being initiated into successively higher levels within a subject by those who already 'know'.

(7) Educational knowledge (high status) is kept separate from common sense knowledge (low status)—except for the less able children whom the system has given up educating. (1990a: 38)

Given the pervasiveness of the underlying conceptions which constitute this code within education it is little wonder then that 'ethnic additive' approaches to multicultural education (Banks, 1986a; 1986b; 1988; Gibson, 1976; Sleeter & Grant, 1987), as typified in benevolent multiculturalism, have had little effect in changing the educational position of minority children. As Harker concludes concerning New Zealand education, 'if our system is to be multicultural or even bicultural in any real sense, then we should be engaging in a fundamental re-appraisal of the structural features of the school' (1990a: 39). Hulmes comes to a similar conclusion in his discussion of British multicultural education when he suggests that an effective multiculturalism requires *organic* rather than merely *incremental* change within schools. This would include 'a thorough reassessment of curriculum content, of teaching methods and of the dominant [western] philosophy of education' (1989: 20).

A Critically Conceived Approach to Multicultural Education

Hulmes' and Harker's conclusions are echoed in recent developments in the multicultural–antiracist debate in Britain and in recent commentaries on multicultural education in the United States. In Britain the artificial divide set up between antiracist and multicultural education has been brought increasingly into question (Carrington & Short, 1989; Figueroa, 1991). As Figueroa observes:

> It is sometimes said that multiculturalism and antiracism are at opposite ends of a continuum... This metaphor, however, is oversimple and distorting. Admittedly *prima facie* multiculturalism does not *necessarily* imply antiracism... But neither is there any inherent opposition between multicultural and antiracist education. (1991: 50)

Carrington & Short support this argument and also suggest that—at the level of practice—advocates of multicultural and antiracist education are increasingly espousing similar (and, at times, identical) pedagogical and organisational strategies. These strategies include: the appointment of ethnic minority teachers; whole-school approaches to educational reform; collaborative teaching and learning arrangements; peer tutoring; child-centred and process approaches to learning; promoting (minority) parental involvement; and fostering bilingualism and multilingualism (see Carrington & Short, 1989: 82–101).[13]

This increasing emphasis on adopting holistic processes in antiracist and multicultural education is also reflected in recent arguments for a more critical and holistic approach to multicultural education in the United States (see, for example, Grant, 1992; Nieto, 1992). As Beverly Gordon argues, in Carl Grant's edited collection, 'throughout this volume there is expressed a pervasive belief that the success of multicultural education depends on at least two conditions: first, that such education makes an analysis of the social context of society; second, that teachers along with other interested persons who wish to have influence on the contested terrain, work within it to build conditions for change' (Gordon, 1992: 25). Elsewhere in this volume, Ellen Swartz argues for the construction of a framework of knowledge for multicultural education 'that has the capacity to produce non-hegemonic emancipatory narratives built upon a scholarly foundation' (Swartz, 1992: 34). She goes on to describe what multicultural education might be like within such a framework:

Multicultural education is an education that uses methodologies and instructional materials which promote equity of information and high standards of academic scholarship in an environment that respects the potential of each student. An education that is multicultural conforms to the highest standards of educational practice: the use of well researched content that is accurate and up-to-date; the presentation of diverse indigenous accounts and perspectives that encourage critical thinking; the avoidance of dated terminologies, stereotypes, and demeaning, distorting characterizations; the use of intellectually challenging materials presented in an environment of free and open discussion. *In short, multicultural education is a restatement of sound educational pedagogy and practice that requires the representation of all cultures and groups as significant to the production of knowledge.* (1992: 34–35; my emphasis)

Swartz's formulations are very similar to those advocated by Sonia Nieto (1992) in her excellent book *Affirming Diversity*. Nieto argues that multicultural education cannot be understood in a vacuum, divorced somehow from the policies and practices of schools and from the society in which we live, as is the case in benevolent multiculturalism. Rather, if multicultural education is to redress the educational disadvantages faced by ethnic minority groups, it needs to directly address issues of stratification, empowerment and inequity. For this to occur, multicultural education needs to be conceptualised as 'broad-based school reform' (Nieto, 1992: 207). The specific elements of multicultural education as broad-based school reform, advocated by Nieto (1992: 208–22), include a multicultural education which is:

antiracist education: the recognition of unequal power relations in schools, and in the wider society, is central to a critically conceived approach to multicultural education.

basic education: multicultural education should be concerned with teaching the common or core curriculum; what I referred to in Chapter 2 as the 'cultural necessary'. However, this need not be confined to a monocultural perspective, as it is so often in popular 'back to the basics' debates, and should include the notion of multicultural literacy.

important for all students: multicultural education, while concerned with educational parity for ethnic minority students, should not be directed solely towards minority students. In fact, this would be self-defeating since it lends itself to the pathological conceptions of the past. Rather, multicultural education should be expansive. After all, it can be convincingly argued that students from the dominant culture need multicultural education more than others, for they are often the most miseducated about diversity in our society.

pervasive: multicultural education should permeate the whole school environment; the physical classroom environment, the curriculum, the staffing composition of the school, the instructional strategies adopted, and the relationships among teachers and students and community. The school should be a learning environment in which curriculum, pedagogy, and outreach are all consistent with a broadly conceptualised multicultural philosophy.

education for social justice: all good education connects theory with reflection and action, what Paulo Freire defines as *praxis*. To be able to contest the power relations reflected in education, schools need first to be able to identify and discuss them.

process: process is as important as content, if not more so, in multicultural education. It should involve the complete restructuring of the curriculum and the total reorganisation of the school. Such a process is, of course, complex, problematic, controversial, and time-consuming. However, it is one in which teachers and schools must engage in order to make their schools truly multicultural.

critical pedagogy: because 'transmission' models of education exclude and deny students' experiences they cannot be multicultural. In contrast, critical pedagogy is based on the experiences and viewpoints of students rather than on an imposed and often alien culture. It is therefore multicultural as well because the most successful education is that which begins with the learner. Students themselves are the foundation for the curriculum, although the curriculum should not be limited to their experiences.

Nieto's conception is a powerful one, both for its critical insight and its potential for practical application. It does not view multicultural education as a panacea since central to the analysis is the recognition that 'schools are part of our communities and as such reflect the stratification and inequities of the larger society'. Accordingly, 'no school program, no matter how broadly conceptualized can change things completely' (Nieto, 1992: 207). However, it does provide an approach which offers significant hope for change. In the final analysis, Nieto concludes that multicultural education, as she defines it above, *is simply good pedagogy* (1992: 222). This is a position I also hold.

Nieto's analysis brings us much closer to combining critical theory and practice in multicultural education. However, having outlined such a clear approach for organisational and pedagogical reform at the school level, she concedes—as do many contributors to the British debate—that most schools have yet to undergo (or even attempt) these changes. Accomplishing such a fundamental reorganisation at school level in order to establish a genuinely 'multicultural' education is enormously difficult. It requires a critical macro-sociological conception of schooling to be realised in the micro-sociological practices of the school; a combination which has evaded many theorists (see Chapter 2) let alone practitioners. That so few schools have as yet attempted the task is indicative of the difficulties involved—organisationally, pedagogically and relationally. But, as with the broader conception of emancipatory education outlined at the end of the previous chapter, *it should be possible*.

Unlike previous accounts then, what follows is an examination of a school—Richmond Road School in Auckland, New Zealand—which has implemented a critically conceived approach to multicultural education. Richmond Road has undergone a process of change which has seen the total reform of its school environment—curriculum, pedagogy, assessment, and school organisation and relations. As it happens, all the elements outlined by Nieto in her analysis of a critically conceived multiculturalism are incorporated into the school's approach. Richmond Road provides us with a model of education that, perhaps for the first time, successfully combines critical theory and practice in the field of multicultural education. It may have been a long time in coming—but I hope to show that it's been worth the wait.

Notes to Chapter 3

1. Some of the following arguments are developed from May (1993).
2. Interestingly, Porter's aim in advocating assimilation was actually a progressive one. He wished to see ethnic hierarchies dismantled in Canadian society and a more egalitarian society emerge as a result. Ironically then, his advocacy of assimilation worked against these egalitarian intentions, albeit unwittingly.
3. In New Zealand it has been the indigenous Māori who have borne the brunt of assimilation (in contrast to the British assimilation policy described by Mullard, which was directed primarily at Black and, subsequently, Asian immigrants). Māori were in fact the only minority group for which a specific policy was developed in New Zealand since the immigration of so-called 'coloured' persons was strictly controlled until the 1930s and non-British immigrants were simply expected to conform to Pākehā (see glossary) cultural norms (Metge, 1990). Assimilation was formally endorsed as an educational policy for Māori from the time of the Native Schools Act, 1867, and was pursued with little deviation until the early 1960s when the Hunn Report (1961) ushered in a brief 'integrationist' period (see below).
4. 'Equality of opportunity' is a problematic term in educational discourse. In much of the research on minority education it has been assumed to mean the same as 'equity'. This is not the case. Rather, as Grant & Millar argue, '"Equal opportunity", meaning having equal access [to education] is not synonymous with "equity" which means having fair and just opportunity' (1992: 14). Figueroa argues, along similar lines, that if the term 'equality' is to be rehabilitated to include a real notion of equity it 'should include equal respect and equitable treatment for *difference*... Rather than sameness, equality means fairness—that is, giving full recognition to everyone's rights and legitimate needs, and inseparably taking into account relevant similarities and relevant differences, relevant resources and relevant disadvantages' (1991: 59).
5. The terms 'cultural pluralism' and 'multicultural education' are not synonymous, although the promotion of cultural pluralism is often advocated by exponents of

multicultural education, and distinctions between the terms consequently become vague. The conceptual overlap of these terms is characteristic of the terminological vagary associated with the field (see below).

6. While focusing primarily on the plight of ethnic minorities, the term in North American discourse has also come to include, for some protagonists, members of all marginalised groups. What constitutes the basis of marginalisation, however, is not always made clear (see Banks, 1988; Banks & Lynch, 1986; Gibson, 1976; Sleeter & Grant, 1987).

7. A later, and more prominent, articulation of this multiculturalist position in Britain can be seen in The Swann Report (DES, 1985), *Education for All*. The report actually began life in 1977 when the then Labour government asked for 'a high level and independent inquiry into the causes of the underachievement of children of West Indian origin'. This investigation was initially chaired by Anthony Rampton until he resigned in May 1981 (an interim report—the Rampton Report—was published in 1981) and then by Michael Swann. Regarded, even by its opponents, as the 'most important document within the discourse of race and education [in Britain]' (Brandt, 1986: 61–62), the report gave official sanction to multicultural education. Subsequent criticisms of *Education for All* have come principally from antiracist educators (see below). For an excellent summary and critique of the report, see Troyna (1993: 61–71); see also Verma (1989).

8. Taha Māori attempted to formalise the inclusion of aspects of Māori culture into New Zealand's common curriculum. The initiative quickly foundered, however, because of the demonstrated ambivalence of both Māori and Pākehā towards it, albeit for different reasons. The former were ambivalent because of its exclusion of Māori language, its additive approach to the curriculum (see below) and its peripheral position in most schools. The latter viewed it, more often than not, as a threat to or at least a distraction from the 'real' concerns of a Pākehā education.

9. I will use this notion of 'benevolent multiculturalism' to structure the ensuing discussion. There are, however, numerous other typologies of multicultural education which could equally have been applied (see, for example, Gibson, 1976; McCarthy, 1990; Sleeter & Grant, 1987; see also Chapter 11).

10. An emphasis on lifestyles in multicultural education has seen the rapid development of 'heritage' approaches to culture and cultural difference(s). As Bullivant argues, there is nothing intrinsically wrong with such approaches as long as their limitations are realised. Heritage approaches tend to emphasise the expressive over the instrumental in conceptions of culture. They also emphasise the histories of ethnic groups but have little to say on their current circumstances and concerns within society (and the real nature of that society). In so doing, they promote the preservation of a fossilised view of the culture(s) of ethnic groups in the minds of both minority *and majority* groups.

11. An emphasis on cultural differences as a means of educating *all* children, rather than reducing racism and discrimination as is its intention, may in fact act to confirm them by entrenching the perceived differences between 'us' and 'them' (see Bullivant, 1986; Crozier, 1989).

12. As I outlined in Chapter 2, Bernstein argues that collection codes arise from strong classification and framing rules. They are clearly demarcated by subject and imply didactic teaching. Bernstein contrasts these with integrated codes which are more relational, integrative, and child-centred.

13. Each of these strategies will be explored more fully in the ensuing account of Richmond Road School.

4　A Critical Ethnography

The methodological approach I use in the following account of Richmond Road is that of critical ethnography. Critical ethnography is a relatively recent development in social science research methodology (see Anderson, 1989 for an excellent summary) and arises out of a concern to combine a critical conception of social and cultural reproduction with the study of particular organisational or social settings. As Angus describes it, critical ethnography aims 'to develop an understanding of the processes and mechanisms by which macro forces are mediated at the level of a single institution' (1988: 4). As such, it is admirably suited to exploring the issues of structure and agency— particularly as they relate to multicultural education—which I have outlined in the preceding chapters. Before doing so, however, it may be useful to provide some background on the ethnographic tradition within educational research.

School Ethnographies

Ethnography and ethnographic methods have become increasingly popular with researchers in the social sciences and, in education particularly, the use of ethnography in the study of classrooms and schools has burgeoned in recent years. Originating in anthropology, ethnography has been associated most prominently with the work of Malinowski in the 1920s. In this classic sense, it has been described as 'the process of constructing through direct personal observation of social behaviour, a theory of the working of a particular culture in terms as close as possible to the way members of that culture view the universe and organise their behaviour within it' (Bauman, 1972; cited in Erickson, 1979: 182). Put more simply, one's goal as an ethnographer is to focus on a setting and discover what is going on there (Wilcox, 1982). This can be achieved by describing the norms, rules and expectations which identify people with a particular culture, setting, or institution. In other words, the ethnographer attempts to find out the 'essential characteristics' of a particular group or setting. However, if the ethnographer wants to ascribe meaning to behaviour in a fuller sense, she or he needs to *share* in the meanings that participants take for granted in informing their behaviour, and to *describe* and *explain* these meanings for the benefit of the reader. Geertz (1973) has described this process as 'thick description' which seeks to discover the important and recurring variables in a setting—as they relate to one another, and as they affect or produce certain results and outcomes within it. The aim of ethnography, in this sense, is an interpretive one; to systematically learn reality from the point of view of the participant(s). The result, as Angus observes, is 'to place human actors and their interpretive and negotiating capacities at the centre of analysis' (1986a: 61).[1]

The use of participant observation—where the researcher is both a participant and observer in the research setting—is a prominent feature in any ethnographic account. Ethnography is not limited to participant observation, however, since other methods such as document collection, field note taking and the use of interviews are also commonly used. Research methodology is not defining in ethnography because particular settings will determine the range of research methods employed.

Criticisms of Conventional Ethnography in Educational Research

The popularity of ethnographic accounts in educational research (some would say an excessive popularity!) has led to two major criticisms of the approach. The first, concerning ethnography's preoccupation with detail, actually derives from one of its major strengths. The second, has to do with the attempt in conventional ethnography to abrogate a theoretical perspective for the 'open-ended' collection of data.

Chilcott, addressing the first concern, argues that much of what has passed as school ethnography 'appears to be mere description' (1987: 209). As such, he suggests, it is non-contextual. The problem seems to lie with what Erickson, another ethnographic commentator, has described as the inevitable tension between descriptive *specificity* and *scope* in ethnographic research; 'between precise and adequate amounts of research data relevant to research questions of small compass, and the general comprehensiveness of a more synoptic view' (1979: 183). Previous ethnographies of schooling have, it seems, predominantly attended to the former at the expense of the latter. This trend has come to be known as *micro-ethnography* and while it may generate some important knowledge about a particular school setting its narrow focus fails to shed light on the more complex issues that account for much of what goes on in schooling and in the wider society (see Chapter 2).[2] Lutz argues, along these lines, that 'the narrower the focus of a study of schooling processes, the more likely important, perhaps necessary, variables are to be unseen and unaccounted for' (1984: 110).

The reason why ethnography, at least in education, has ended up largely addressing micro concerns is because of its commitment to what Hammersley (1992) describes as a 'reproduction model'[3] of research. Such an approach concerns itself with 'describing' a social setting 'as it really is'; assuming this to be an objective, 'common sense' reality. As I have already discussed in the preceding chapters, however, things are not nearly this simple. Wider power relations in society affect and shape both the setting itself and the 'common sense' interpretation that participants (and we as researchers) have of it. As Hammersley argues,

> Ethnographers' commitment to the reproduction model obscures, from readers and perhaps even from ethnographers themselves, the relevances that structure their accounts. As a result, the rationales for those accounts may be incoherent; and, wittingly or unwittingly, ethnography may become a vehicle for ideology. What is required is that the relevances and the factual and value assumptions that underlie ethnographic descriptions and explanations are made explicit and justified where necessary. (1992: 28)

This leads us to the second principal concern with conventional ethnography. Ethnographic accounts need to recognise and acknowledge their theoretical perspective(s). While the interpretive emphasis on human agency and local knowledge is an important strength of ethnography, it has also led many ethnographers to the false conclusion that they can dispense with 'theory' by simply letting meanings 'emerge' from the data.[4] This attempt to divorce theory from data collection is specious. As Hughes argues,

> whether they may be treated as such or not, research methods cannot be divorced from theory; as research tools they operate only within a given set of assumptions about the nature of society, the nature of man [sic], the relationship between the two and how they may be known. (1980: 13)

Angus observes, along similar lines, that 'there is no sensible distinction between theory and data—for the generation of data through observation and participation involves selection and interpretation that must reflect judgements that are theoretically based' (1986b: 72). All research is theory laden and, as such, a researcher *must* begin from a theoretical position of some description— whether this is articulated or not in the ensuing study:

> Researchers never *simply* hang around waiting for something to happen. They invariably and inevitably carry so much theoretical (and cultural) baggage inside their heads that what they look at, what they look *for*, and how they interpret what they 'see' can never be totally impartial. (Angus, 1986b: 71–72)

What is needed is a more *critical* ethnographic conception—a conception which specifically recognises the interrelationship between theory and data, and which recognises and examines the broader social and cultural processes that affect the school setting under study. Lutz suggests such an approach when he argues for a *macro-ethnography* which 'seeks explanation within a broad social context, regardless of where the focus begins, and couches that explanation in an even broader cross-cultural approach' (1984: 112; see also Ogbu, 1987).[5] In adopting the notion of a cross cultural perspective, the school can be observed as a social and cultural system situated within the broader social and cultural systems apparent in society. Chilcott argues, along similar lines:

> the focus of school ethnography needs to be more diachronic, focusing on the socio-cultural processes within and outside of the school that create the situations within the school... A school culture can no longer be understood by contemplating its navel... The ethnographer must develop more of a holistic perspective that focuses upon the interdependence of variables affecting the school—upon structural causes of change within the organization... (1987: 209)

This is where critical ethnography comes in.

Critical Ethnography

Critical ethnography has emerged from the ethnographic tradition because of concerns with conventional ethnography's preoccupation with micro-level analyses, and with its unwillingness to engage with theory. As Masemann— one of critical ethnography's early proponents—summarises this development: '"Critical ethnography" refers to studies which use a basically anthropological, qualitative participant observer methodology but which rely for their theoretical formulation on a body of theory deriving from critical sociology and philosophy' (1982: 1). The role of critical theory is central to critical ethnography, and is acknowledged as such. My own advocacy for a critically conceived approach to multicultural education is indicative of this. For the critical ethnographer, 'common sense' knowledge in a school setting is not taken for granted but is seen as a social and cultural construction which privileges some (and disadvantages other) participants. The critical perspective brought to the research is thus linked to a general theory of society and a concept of social structure which exists beyond the actors' perceptions of it (Masemann, 1982; Angus, 1987). Indeed, if a school ethnography is to become more than simply a reporting process it must direct the reader to the cultural theory and problem orientation that provide the focus for the research (Chilcott, 1987). As Angus argues,

> Investigations of schooling...should attempt to specifically illuminate the process and mechanisms by which the macro-forces of the society-wide education system are both produced and mediated, through the everyday lived experience and perceptions of human agents, at the level of specific institutions. Such mediation, given the essential human agency of school

participants, will never be simple, enabling the automatic reproduction of prior arrangements, but will instead allow for moments of contradiction which will signal new social or institutional forces, or the beginnings of new organisational forms. (1986b: 75)

Critical ethnography also addresses the limitations of earlier structuralist accounts (see Chapter 2) where—in emphasising the role of social structures— human actors seldom, if ever, appeared. Critical ethnography, with its focus on human actors *and* its recognition and use of critical theory, overcomes this difficulty. As Anderson argues, 'critical ethnographers seek research accounts sensitive to the *dialectical* relationship between the social structural constraints on human actors and the relative autonomy of human agency...' (1989: 249; my emphasis). This emphasis on the dialectical relationship between human agency and institutional structure enables a critical ethnography to explore the nature of the intersection between choice and constraint, and to centre on questions of power (Lather, 1986a). As such, it is intrinsically concerned with relating critical theory to practice—and particularly, to *political* practice (Hammersley, 1992).[6] The overriding goal of critical ethnography is to free individuals from sources of domination and repression.

By attempting to add prediction and explanation to thick description, critical ethnography can be regarded, admittedly, as 'openly ideological research' (Lather, 1986a; 1986b). But then, so must any exploration of emancipatory education. Issues of validity, particularly from the explicit use of *a priori* theory do, however, need to be considered. As Anderson concedes, critical ethnography's 'agenda of social critique, [the] attempt to locate... respondents' meanings in larger impersonal systems of political economy, and the resulting "front-endedness" of much of [the] research raises validity issues beyond those of mainstream naturalistic research' (1989: 253).

To counter these concerns with validity, a number of research characteristics are regularly employed in critical ethnography. There is an emphasis on reflexivity—the ability to reflect on the research process. For critical ethnographers, this involves a dialectical process among (a) the researcher's constructs, (b) the informants' 'common sense' constructs, (c) the research data, (d) the researcher's ideological biases, and (e) the structural and historical forces that inform and shape the social setting under study (Anderson, 1989). There has also been a move towards more collaborative research in critical ethnography, including the negotiation of research outcomes with participants. This kind of researcher/practitioner collaboration attempts to democratise the research context, and is consistent with the emancipatory aims of critical ethnography. Standard research procedures such as member checking, and triangulation of data sources and methods, are also applied.

The Richmond Road Account

The following account of Richmond Road demonstrates these characteristics of critical ethnography. The starting point of the analysis is my belief that a critically conceived approach to multicultural education is both desirable and achievable. This is the critical theoretical position I bring to the research and the perspective which frames the following account. You may or may not agree with this, but at least you know where I stand. Accordingly, I am also committed to (although not uncritical of) the educational purposes and practices of Richmond Road School. I believe that Richmond Road provides us with a successful model of critical educational practice in the field of multicultural education.

My research at Richmond Road has been conducted, as a visiting researcher, over a three year period (1990–1992) and has seen me closely involved in the communal life of the school over that time. This has included regular involvement in staff meetings, team meetings, Board of Trustees[7] meetings, and various school/community events. It has also seen me observing and participating in all the teaching programmes within the school. As well as this, I have also directly contributed—along with other staff members—to policy development: firstly, in response to a school review from the local education review office; and secondly, in formalising various policy documents for the school as part of a second review process (see Chapter 9).

Additional information on Richmond Road has been derived from extensive informal discussions, and tape-recorded interviews. I have both talked with and interviewed: present and past staff members (including non-teaching staff); parents; present and past pupils (including a cohort who were at the school in the mid–1980s); Board of Trustees' members; and national and local Department of Education officials who, in one capacity or another, have been associated with the school.[8] Tape-recorded interviews were open-ended and ranged from 1–3 hours in length. Except on three occasions, when respondents asked for particular comments to remain anonymous, all interviewees' responses have been identified in the following account. Permission was obtained for this from all those interviewed. Also, all interviews—along with the other sources of information acquired—were verified with participants and, if necessary, corrected before being drawn upon. My subsequent interpretation of these data, as outlined in the following pages, has also been subject to discussion and criticism by participants although it remains inevitably my own account. The school's extensive documentation—which outlines both past and present developments in the school's ethos and operation, and includes source articles drawn on by the school—also provided me with a rich source of information, as did material already written on Richmond Road by others (see, in particular, Cazden, 1989). Finally, while most of my account is qualitative in nature, I have also undertaken a statistical analysis of the reading records of a cohort of children within the school (see Chapter 8).

Extending Critical Ethnography

In using the research strategies outlined above, my account of Richmond Road is consistent with critical ethnography as I have discussed it. However, I have also tried to extend critical ethnography in two further directions. First, I have highlighted the role of language in legitimating power relations in schooling.[9] Previously, sociolinguistic analysis has not featured prominently in critical ethnographic accounts (Anderson, 1989). Second, I have attempted to account for the persistent criticism levelled at educational critical theory that I discussed at length in Chapter 2—'its tendency toward social critique *without developing a theory of action* that educational practitioners can draw upon to develop a "counter-hegemonic" practice in which dominant structures of classroom and organisational meaning are challenged' (Anderson, 1989: 257; my emphasis) Most critical ethnographies have simply critiqued the malign influence of power relations in education; and have consequently given little practical advice, or much hope for change, to practitioners. Richmond Road, however, offers us a critical model of multicultural education which does both. As Anderson concludes:

> Although many critical ethnographies have attempted to address implications for practitioners...few have taken critical practitioners as objects of study...if educational critical ethnography shares with applied educational research the goal of social and educational change, then it must address its impact on educational practitioners. (1989: 257, 262)

It is with this in mind, that a critical ethnographic account of a 'critical school' such as Richmond Road seems both appropriate, in its exploration of critical theory *in practice*, and timely, in its extension of the field of critical ethnographic research along these lines.

Notes to Chapter 4

1. The interpretive research tradition originally developed as a reaction to positivist approaches to research adopted from the physical sciences. Positivist approaches emphasise the 'objective' nature of research and try to exclude the influence of individuals in search of the 'facts'. In contrast, interpretive approaches, like ethnography, attempt to understand a given situation from the perspective of the actors involved—hence, the emphasis on human agency. Accordingly, a 'theoretical divide' developed between positivism—associated primarily with quantitative or experimental approaches to research, and interpretive accounts—which are generally more qualitative in nature. More recently, however, some commentators have suggested that this divide is unhelpful and unnecessary (see, for example, Hammersley, 1992:

159–173). Research can combine both quantitative and qualitative dimensions, as is the case in my account (see Chapter 8), and need not be confined to past typologies.

2. A proviso needs to be made here. While this criticism still applies to many school ethnographies, micro-ethnographies are beginning to be critically reconceived in other areas, particularly in discourse analysis (see, for example, Clark *et al.* 1990; 1991; Fairclough, 1989; Gee, 1990; Young, 1992).

3. Hammersley's use of 'reproduction model' in this particular context should not be confused with the term as used elsewhere in this book.

4. From this perspective, the aim of the ethnographer is to explore the setting from the point of view of the participants and the principal concern is how her or his preconceptions and expectations might be set aside to allow this information to be gathered 'untarnished'.

5. John Ogbu has been particularly influential in his advocacy for macro-ethnography, and his critique of micro-ethnography, in the field of minority education. In critiquing the latter, he argues: 'practitioners [of micro-ethnography] basically accept the assumption that minority children's social adjustment and academic performance difficulties are due to cultural and language differences. The focus of [these studies] is process, how the assumed cultural/language differences interact with teaching and learning to cause the problems experienced by the minorities…they cannot provide *a general explanation* of the school success or failure of minority children…' (1987: 313; my emphasis).

6. While Hammersley's description is drawn upon here, he is actually quite dismissive of critical ethnography (see 1992: 96–134). His critique does raise some valid concerns. However, in the end, I find it unconvincing. Of particular concern in his account is the way that he actually dichotomises theory/research and practice/policy. At one point, for example, he argues that there are clear differences between 'the sorts of knowledge that research can produce and those required for practice…' (1992: 129). In other words, theory is distinct from the kinds of 'practical' knowledge which inform practice and this limits, for Hammersley, ethnography's potential influence on policy and practice. I disagree with this entirely. Rather, as I go on to outline in the account of Richmond Road, practice is at its most effective when it is *informed* by theory. While much of educational practice does comprise *ad hoc* and 'common sense' responses from practitioners—something Hammersley correctly identifies—it need not always do so. In fact, Richmond Road shows what a critically conceived (and eminently 'theoretical') approach to practice *by practitioners* can actually achieve.

7. Boards of Trustees, elected from local school communities, were established in New Zealand in 1989 to formally administer primary (elementary) schools. They formed part of a national reform (and devolution) of school administration at that time (see Chapter 9).

8. I acknowledge that the following account may appear to be dominated by these discussions and interviews. However, the extent to which they have been drawn upon relates to the degree to which Jim Laughton, Richmond Road's previous principal, features in the development of the organisational and pedagogical changes that now characterise the school. I had initially envisaged simply exploring the school's present educational circumstances but it soon became apparent that this would prove of little value unless the school's history under Laughton was also detailed. Because of Laughton's death in 1988, I have inevitably had to rely on others' perceptions of him in outlining the process of change undergone by the school during his tenure as principal.

9. See also the discussion in Chapter 2 of Bourdieu's analysis of language.

5   Richmond Road School

Real educational reform is so especially difficult and unlikely that a model such as Richmond Road is precious both locally and internationally as a statement of what is really possible. (Holdaway, 1984)

Richmond Road School is situated in the inner-city area of Ponsonby in Auckland, New Zealand's largest city. It is a multiethnic state primary (elementary) school with approximately 200 pupils and 18 (full-time and part-time) teaching staff. Most of the pupils at the school represent non-dominant groups in New Zealand society, principally of Māori and Pacific Island origin (see Table 5.1). Of these, 48% are students for whom English is not their first language (Richmond Road School, 1992). There is a similarly multiethnic staff, including representatives of most of the cultural groups to which the majority of pupils belong.

Table 5.1 Ethnic composition of Richmond Road Primary School

Ethnic Origin	March 1993
Samoan	22%
Cook Islands	18%
Māori	17%
Pākehā (European New Zealanders)	15%
Tongan	9%
Niuean	9%
Indian	5%
Chinese	4%
Other	1%

Cultural and ethnic differences permeate every facet of school life at Richmond Road. The multicultural nature of the school is evident as soon as one enters the door. Māori and Pacific Island motifs and displays feature prominently throughout the school. Māori and Pacific Island pupils and staff are also clearly visible and, along with English, Māori and a variety of Pacific Island languages are heard regularly in rooms and corridors. While this might appear little different from many other inner-city schools, what distinguishes Richmond Road is that this diversity of language and culture is formalised within the structures of the school. The school has on site, for example: Ritimana Kōhanga Reo (a Māori language pre-school immersion unit; see glossary) that has been operating since 1985: an *A'oga Fa'a Samoa* (Samoan language pre-school) that started in 1989; and *Te Apii Reo Kuki Airani* (a Cook Islands language pre-school) that began in 1990. These pre-school units aim to foster their respective minority languages through full-immersion teaching and are part of the recent emergence in New Zealand of such programmes. Other English-speaking pre-school units in the area also contribute to the school's clientele.

The school itself offers a range of language-based programmes. In addition to two English-language programmes, a Māori bilingual programme was established in 1984, a Samoan bilingual programme in 1987, and a Cook Islands bilingual programme in 1991. An inner-city second language unit, established in 1976, also caters for recent arrivals to New Zealand and teaches English, where possible, through the home languages of its students. All these programmes are arranged in vertical rōpū (the Māori term for group(s)) which are based on the whānau (extended family) model and of the non-graded New Zealand rural school. Each rōpū consists of the entire range of pupils from New Entrants through to Form 2 (NE-F2; 5–13 years old) and children stay in the same rōpū, with the same teachers, right through their primary schooling. The largely open plan setting of the school allows for most of the rōpū to be taught in 'shared spaces' and a principle of the school is that there always be two teachers in every room. This allows the rōpū to be further divided into 'home groups'. Home groups are the basic teaching groups and it is the pupils in them that are monitored and reported on to parents by individual teachers. The presently favourable staff to student ratio sees these groups comprise approximately 20 pupils. However, the rōpū can effectively operate with greatly increased numbers (as they have done in the past) because of the varied individual and collective teaching arrangements, and the variety of resources available at all levels (see Chapter 7).[1]

Within these organisational structures responsibility is shared and non-hierarchical relationships are emphasised. The collectivity which is fostered among staff as a result also encompasses the management of the school where the principal and the two associate principals work collaboratively as an administrative team. The associate principals rotate this responsibility— spending two weeks in a class which they share with another teacher, and two weeks in the office. This ensures that the administration does not lose touch with what is happening in the classroom and is aimed at preventing potential isolation between those who administer and those who teach in the school. As the current principal, Lionel Pedersen, argues, the aim of the school is to break down pedagogical isolation—by rejecting artificial class grouping by age, and through shared administration and teaching (Field Notes, 26 February, 1990).

This collaboration is closely allied with staff development generally and curriculum development in particular. The collective approach to teaching allows individual teachers to be released every morning to look at curriculum issues. Likewise, staff meetings—which are held every Tuesday after school and regularly continue into early evening—focus on cooperation and staff development. This involvement in curriculum development by staff is also supported through the organisation of staff into curriculum teams which deliberately cut across the rōpū teaching teams. Curriculum teams develop resources for the curriculum during the course of the year (these resources must include all ethnic groups represented in the school community), supervise these materials, and provide support for staff working in other areas. The involvement of all staff in this process leads to a significant coherence and consistency across the curriculum and a great deal of mutual support among teachers (Cazden, 1989). This participation is extended to the school community through an open door policy which encourages full community consultation and involvement in the discussion and development of school policy (see Chapter 6). Parents are welcome at Richmond Road to contribute to all facets of school life and, moreover, readily do so.

The multicultural population and character of Richmond Road are a reflection of the local Ponsonby community that the school serves, and the close and reciprocal relationship between the school and its community. However, as a brief history suggests, neither the school nor the community have always been as they are now.

The Historical Background

Richmond Road is one of the oldest remaining primary schools in Auckland; being first established as a temporary school in February 1884 to alleviate the overcrowding of other Ponsonby schools at the time. Its temporary character soon became permanent, however, as the inner-city began to expand. This expansion was also to pose similar difficulties of overcrowding for Richmond Road. In 1922, for example, Villers *et al.* (1984) note in their centenary booklet that the largest class contained 82 Standard 5 (Form 1; 11 years) children. Additions to school buildings in the 1930s, and a remodelling of the school in 1972, were undertaken to alleviate these extremes but conditions did not markedly improve. Colleen Belsham, who first began teaching at Richmond Road in the early 1970s, recalls her initial reaction to the school's overcrowding: 'The thing that shocked me most was the space for kids... There was only a strip of grass at the end of the concrete. There was just classrooms everywhere...and it just used to look criminal because there was so much concrete and so many kids...' (Interview, 25 May, 1991). Similarly, Jim Laughton, in the school's centenary publication, recalled conditions on his arrival as principal in September 1972:

> 830 pupils, 34 teachers, and other ancillary staff crowded the school. Instant classrooms were crammed into the meagre, 2¼ acre site, perched on the old bomb shelters, squeezed into corners, occupying nearly all of the area... Playing space was at a premium, every square metre valued. Some duty teachers supervised young children's play on the front lawn and along the narrow strip between buildings... (1984: 37)

Conditions at Richmond Road only improved when the school was decapitated to a contributing primary school in 1976, and its senior pupils were syphoned off to the newly established Ponsonby Intermediate.[2] Ironically, decapitation, which saw the school's roll drop by a quarter of the 1975 figure, was also to coincide with changes in the local community that were to lead to the rapidly falling roll situation currently faced by the school.

Up until the 1950s, Ponsonby had been a dormitory suburb for a predominantly Pākehā working-class. From the 1950s, however, the confluence of other ethnic groups in the area was to become increasingly apparent. An influx of Māori families moving from rural communities to the cities in search of work, coupled with the migration of Pacific Islanders, saw the area emerge as the 'Polynesian heart of Auckland' (Hucker, 1984). The emerging Māori and Pacific Island communities came to provide the focal point for the newly reconstituted suburb. This multicultural milieu, however, was followed by developments in the 1970s and 1980s which heralded the decline of the inner-city. Middle-class Pākehā began moving back into the area, and the process of gentrification which ensued has resulted in a population decline from which the inner-city has not recovered. Subsequent property speculation resulted in the rapid increase of inner-city housing prices, forcing Māori and Pacific Island families—who were predominantly living in low-cost rental accommodation—to move out of the area as landlords took advantage of changed circumstances. As these families left the area, they were replaced by Pākehā who were either childless or had small nuclear families. This gentrification of the inner-city, along with an attendant process of 'white flight', has contributed to the decline in school numbers at Richmond Road and other multicultural inner-city schools. Nicola Legat—writing in the Auckland magazine *Metro* on the phenomenon of 'white flight' in the inner-city—notes that Pākehā parents, in their preoccupation with finding the 'best' school for their children, are often taking them to a school out of the area, or into the private system. This is, she suggests, 'a peculiarly middle-class obsession, presupposing the assertiveness to question and challenge, the time to observe, and the access to a car to drive children to schools further afield... Typically, in the search, they are giving the schools with high Polynesian rolls the big swerve' (1991: 63). Steve Williams, a local electrician and parent at Richmond Road, makes a similar observation: 'I hate to say this...but because there are a lot more Pākehā than Māori or Polynesian now in the area, they have a tendency to stick to certain [predominantly white] schools... [and] that's the reason why the roll [at Richmond Road] is dropping' (Interview, 17 November, 1992). 'White flight' compounds the falling rolls which face multicultural inner-city schools like Richmond Road. The result, as Legat concludes in her article, is that 'the gap between who sits in the inner-city classrooms and who actually lives in the neighbouring streets looks likely to continue' (1991: 70).

Pākehā scepticism of the educational merit of Richmond Road and its neighbouring schools reflects the wider process of racism at work in New Zealand society. Shona Matthews, a Pākehā parent at Richmond Road, comments that while she sent her child to Richmond Road because 'from the outset I was just really impressed by the atmosphere of the school', she also 'could see all of the other Pākehā parents at the kindergarten [pre-school] that we were at, heading in the opposite direction as fast as possible' (Interview, 17 November, 1992). However, the evident scepticism among many Pākehā parents about Richmond Road is ironic, particularly in light of its exemplary educational pedigree. Holdaway (1984) outlines, for example, how Richmond Road had a pivotal role in the late 1960s and early 1970s in the development and trialing of Marie Clay's internationally renowned work on early reading practices (see Clay, 1979; 1985). The development of 'Big Books' and 'Shared Book Experience' undertaken by teachers in Richmond Road's junior school was central to this project and has formed the basis for much of the subsequent development of 'reading recovery' in New Zealand schools and elsewhere. This involvement in educational innovation was to continue under the subsequent principalship of Jim Laughton. Laughton's concern to establish a critically conceived approach to multicultural education, and the means by which he achieved this, inform much of this present study of the school. Since his death in 1988, the school has continued to develop the multicultural systems which Jim Laughton set in place within the school, and for which the school has become nationally and internationally known. While Richmond Road cannot be the same without him, it has not been left bereft, since Laughton's intention was for these systems to be 'self-sustaining and self-generating' (Richmond Road School, 1983). The degree to which this aim has been achieved is reflected in the present structures and philosophy of the school.

The Present Context

Laughton's tenure at Richmond Road (1972–1988) has seen the school develop and sustain a critically conceived approach to multiculturalism. In this regard, Laughton was concerned with developing at Richmond Road both *cultural maintenance*—the fostering of identity and self-esteem through the affirmation of cultural difference, and *access to power*—equipping minority children with the skills necessary to live in the wider society. Both aspects are necessary, he believed, if unequal power relations in society are to be effectively contested (see Chapter 2). In implementing these ideas, he saw certain values as prerequisite: difference is never equated with deficiency; cooperation is fostered not competition; cultural respect is seen as essential to developing a pluralistic society; and the school's function is directed towards increasing a child's options rather than changing them:

> There is a tendency in education, it seems to me, to recognise competent students in ways that set them apart from their peers...; to value conformity too highly at the expense of individual and cultural identity; to put all learning in competitive contexts; to emphasise what children learn without realising that the contexts of learning may carry the most important lessons... Not that our concern for competence in the basics of education is in any way diminished. Indeed it is our belief that this can be achieved best by encouraging children to hold onto their cultures, their languages, their identities as contributing members of a richly diverse community; by emphasising co-operation rather than competition and by valuing human relationships above all as a vital source of knowledge and wisdom. Education in our view is not a preparation for living, it *is* a living experience. We come to school to learn from each other, to learn about each other, and through those learnings to begin to envisage the world at large. (Laughton, 1984: 39)

As I argued in Chapter 3, the concern for fostering cultural pluralism within the school environment, exemplified in Laughton's comments, has been advocated by an increasing number of educationists under the rubric of multicultural education. However, unlike the vast majority of these initiatives, Richmond Road does not stop at this point. Rather, the school bases its educational endeavours on an 'informing theory' of education which recognises the power relations implicit in the multicultural equation. Emphasis may be placed on the value of all children at Richmond Road, but cognisance is also taken of the particular processes of institutionalised power which often limit the choices and life chances of minority children. Accordingly, the school sets itself the task of increasing the latter's alternatives—hence the emphasis, along with cultural pluralism, on 'access to power'. Secondly, and in order that these wider alternatives are achieved, this critically informed approach to multicultural education has been realised through structural diversity at the school level. Jim Laughton recognised that establishing cultural pluralism in any serious manner requires structural pluralism; the reform of the school's organisational structures.

Richmond Road consciously aims to resist hegemonic forces within education by promoting the recognition, affirmation and celebration of cultural difference *within the institutionalised structures of the school*. The school also rejects the assumption that the 'cultural necessary' in schools has to be tied to a single 'cultural arbitrary' (that of the dominant group).[3] Richmond Road demonstrates, as I will show, that structural alternatives can be employed for delivering necessary school knowledge which are not only inclusive of the values and practices of both minority and majority cultures but are non-hierarchically construed. In this process, minority students are empowered by a recognition and affirmation of their language(s) and culture(s) within the context of the school, along with a provision of the skills necessary to live in mainstream society. Majority students are similarly provided for, and responsibility is imputed to both groups to realise this process of cultural difference and mutuality (Richmond Road School, 1983; 1985; 1986). A whakataukī (proverb) often quoted by the school encapsulates this ethos:

Nāu te rourou, Nāku te rourou, Ka ora te tangata

Your food basket, My food basket, Will give life to the people

What has resulted at Richmond Road is an approach to multicultural education that recognises the identities and claims of groups *as groups* and attempts to represent and legitimate their collective identities (Olneck, 1990) in its delivery of education. In so doing, the school has sought to reconstitute the school environment to the *real* educational advantage of minority children. As Laughton often said of previous policies in minority education, 'I don't know what's right in education, but over the years, these things have proved to me that at least for minority people, they haven't been successful. So what is the point of pursuing those same things?' (cited in Cazden, 1989: 145)

The Structure of the Account

The different directions which Richmond Road has pursued—both in establishing a coherent and powerful critical educational theory, and in realising this through structural diversity at the school level—mark the school as a site of educational and social change. In the following account of the school I have used Bernstein's (1971; 1990) categories of curriculum, pedagogy and evaluation as a broad framework for analysis, and have added the category of school organisation.[4] How the school's educational philosophy and practice came about, how it developed, and how it is currently understood and practised within the school are explored. Specific policies are detailed and, within my theoretical orientation, general conclusions and recommendations for practice are outlined. Jim Laughton figures prominently in much of what follows, but while Richmond Road is very much a testimony to Laughton's educational vision, perhaps the greatest testimony is that the school has continued on without him. By all accounts, it is what he would have wanted.

Notes to Chapter 5

1. The currently favourable staff to student ratio is a product of the historical provision of extra staffing for multiethnic schools like Richmond Road, and the falling roll situation the school now faces (see below). Richmond Road is officially designated a special staffing school and is consequently staffed on a notional roll 20% above normal staffing entitlement because of the high percentage of Māori and Pacific Island children at the school. In addition, Richmond Road's status as an officially designated bilingual school provides a ministerial Māori bilingual staff appointment and a kaiārahi reo (see glossary). The school also has two 1:20 staffing allocations which are provided by the government to lower class sizes and facilitate the reading recovery programme developed by Marie Clay (see Clay, 1979; 1985) and used nationally in New Zealand primary schools since 1988. This additional staffing obviously advantages the school. However, as I will argue, these benefits are not *necessary* for the success of the school's educational approach and programmes.

2. There are two types of primary school in New Zealand: full primary schools (usually rural) which have children from 5 years until they enter high school at 13 years; and contributing primary schools which only have children up until 10 years (Standard 4) when they then enter a two year intermediate school system prior to high school. Up until 1990, most primary schools were the latter. The policy of promoting the intermediate school system in New Zealand meant that unless a population area was too small to warrant a local intermediate, all primary schools in a given area were required to contribute to one. This saw the 'decapitation' of many full primary schools to contributing status. Richmond Road School underwent this decapitation process in 1976 when Ponsonby Intermediate School was established. It has only been recently that legislative changes have allowed primary schools to 'recapitate' to full primary status again if they so wish. Richmond Road has since done so; extending to Form 1 in 1992, and to Form 2 in 1993.

3. See the section on Bourdieu in Chapter 2 for a discussion of these terms.

4. I have used these categories because of their usefulness as an heuristic device. The categories need to be recognised, however, as inevitably somewhat arbitrary, particularly in light of Richmond Road's emphasis on an holistic educational approach. The distinctions drawn in the following chapters reflect this arbitrariness and exhibit, as such, a degree of overlap.

6 School Organisation: Achieving Structural Change

The whole business about diversity is obvious as soon as you look at Richmond Road School... Now at a superficial level a lot of schools then say 'well, we've got a multicultural school' [but] Laughton didn't say that. He said, 'well now we've got the material to make a multicultural school, whatever that means'. And the way he interpreted it... was [by]... creating structural diversity within the school. Now I think that's always to me been the... major difference... (Wally Penetito: Interview, 14 October, 1991)

The emergence of the school structures briefly described in Chapter 5 occurred during the time of Jim Laughton's principalship at Richmond Road. Prior to his arrival, the school had gained recognition for the innovations in reading associated with its junior school. However, like many other schools in New Zealand at that time, it had otherwise made little effort to accommodate for its multicultural clientele in its teaching and learning practices. Jim Laughton was to change all this.

Jim Laughton: Principal as Educational Visionary

Jim Laughton was an educational visionary. There is a remarkable consensus about this from those who knew him. The well known linguist Bernard Spolsky, writing on New Zealand education in the late 1980s, described Richmond Road as 'an innovative school...that has already attracted international attention; the principal, Jim Laughton, is a charismatic leader with a compelling vision of what elementary schooling can accomplish' (1989: 97). And Spolsky is not alone in his assessment; teachers, students, parents and educational officials consistently paint a similar picture of Laughton.

Interestingly, though, Laughton's beginnings in education, as a teacher trainee, were not particularly auspicious. Eric McMillan, who was deputy principal at the school from 1977–1982, and his contemporary, recalls that Laughton's enthusiasm for teacher training was variable at best and, at worst, nearly saw him removed from the course. That Laughton had come into teaching at all was due, as McMillan observes, to the teacher selection process in New Zealand 'reaching down for the first time into the working-classes and the Māori community...it hadn't done that [before]... We were paid therefore we could afford to go to College and we were left alone so we could be lazy, not get locked into too many things.[1] And then the sleepers forty years later, suddenly you have got a contribution to make...' (Interview, 26 February, 1991).

Laughton's contribution was to be seen most clearly at Richmond Road. However, in the interim, he taught in a range of country schools, including two sole-charge schools, and spent a period of time teaching in the secondary department of a rural high school as well as a period outside teaching. He was subsequently appointed as a Māori reading advisor and, immediately prior to Richmond Road, spent 5½ years as principal of a residential school for emotionally disturbed children. The collective ideas and experiences which he gained from these varied positions, most of which had involved teaching Māori children, were to form the basis of what he was to go on to establish at Richmond Road. As McMillan again comments: 'He got Richmond Road when he was quite young. He wouldn't have been much more than 40. And he was able to stay there for nearly 20 years and actually put into practice the developing ideas that he had' (ibid.) Those ideas, and the characteristics of the man behind them, bear closer examination.

'He had a very powerful presence and a fine mind'

Frank Churchward who followed Eric McMillan as deputy principal at Richmond Road specifically came to the school because of Jim:

> I think what greatly impressed me with Jim was his tremendous knowledge of people and education—of education in particular. Of many principals I've met he's probably the most widely read... A lot of principals, they're good people—ignorant's not the word—but they're narrow. You don't talk about philosophy with a lot of principals because they don't know what you're talking about anyway. *Jim was a philosopher and an educationalist.* And that's what impressed me about the man. He thought about what it was that he was doing. (Interview, 28 May, 1991)

Wally Penetito, a prominent Māori educationalist, ran numerous courses with Jim in the 1980s on multicultural education and developed a close friendship with him over that time. He recounts a similar response on first meeting Jim at an in-service course in the mid 1970s:

> I was impressed by the man's knowledge at that stage...the way he talked about things... When Jim talked about education he talked about it as

somebody talks about something which they know intimately, that they know very well—they've got a depth of knowledge and a depth of experience as well... Just the way he spoke about education, I knew that he wasn't an ordinary run-of-the-mill principal of a school. (Interview, 14 October, 1991)

Talking (and arguing) came naturally to Laughton. He had a formidable intellect, he had thought deeply about educational issues, and he had a remarkable capacity to articulate his considerations. As Penetito again observes:

Jim actually had an extraordinary way of latching on to things... He had a way of getting to the heart of...an issue, and dragging that out and putting it right up clear as hell... It was actually the insights into what he took that were incredible I used to find. Extraordinary...his handling of the English language, but...really his perception about ideas... (ibid.)

That knowledge, and the capacity to articulate it, feature prominently in others' accounts of Jim also. Steve Williams, a parent at Richmond Road, describes Laughton's intellectual ability as 'magical really—he just had so much knowledge...everything he did he thought out' (Interview, 17 November, 1992). Likewise, Judy Hucker, an ex-teacher at Richmond Road and now a principal herself, recalls:

Jim's personality was a major thing... You cannot talk about Richmond Road without talking about Jim Laughton. You ask me what I carry with me, I carry the bold, bearded bugger sitting on my shoulder talking about bilingual education, because I remember you'd get into the office and then you wouldn't get out for two hours because you'd end up with a discussion... (Interview, 15 August, 1991)

Helen Villers, who taught at Richmond Road from 1980–1986, recounts a similar experience on her first meeting Jim:

I just walked in off the street virtually one morning at the beginning of term and he spent most of the day with me. He was that sort of person—he'd just...put aside what he was probably supposed to be doing. And he and I just clicked, philosophically, just at that moment and he talked to me most of the day... I didn't get much of a word in! (laughs) Other people tell me they didn't either, and when you did get a word in it seemed pretty inconsequential! Anyway, I went away and I thought this is amazing...he can articulate the sorts of things that run round in probably a lot of people's heads at random and he takes them out and cleans them up... He could neatly sort out the strands of your thinking and lay them out on the table in the most exquisitely logical order, and you'd think 'yes, right, that's what I always thought'. But you never quite got it as straight as he was able to.

But, given the opportunity to talk with him and listen to him for long enough, you actually improved your own ability to articulate the sorts of...issues that he made us deal with. (Interview, 29 May, 1991)

As Villers suggests, talking with Jim facilitated the development of her own ideas (as it did others), but there is also an admission that his considerable intellect could intimidate at times. Penetito reiterates this point: 'I mean Jim, when he spoke about matters, he'd already given a great deal of thought to them. And he just loved to argue. A lot of people actually didn't argue with him I don't think. Because in some ways what he said sounded like the last word on the subject' (Interview, 14 October, 1991). Having said that, it is also clear from accounts of Jim that his thinking was not closed. As the current principal, Lionel Pedersen,[2] observes:

...if you actually knew Jim, he knew everything but it was always open. What developed with some staff members was a pathology—if you ask him he won't listen. It's 'no'. And that wasn't the case. What he did was he really spotted you. 'Well you believe that, now sit here and tell me why'. And of course in a lot of cases they couldn't because it was an emotional judgement... (Interview, 11 February, 1991)

Frank Churchward, a former deputy principal, also endorses this point strongly:

He was very firm in his beliefs, and if you had a point of view, where maybe it was a little different from the one he held, then he would argue it with you...but if you presented substantial arguments that were strong I know he'd go away and think about it...and if he was convinced by your arguments, then these things would be included into the way the school thought. (Interview, 28 May, 1991)

A key to the development of Jim Laughton's educational philosophy, in fact, was this ability to incorporate the knowledge of others. While holding strong views of his own he was always looking for ways to expand, and where necessary, change his own thinking. Eric McMillan, who preceded Churchward as deputy principal, comments about his experience of Laughton's willingness to explore new areas of knowledge:

McMillan: ...at that stage I was doing some work through Massey [University]—a curriculum theory paper, which was a very important paper, it brought a whole lot of ideas to the [current school] structures—so I took with me the texts of this material. He'd just come back from the Dip. Tesl.[3] He was very attracted to the ideas that had come through there—they appeared logical, Courtney Cazden's [work] on language for example—and he was putting together a whole lot of these views...

Interviewer: Had he read Freire?

McMillan: No, Freire came with my texts. He found that most interesting of course (laughs)—education of the powerless... Illich interested him too. He loved much of the texts that I took but what interested him... particularly, was the British school—R. S. Peters and Stenhouse.

Interviewer: Is it unusual though for a school principal to be so conversant with educational theory?

McMillan: I don't know. There are a lot of school principals who have come to face that material but whether they accept it or not, whether they could use it... I'm not at all convinced. But in his case, he was looking for things to fit to those ideas that he had developed... So all that I took was just added. Stuff that I had battled my way through and focused on to try and integrate something for myself...it then became a part of a coherent view of education [that he had]. That's what it was. Everything was consistent and not many people ever achieve that. *I think that he made an education philosophy work.* (Interview, 26 February, 1991)

It was this ability to articulate and make coherent a working philosophy of education which distinguished Jim Laughton as an educator, and an educational innovator, and has gained for his school a growing international reputation. What is apparent in reading through the school documents, and in talking with teachers and others associated with the school, is just how many visiting educationalists the school has hosted over the years. These educationalists have come to be associated with Richmond Road principally through Laughton and many have subsequently continued a long-standing involvement with the school.[4] Joy Glasson, who began at Richmond Road as a teacher in the language unit in the mid–1970s and proceeded through to deputy principal by the mid–1980s, comments concerning this:

Each of those people...respected him as an educator, I think almost uniquely. These people are recognised as world experts in their fields—the people he encountered—and I can't think of anyone who didn't come away from the encounters talking about him as an educator. That's true of people like Spolsky and the Goodmans, Courtney [Cazden] of course... All of those, and over the years there were a lot. There were times when it got so busy at school I threatened to put a sign outside that said, 'tours leaving at 11.00'! (Interview, 29 May, 1991)

McMillan reiterates this in his observation:

He could talk with and discuss with anybody who came. That's why people came. That's why Courtney kept coming. And she didn't go there to explain things. She went there to listen and so did people from all over. And sometimes the string of people flowing through was quite remarkable. *She claimed that he ran, had the most important primary school in the world, and he probably did.* (Interview, 26 February, 1991; my emphasis)

And yet Laughton was also careful, if not reticent, to tout the school as an educational model. As Penetito observes, 'he was keen to say to people, and I think he was absolutely genuine about it, "don't come asking me how we do what we do, I mean that's the way we do things... Don't take the whole thing away and transplant it. This is where it belongs"' (Interview, 14 October, 1991). He was also, as Penetito comments, quick to dismiss the superficial; those who were only interested in the easy answer:

he was equally passionate about people who were, I think Jim's term [was] charlatans—that were educationalists but didn't actually want to know, didn't want to get too detailed...didn't want to theorise about things, who wanted to know *the answer.* 'OK, you've been successful with Richmond Road School, tell me in ten words how you got there'... Now Jim, he'd read some of Paulo Freire so he knew about banking knowledge...and [he] went out of his way to tell people who wanted to muscle in on his place with these superficial understandings that they [had] to go away and do some homework. I don't really think Jim had any patience for that really. He... eliminated his opposition by not talking to them. But anybody who really wanted to talk education, whatever your philosophy of education was, had a willing ear every time. But you'd be in for a debate... (ibid.)

This debate, and the educational practice that resulted at Richmond Road, has been the focus of the interest shown towards the school:

Interviewer: It had a lot of international interest. Why do you think that was?

Helen Villers: Well there's the network isn't there—of ideas. There's all those theories about how ideas [don't] generate independently, they generate simultaneously. I think people were generating ideas at the time, and Jim a) articulated it and b) had a model, an operational model of the sorts of ideas that were beginning to—which *were* effective. (Interview, 29 May, 1991)

'I think...conflict theory was what interested him'

The operational model that Laughton developed at Richmond Road, and which has generated such interest, arose from his passionate concern for social justice. This concern extended to all disadvantaged groups, but is exemplified in his view of Māori (his own people) within education:

He was concerned about Māori children because he used to say that [they] sat on the inside of that brown skin—and whenever he spoke with Pacific Island or Māori children he was very aware of being inside the skin looking out. It was—he said it many times—about children coming for education cap in hand. That was the patronising system that schools [represented]. He said you've got to get the cap out of their hand and stick it where it belongs on their heads! (laughs) (Eric McMillan: Interview, 26 February, 1991)

Folole Asaua, a Samoan student who went through Richmond Road in the 1980s and is now nearing the end of secondary school, still vividly remembers that interest and concern:

There was something about him that we really liked. I guess it was his manner, his personality, his attitude towards us children when we were young…his way of approaching us. We would usually be afraid of principals, but he was more like a down-to-earth person. He was very caring—encouraging. He was like another teacher, like another parent to us, which was really good… He was a really great principal. (Interview, 21 November, 1992)

This might not be particularly remarkable in itself (there are, no doubt, many principals who could be described with such affection), except that Laughton went on to actualise this concern for minority students by completely changing the institutional culture of his school. Asaua also makes this point: 'When he died, I think his wife mentioned at his service that 95% of him was for the school—he spent a lot of that time with the school… He did a lot of things for us—there was a lot of change throughout the years. I guess he would do things for us—what we wanted—he'd do what we want, as best for our school' (ibid.). Joy Glasson, who worked closely with Jim in her time at the school, elaborates further:

Interviewer: What was Jim wanting to achieve?

Glasson: Something that empowered kids and empowered their families in a true sense of the word, so that it wasn't lip service…that says, 'OK we'll empower you, but we'll still fit you into the system, into the majority middle-class white system'. Empowerment actually comes from knowledge and becoming independent…that's why everything else in the school was always geared to…making kids independent…so kids could actually walk out the door and not look back. Because everything about our school system tells kids they're dependent—on teachers, and on schools, and on all of those bureaucratic structures. It says you can't operate without them, and [this] school is about the opposite. It's about telling people that you *can* make decisions, and they're yours to make—you have the right to make them...because you are important, you've got strengths, you've got knowledge. (Interview, 29 May, 1991)

This emphasis on empowerment and the fostering of independence, however, was not limited to the realm of idealism or good intentions. It had a hard edged pragmatism as well:

> One of the things that Jim always quoted was from Tolstoy... 'I sit on a man's back choking him and making him carry me and yet assure myself and others that I'm sorry for him and wish to lighten his load by all possible means except by getting off his back'. The other one was C. Wright Mills in *The Sociological Imagination* [1959]—'To those with power and are aware of it impute responsibility. To those with power but who are unaware of it, educate them and then impute responsibility. To those without power, inform them about what the others are up to!' So for him a lot of what we did was really all about *access to power*...so that when you ask how children did that was actually one of his overriding concerns—that children went out with all the self-esteem things and everything else, but *it wasn't a soft woolly headed liberalism*... in as much that the skill base of things was very important to Jim as well. It was certainly important. (Judy Hucker: Interview, 15 August, 1991; my emphasis)

The result can be seen in the twin emphases of 'cultural maintenance' and 'access to power' (see also Chapter 5) which characterise the school today. This dual emphasis addresses the concerns I discussed at length in Chapters 2 and 3 of providing an approach to education which is culturally pluralist but not academically isolationist. That is, an approach which achieves both cultural and language diversity *and* academic excellence through structural change at the school level. It developed from Laughton's engagement with the work of the Victorian Institute of Secondary Education in Australia and, in particular, their report on developing 'socially critical' schools (Kemmis, 1983). The report had argued for curriculum debate and innovation as a means to achieving social change. Laughton, however, wished to extend this to include, not only curriculum, but also 'the process of learning, teaching interaction and communication, policy formation, community participation, evaluation and counselling' (1985: 17; cited in Churchward, 1991: 42). How he went about this radical and comprehensive process of change within the school is where I now want to turn.

The Process of Change

Maybin (1985), in her discussion of whole-school language policies, argues that establishing school-wide change means talking about and working through curriculum change, and that this is neither a short nor easy process. Richmond Road demonstrates the truth of this observation clearly because while Laughton had specific educational intentions for the school that he came to as principal in 1972, his plans for change were gradual and carefully managed over the ensuing sixteen years of his principalship. At all times in this process Laughton acted as a facilitator—working with his staff, rather than imposing change upon them, and being sensitive to individual staff members' capacity for change. Accordingly, while some staff left, and some adapted more quickly than others to the changed structures, curriculum, and pedagogy which were implemented at the school, all staff who remained came eventually to own these changes for themselves. This enduring sense of ownership remains one of the school's key strengths today, as does its capacity after Laughton's death to continue to initiate and respond to change.

The establishment of the family grouping or rōpū structure[5]—the principal area of reorganisation upon which Laughton embarked—provides us with an example of this process at work. Laughton only began to move towards significantly changing the traditional single cell classroom structures at the school towards the end of 1977. Prior to then he had made only minor changes in classroom structures. He had introduced open plan organisation for year 1 & 2 infants and had distributed New Entrants (NE; year 1) across junior classes. The establishment of the Inner-City Language and Reception Unit in 1976 had resulted in a two teacher Standard 1–4 (S1–4; 7–10 yrs) class. And, in 1977, he had set up two-year open plan groupings in infant classes, and a composite S1–2 and composite S3–4 class. The arrival of a new deputy principal, however, with a similar commitment to change, saw Laughton move to establish a family group which included the full range of pupils, using the new deputy principal and the assistant principal to model the development.

> So I went to see him on being offered the…job, to see what the job was to be… and he talked about wanting to rearrange the place in ways that not too many—*any* schools had tried before. He wanted to operate a single class covering the whole range of kids…with me running the class together with [the assistant principal] and teaching it half time. At that time I was very dissatisfied with teaching…and I'd just about had a gutsful…but the idea of this particular [way of teaching], I hadn't done that, so I thought I'd give it a shot. (Eric McMillan: Interview, 26 February, 1991)

The use of senior teachers who were willing to model such an approach was a clearly thought out strategy to give the organisational changes status within the school. As McMillan recalls:

> I was there long enough to bring through the first kids that we had—they came right through. It wasn't randomly selected early on, we got the two most experienced teachers in one class together and we put in [the whole range of children with them]. So a lot of our older kids weren't there long but to counter that we put in at the bottom end some of the brightest children

and it was watching them come through, I think that's what kept us there (laughs)—to see how they would go! (ibid.)

By 1981 the school had been divided into two basic teaching levels—Level 1, NE-S1 (5–7 yrs), and Level 2, S1–4 (7–10 yrs)[6]—to complement the development of the initial NE-S4 family group. It was from this time that Laughton went on to establish family groups across the whole school; gradually encouraging teachers into fully extended age groups. In 1984 another three teacher NE-S4 group, as well as a four teacher NE-S4, were set up. In 1985 the Māori bilingual programme was established as a Level 1 class and extended to NE-S3 in 1986. And in 1987, the whole school, including the Māori bilingual unit, was organised into six NE-S4 family groups. At that stage, a Samoan bilingual unit was also begun as an NE-S1 class and incorporated into a larger family group.

After Laughton's death, the process of change has continued. The Samoan bilingual unit was extended to NE-S3 in 1989, and to NE-S4 in 1990, and remains a part of a larger three teacher rōpū. One English-language unit was disbanded in 1990 because of falling rolls and spread across the school—leaving five rōpū—and in 1991, a Cook Islands bilingual unit was established and incorporated into one of the remaining English-language rōpū. With the school's recent recapitation to Form 2 (12 yrs), the rōpū have been further extended in age range. The establishment of Māori, Samoan and Cook Islands pre-schools on site at the school over the period 1985–1989 has also complemented these developments. They provide direct links between the school and local ethnic groups and also provide many of the children who go on to the bilingual rōpū within the school.

At present then (1993), the school has five rōpū or family groups. Rōpū 1, which remains solely English medium; Rōpū 2, which now incorporates the Cook Islands bilingual unit; Rōpū 3, which includes the Samoan bilingual unit;[7] Rōpū 4, the Māori bilingual unit; and Rōpū 5, the Inner-City Language Unit. Three of these rōpū have two teachers and two rōpū have three teachers. The two associate principals (APs) share a teaching role to make up a three teacher group.[8] The current school organisation can be seen in Figure 6.1

In 1983–1984 an architectural remodelling of the school was also undertaken to facilitate the transition to teaching in family groups. This remodelling created the four 'shared spaces' (SS1–4) from which Rōpū 1–4 now operate.[9] The variable teaching spaces which have resulted provide an open and interactive environment well suited to family group organisation. A description of SS1 closely reflects the organisation of other shared spaces:

> SS1 can be divided down the middle. On one side are two carpeted teaching spaces (home group rooms) which, while open plan (there are no doors or partitions), are clearly distinguishable. The other side consists of an open

```
                                      ┌─ Te Apii Reo Kuki Airani ─┐
┌──────────────────┐          ┌──────────────────────────────────┐
│ Rōpū 1           │          │                           Rōpū 2 │
│ NE-F2            │          │                             NE-F2 │
│ English Language │          │        English/Cook Islands Bilingual │
│ (2 Teachers)     │          │                       (2 Teachers) │
└──────────────────┘          └──────────────────────────────────┘
```

```
              ┌──────────────────────────────────────────────┐
              │ Rōpū 5                                         │
              │ Inner City Language Unit                       │
              │ (3 teachers, including teaching assistant)     │
              └──────────────────────────────────────────────┘
```

```
┌─ A'oga Fa'a Samoa ─┐                    ┌─ Ritimana Kōhanga Reo ─┐
┌─────────────────────────────────┐   ┌──────────────────────────────────┐
│ Rōpū 3                          │   │                           Rōpū 4 │
│ NE-F2                           │   │                             NE-F2 │
│ English/Samoan Biligual         │   │                    Māori Bilingual │
│ (3 teachers, including APs rotating) │ │ (3 teachers, including Kaiārahi reo) │
└─────────────────────────────────┘   └──────────────────────────────────┘
```

Figure 6.1 Richmond Road Primary School Organisation, 1993

linoleum area which includes children's lockers, resources, art table and sinks and, in one corner, a kiva (a raised area where children can go for time out). Colourful posters and tapestries (all children's work) adorn the walls. There is a book corner in each home group room but books are numerous throughout the classroom—a table with open books is also prominent. There are no teacher desks in either home group room and no hierarchy of organisation (rows etc.). Children sit together at desks or independently on the floor... (Field Notes, 22 August, 1990)

'Jim said...there are features of the ideal family that could be emulated in the school'

The structural changes which Laughton undertook in establishing family groupings at Richmond Road were underpinned by his belief that school relationships, as traditionally construed, undermined and excluded minority group children. The family grouping approach—with its emphasis on inclusiveness and mutual support, and its development of extended relationships—was for him a means of redressing this. As Frank Churchward recalls: 'One of the things [Jim] said to me was that if we look at the ideal family...he wanted to see that in operation, to come alive within the school itself... That I found a very powerful argument' (Interview, 28 May, 1991). A teacher interviewed in Cazden's study of the school states a very similar position: 'Jim said there are many things from the family that can't be replicated in the school; but there are many things that can be. That was his urgent drive: to see what *could* be replicated' (cited in Cazden, 1989: 150).[10]

The family group concept highlighted for Laughton the notions of collectivism, collaboration, democracy, and interdependence among both students and teachers. He wished to create interactive and democratic teaching and learning environments in which students (particularly ethnic minority students) could feel comfortable and could thrive academically. His reasoning rested on the cultural continuity of this learning environment with the backgrounds of many of the minority students at the school, and on his belief in child-centred and process-based learning (see Chapter 7). Establishing the rōpū structure was for Laughton a means of increasing the alternatives available to minority children by:

(1) increasing the age and ability range with which children were in contact;

(2) providing children with opportunities to experience a variety of roles and to develop an appropriate range of social skills; and

(3) assisting the growth of self-respect through the recognition of ethnic diversity and the wide range of skills, interests and cultural perspectives children would bring to the group as a whole.

The concept had arisen from Laughton's experiences in sole-charge country schools where multi-level teaching was a necessity. The implications of developing these long term relational structures in a diverse urban school, however, required a significant realignment in the thinking of both teachers and pupils: 'It soon became clear that there were a whole lot of things that happened once you put children in a vertical group—that it more approximated the [extended] families that those children knew. And so the description of an extended family model, taking some of the qualities of the extended family and applying them to schools, [saw] a whole lot of things come together' (Eric McMillan: Interview, 26 February, 1991). McMillan, who initiated these changes with Laughton, goes on to observe:

> The moment you take children out of that single year range [there are] a whole lot of other things that you then have to identify—the obvious things are that you make for a longer term relationship with the teacher. That was the first thing that Jim ever said—that if you have kids for a year, then for the first term you can scare them into submission, for the second term you can watch while the roof comes off, and for the third term you contain them before you'll be moving them on. So you've only got ten months and that's not long enough. If you've got them for two or three or...six years—then you've got to come to grips with the reality of it. You can't hide anything. You can't suppress things. It's *got* to work. But also, importantly, it takes away a large chunk of the competitive element [between kids] because [Jim]

always emphasised that it was cooperative not competitive... You've got competitive structures in the school and it was to break that down. (ibid.)

Joy Glasson elaborates on this point:

That's why multi-level was so important, because it brought kids together, and it showed that they all have strengths. They all have areas where they need support, that everybody's important and everybody has responsibilities... The vertical grouping [also] actually made teachers operate in different ways. They no longer could stand at the front of the class and berate kids for six hours a day. They went mad, so did the kids. They had to find ways that they could allow kids to operate for themselves—where teachers couldn't take control of it. And then they had to find ways to work with kids in small groups or to work with kids as individuals. What that did, of course, was it actually allowed people to operate with kids at every different level that they were at. To do it they had to know where the kids were, and so that resulted in very deep systems of knowing kids, of watching kids, monitoring kids, being able to very accurately match kids to materials. (Interview, 29 May, 1991)

For Laughton, family groupings give more power and choices to everyone. There is more room for independence but this is paralleled by the expectation that responsibility towards the whole group be accepted:

Inherent within the [family group] organization is the integration of belief systems which emphasize group rather than individual values. If cultural maintenance is to be a priority at Richmond Road School then stress must be placed on values which contribute to the strength of the group as a whole rather than on those which are individualistic. This kind of system is necessary to support cultural transmission in the curriculum. (Richmond Road School, 1986: 3)

Cultural features which emphasise collectivism take precedence over those which are individualistic, thus forming the basis for the characteristic ethos of the school—cooperation rather than competition. Acceptance of this kind of responsibility is inherent in rōpū organisation; socially, by demonstrating care for others, and educationally through peer support activities such as paired reading. The latter activity, for example, sees children with competency at any particular reading level—not necessarily the best in the group—involved in working with children who are at other stages of development (see Chapter 7). This encourages the growth of skills which will lead to independence within a supportive, cooperative environment and, as I have already suggested, is consistent with the values of the minority cultures of many of the students. Individualism is not diminished within a cooperative learning approach. Rather, individualism *as competitive isolation*—a peculiarly western conception (see Chapter 3)—is reconceptualised at Richmond Road within the broader context of mutual accountability.

Laughton was aware of the educational benefits of cooperative learning arrangements for all children (see Slavin, 1983; Yeomans, 1983) but, particularly, for ethnic minority children. In subsequent multicultural and antiracist literature, cooperative learning has also been recognised as a key pedagogical strategy (see Lynch, 1987; Nieto, 1992; Troyna, 1993). Sonia Nieto argues, for example, that 'providing an educational environment that emphasizes cooperative learning rather than individual competition is [an] important culturally appropriate strategy to consider' (1992: 104). Moana Saulala, a Tongan ex-student of Richmond Road, clearly endorses this conception: 'It's the same as working at home, because at school you work sort of like a family. And then you go home and you do the same thing' (Interview, 21 November, 1992). Similarly, a teacher in Cazden's study observes:

> I like vertical grouping; I think it's excellent. I would *not* like ever to go back to a straight class. I like the way children fit in. I think of Māori in particular. In a regular school, they start school as 5-year olds, probably with no pre-school education. So straightaway they're on a sort of back foot, compared with others. Whereas here they could gain confidence. They fitted in perhaps way down here. But then in their own time, they could work up, without the feeling of always not making it. For me that was great—not only for Māori children, but for *all* children. (cited in Cazden, 1989: 151)

Two strands of the family group process are highlighted here: the recognition of cultural difference, and the supportive and integrative family environment which frames such recognition:

> Family grouping...rests on the idea of integration of differences—differences of ethnicity, age, ability, gender, interest and knowledge. These factors are brought together so children may grow in knowledge, appreciation and respect for themselves and others...they are encouraged to take responsibility for their own learning and [to] support the learning process of those around them. (Richmond Road School, 1986: 4)

The combination of recognising both cultural difference and cultural inclusiveness does not, as one might expect, diminish the fostering of cultural maintenance. Rather, the centrality of cultural *recognition* is complemented by an emphasis on cultural *interaction*. All children at Richmond Road are imputed with responsibilities in the process of working out intercultural relationships. However, recognition is still accorded to the processes of power relations which usually weight the equation against children from minority groups. In effect, the notion of integration is critically reconstituted in family grouping. As the school argues, the aim of the rōpū structure is 'to *integrate* the many diverse elements for the benefit of all without diminishing the distinctiveness or the status of each; in the definition of the Concise Oxford Dictionary "to complete by the addition of (all) parts"' (Richmond Road School, 1986: 2).

The atmosphere of collaboration and mutual support which has resulted from family grouping is consistently mentioned as a key characteristic of the school; by parents, teachers and pupils. All the ex-pupils I talked with, for example, who are now in Form 6 (16 yrs) at secondary school, emphasised the family atmosphere of the school in their recollections. One of these students, Papa Lane, compared Richmond Road with another primary school she went to briefly: 'it was more of a family, more comfortable at Richmond Road...you felt more comfortable around your own people [Lane is Māori] and you had more confidence at Richmond Road because you had that kind of [family] support from other children and teachers as well' (Interview, 17 November, 1992). Parents, too, are enthusiastic about this cooperative and supportive atmosphere, and not only those parents from minority groups. When I asked Shona Matthews, a Pākehā parent, what particularly appealed to her about Richmond Road she argued strongly for the social as well as educational benefits of rōpū: 'The children are just enormously friendly...my oldest daughter was very very shy at five [yrs old], and yet she just settled in [to a family group] beautifully. The older children were wonderful—they really cared for her and looked after her. And I think she settled in much more readily than she probably would have into a [standard] New Entrant situation' (Interview, 17 November, 1992). But the process of change in establishing these relational structures, at least for teachers initially, was not always as well received.

'People have been known to stay until morning tea and disappear'

The establishment of family groupings required a radical reconceptualisation of the teaching process for teachers at Richmond Road, and that, necessarily, did not come easily. As Graeme Page, a parent with a long-standing involvement in the school, comments:

> You've got to change staff. To organise this [school] from a single cell organisation to what it is now must have been a difficult task when individual teachers believed they should be autonomous within the classroom. You're actually changing these people's concepts. It wouldn't be an easy feat. Obviously every time you do those things you're going to have drop outs. A lot of people see cooperative [arrangements] as interference, because they know better. Yet we all know that [traditional] systems never work for minority groups. (Interview, 14 August, 1991)

Inevitably, there were 'drop outs'. As Wally Penetito observes:

> ...there have been those who came to Richmond Road who haven't stayed long. There have been those who've come to Richmond Road who the school hasn't wanted to keep long! I mean Jim was never bashful about that either if people didn't belong there. He wanted people to *choose* to be there—the same way he wanted kids to choose to be there, and their parents—by showing them the diversity that Richmond Road was. And his philosophy again was 'this is what's here—it's yours, you're welcome to it. If you don't want it, go to wherever it is—whatever it is you [do] want'. (Interview, 14 October, 1991)

Lionel Pedersen, the current principal, reiterates the cost of this change process for teachers: 'when [Jim] first came here it was a tremendously generative time. A lot of people left because they couldn't hack it, but those who stayed were part of the changes' (Interview, 11 February, 1991). However, even those who stayed did not necessarily find adjusting to the new organisational and teaching arrangements easy. Helen Villers clearly recalls the difficulties involved in first learning to teach extended family groups in shared spaces:

> Every area [SS1–4] found their own way of coping with it. Jim was very patient about that too. Again he saw it as a process, and he wouldn't intervene unless it was critical, but often people wanted to crawl off into their corner with their own little group of children. And for a while, while people found their feet, or a team found their feet, that was probably OK. But then he would start talking about and generating ideas about how to be more integrated... (Interview, 29 May, 1991)

Laughton's role in facilitating the development of family group organisation was central to its success. He provided strong direction and had high expectations of his staff but was also aware of the need to give those willing to change sufficient time to do so. As Judy Hucker argues: 'I think you've got to realise that Richmond Road was something that actually spanned 14–15 years of development. The actual physical organisation into family groups would have taken five or six years' (Interview, 15 August, 1991). More crucially perhaps, he was also able to provide his staff with ongoing development and support within this process—principally through an intensive programme of staff development. Staff *learnt* about teaching at Richmond Road, in ways they would never have otherwise, and in ways they never had before.

Ko te hunga hanga whare na te whare ano rātou i hanga: 'They who build the house are built by the house'

Staff development was the key strategy Laughton employed at Richmond Road to create a cohesive, informed and committed staff, and the fulcrum of that development was the staff meeting. As Margaret Leaming, a local education department official, comments:

> One of the things that I saw there that I never saw anywhere else, was the (pause)—here was a school with an in-built staff development programme...so that the staff meetings there, for instance—staff meeting seems such a pathetic name for what they did there—were such that there was this enforced sharing of knowledge... I never saw that anywhere else at all... I saw schools that had professional components in their staff meetings, but I didn't see one where it was built in...absolutely built in and implicit into the structure, totally into the structure of the school. (Interview, 28 May, 1991)

Frank Churchward describes what would happen in staff meetings:

> Say, for example, you had put in front of Jim [an academic] paper. You would initially describe things that were in this paper and arguments that were being presented [in a staff meeting], and then we'd all take it away, read it thoroughly, and come back several weeks later for more in-depth discussion...a trivial example of this [might be] that kids write better with blue ballpoint pens than with red ballpoint pens. Jim would say 'let's find out why that is thought to be true'. So we would get all the information and we'd read and read and read, and then...in the end you might say 'right, all the research and all the evidence that we can gather to this minute proves that blue is better than red'. Then we would adopt that. (Interview, 28 May, 1991)

Laughton *made* his teachers learn theory as the basis for their practice and that was an unusual process for teachers to have to undergo. As Churchward again observes, 'a lot of teachers are stunning people—they're hard workers, they're good practitioners, they're good technicians—but they don't always think in depth about the process of learning' (ibid.). Penetito expands on Laughton's cultivation of this theorised approach to practice at Richmond Road:

> Jim was keen that his teachers not only should be good practitioners but that the whole definition of a *good* practitioner meant someone who knew what they were doing—understood their practice. And in order to understand your practice you have to be able to theorise about it... You need to deal with these theoretical things because you need to be able to articulate it—you need to be able to talk about it. You [also] need to be able to improve on it

and you do that by making it real— by taking ideas in the abstract and applying them in real situations. (Interview, 14 October, 1991)

However, while Laughton provided the impetus and expectations for such learning, he did not dominate proceedings. The learning process for teachers came principally through their own active (and interactive) participation:

> I got very excited by the way he thought about things—the things we would discuss at staff meetings. When I went to the school I did Marie Clay's reading papers to complete my Bachelors degree, so I had some things to offer, and I know Jim would pick up [on that] and if he recognised that you had perhaps a bit of skill then he was adamant or anxious that we share it with each other... *He made sure that what we had was shared with the staff.* (Frank Churchward: Interview, 28 May, 1991; my emphasis)

Helen Villers recounts a similar experience:

Villers: He made me talk. He made me discuss a lot of papers in the staff meetings. I was finishing my degree at the time and he knew I was interested in [these] sorts of issues, but shy about talking, and he dropped me in the deep end... We all had to do it. Each of us.

Interviewer: No-one was exempted?

Villers: No, never. And the other thing that you had to do was chair the staff meeting. I think they probably still do that on a rotating basis, and do the karakia [prayer; see glossary]... I'll never forget the first time I had to do that! So you're dropped in it. And I'd have to say that it was harder for teachers in that school than it was for kids, which is probably the way it should be, but there were no soft options for teachers at all. (Interview, 29 May, 1991)

Staff meetings were long affairs and, along with many other aspects of the school, required an unusual degree of commitment from teachers. As Judy Hucker recalls, 'it was a total expectation that Tuesday was staff meeting day and you did not have anything else on that day' (Interview, 15 August, 1991). However, as Hucker goes on to observe, the commitment from teachers to staff development was principally sustained by their ownership of the process: '[Jim] got huge commitment from his staff. Mind you...in terms of staff meetings...it was curriculum, it was staff development—staff were always involved, so they owned it... I wouldn't have, and I don't think many [other] people would actually have done it had it not been useful' (ibid.).

Little has changed at Richmond Road in that regard. Thinking in depth about educational issues remains a characteristic of the school today and staff meetings, which are still held every Tuesday afternoon, follow a remarkably similar format. Lionel Pedersen, the current principal, operates in a similar manner to Laughton; facilitating rather than dominating proceedings. Staff meetings remain lengthy (3–4 hours was not unusual) and the expectations concerning attendance are unchanged. The curriculum content of the meetings also continues to provide the focus of activities. Over the three years of my association with the school, for example, the bulk of staff meeting time has been taken up in revisiting key theorists in the school's educational development. This has been principally for the benefit of staff who have come to the school since Laughton's death in 1988. However, Richmond Road staff have also in that time explored the work of Jim Cummins (whom they have come to know of more recently) and, arising out of my theoretical interests and involvement in the school, the work of Pierre Bourdieu. Staff meetings have also been a collective forum for the appraisal, discussion, and criticism of my own work.[11]

In addition to the staff meeting, other support systems for staff development, also established by Laughton, continue to operate. Each teacher on arriving at the school receives a personal folder, which comprises both the educational articles that have been discussed over the years, and the rationales which the school has developed from these to inform its practice.[12] A teacher release system, combined with the shared teaching arrangements of the rōpū, allow for individual teachers to be released every morning to look at curriculum issues. And curriculum teams which are presently in the areas of Science, Art, Music & Expressive Arts, and Health & Physical Education—and which deliberately cut across the rōpū teaching teams—have also been established within the school to foster curriculum development and to resource student learning (see Chapter 8).

All of these systems set in place for staff development by Laughton aim to foster within teachers an understanding of the processes of teaching and the processes of learning. They have also been central to establishing an approach to education which meets the needs of its ethnically diverse school population. As Lynch argues, 'staff development for teacher educators and teachers in schools is in a very real sense an indisputable fulcrum to progress on educational policies addressing democratic cultural diversity, and each institution needs a comprehensive staff development programme subject to continuing monitoring and review against negotiated criteria' (1986: 192). Richmond Road demonstrably fits such criteria. However, the school has also taken this a step further by cultivating—within its staff development process—a broader understanding of schooling's function in society and the unequal power relations which schooling traditionally perpetuates:

> Richmond Road School...is one of the few places I know of—maybe the only place I know of in terms of schools—that can hold a lucid debate about the way in which power works in the infant classroom. Again most people

think power is something that exists 'outside'. I mean it's (pause)—you've first of all got to be dealing with policy...in education. [Teachers at Richmond Road] can actually talk about it in terms of what teachers do with kids *inside* classrooms and they can talk about it...by taking a theoretical stance on it to begin with. 'What...do we mean by power?' And then, 'how does it work in this place?' 'Is it quantifiable, and who's got it if it is?' 'How do they use it?' The people in that school could talk like that and could deal with all those subjects. And most schools, they don't want to know to start with...that's one of the real problems...it's too hard [for them]. (Wally Penetito: Interview, 14 October, 1991)

Lionel Pedersen endorses this in his observation that there is no substitute for wide teacher knowledge. He goes on to suggest that Laughton's cultivation of this principle at Richmond Road has seen an enormous accumulation of knowledge among staff on the nature and process of teaching (Field Notes, 26 February, 1990). Teachers at Richmond Road are *reflective* practitioners. Their involvement in, and approach to, curriculum decision-making allies closely with the action research paradigm and its particular emphasis on developing 'critically informed action' (Kemmis & McTaggart, 1988).[13] Critically informed action requires that teachers become experts in particular curriculum fields and also asks them to take account of any theoretical knowledge (beyond that normally associated with everyday professional knowledge) that might be of use to them. Once this is achieved, teachers—as participants in the curriculum decision-making process—can plan action together, act and observe individually and collectively, and reflect together. They can also then reformulate more critically informed plans because this cyclical approach allows for flexibility and responsiveness in dealing with continuing emergent concerns, needs and developments (Carr & Kemmis, 1983; Kemmis & McTaggart, 1988). It is this critical and reflective knowledge base of teaching and learning present within the school which acts to contest the hegemonic forces at work within education. The resulting approach to multicultural education is one which 'move[s] beyond theorizing about our practice along the lines of "this works for me" ...to ask questions instead about why we act as we do, and whose interests are served by continuing in this manner' (Smyth, 1989: 57).

'Every time they changed the rules, he took advantage of them'

Theoretical literacy (and the oppositional practices which result from that) is not confined simply to a knowledge of educational research at Richmond Road. The school is also familiar with current educational legislation and provisions, and uses its knowledge fully in the resistance strategies that inform its school practice. Again, this was a strategy first fostered by Laughton. He was aware of the institutional obstacles he was likely to face in implementing educational change at Richmond Road and sought, where possible, to circumvent them:

> I've come to understand as I've come to know the school better and you come to know Laughton better, that...in a multiethnic school where he's trying to do something that fits the multiethnic vision that he's got in mind...that that's actually going to be up against the machinery of the state. It's up against all the conventional wisdom... I think the school got a hard time from all the powers that be over a long [period of] time. I mean Laughton just kind of learnt what the rules were and played right up to the edge of the rules. But I mean he *knew* the rules. I think anybody who's going to play right up to the edge of the rules needs to know them. And that's hindsight. But that's the way they worked. (Wally Penetito: Interview, 14 October, 1991)

In discussing how Laughton was able to set up one of the first inner-city Māori bilingual units in the country at Richmond Road (in 1985), Graeme Page, a parent and Board of Trustees member, makes a similar observation: 'You were allowed to, so he did... A lot of people used to think that Jim did things illegally but he didn't. They changed the rules and he was always the first cab off the rank prepared to do it, and able to make a change' (Interview, 14 August, 1991). Likewise in 1986, Laughton was one of the first to secure a kaiārahi reo [Māori language assistant; see glossary] for the school, on the initial establishment of these positions nationally. As John Matthews, who was appointed to this position, recalls, 'I was one of the early ones. I think there [were] 26 of us appointed throughout New Zealand that year, and that was the first year they were established' (Interview, 25 May, 1991).

Laughton was concerned with access to power, not only for the minority children at Richmond Road but for the school itself, and he knew how to get it. Margaret Leaming illustrates this in her comment on Jim's approach to her in her role as staff inspector to the school:

> I think that the thing that Jim Laughton also did well, if you want to look at things, he recognised power and where it was... He knew what I could do for the school and what I couldn't do, he didn't waste time...asking me to do something that he needed to write to Wellington [the Department of Education's head office] about—he was very good at that. I think it's a point of view, it could be argued, that Māori people have not been good at—knowing where the sources of power are. Of course we [Pākehā] are very good at that, we're brought up to it. And so the whole business of your children finding employment if you like when they leave school... European people, particularly middle-class people, know where to go. (Interview, 28 May, 1991)

To redress this imbalance in power relations to which Leaming refers (see also the discussion on Bourdieu's notions of 'cultural capital' and 'symbolic violence' in Chapter 2), Laughton undertook to know what legislative avenues of resistance were available to him, and the minority groups on whose behalf he worked. As Penetito observes: 'Laughton's way of doing things was that they were more familiar with the legislation than probably most schools are. I mean, they don't only look at that stuff, they actually examine it... You name the legislation...if it has some effect on their school they get down and study it' (Interview, 14 October, 1991). The result has been the additional staffing and resources which the school has enjoyed over the years, and which is reflected in the currently favourable staff to student ratio. Penetito continues:

> ...they seemed to get a hell of a lot more, I mean I think the schools were jealous of what Richmond Road had because Richmond Road was able to get a whole lot of things that other schools never had. That's because, again, [Jim] went to the trouble of finding out what is out there to have and how you get it, and went about getting it...and as far as he was concerned that was the way in which anybody else could operate if they chose to. The fact that they didn't was their problem, not his. (ibid.)

It is a practice that still continues at Richmond Road. Over the course of 1991–1992, for example, the school used its knowledge of current educational legislation to successfully fight to retain its above entitlement staffing provisions. During this same period, Richmond Road used changes in legislation to become one of the first primary schools in the country to recapitate to Form 2 level. However, it has been their recent involvement in a national three year trial for local funding of schools which, perhaps, best exemplifies the school's continued use of current legislation as a resistance strategy. This local funding trial, implemented by a conservative government, has created particular controversy in New Zealand. Education unions have vehemently opposed the move towards local funding; arguing that it will increasingly disadvantage schools that draw pupils from lower socio-economic groups. Richmond Road, however, rejects this position. The school accepts that fiscal devolution is increasingly likely, given the current political climate in New Zealand, and advocates that schools with lower socio-economic populations need to preempt, and circumvent, these developments. This requires, first, learning how to cope with such changes and, second, being able to take advantage of them. As Graeme Page argues, in his role of Board of Trustees member, the educational system is inequitable in whatever form it takes and so the best way forward is to remain as autonomous as possible: 'We want to be in charge of our own destiny and we have always pushed to get as much control as we can under the old system. Self-determination is part of our school philosophy...it is important not to be afraid of it' (*Dominion Sunday Times*, 6 December, 1992: 13).

As Page's comment indicates, Richmond Road has developed a healthy awareness and scepticism of the power relations implicit in wider institutional settings, and a proactive stance in contesting and exploiting these relations. Knowledge of educational provision is one key aspect of this, but it is not the only one. There is also a sense in which, as another form of resistance, Richmond Road is careful not to let the interest it has engendered as an innovative school undermine what the school is wanting to achieve:

> when visitors came [to Richmond Road] they were made to jump through certain hoops to start with...they wouldn't let them loose in the place. All these people want to do is say 'let me loose, I want to see what's going on here and make my own mind up about what I see'. But Richmond Road did actually some of the shaping of what you see... People who are less powerful in society, like minority groups, tend to be more open about the world that they live in—open it up for scrutiny more often... They tend to have open worlds and the powerful people of the world have a closed world. Now if you've got closed-world people coming into [an] open-world institution, what Richmond Road has learned is [not to allow] this. You shape their thinking before they do any of that. You at least make sure they know what you're on about... (Wally Penetito: Interview, 14 October, 1991)

What comes through consistently here is the realist approach that Laughton and Richmond Road have taken on the position of minority groups in a society where the power relations lie with the dominant group. This critical perspective makes their resistance all the more effective. In so doing, of course, they have also undertaken to speak on behalf of the various ethnic communities represented in their school population. This is not necessarily an easy task and they have, as such, been careful to reflect closely the aspirations and concerns of these groups. While I have concentrated in much of this chapter on the internal organisation of the school, I want to conclude by examining this broader relationship between the school and its local community.

The School and its Community: Fostering Reciprocal Relationships

School and community relationships at Richmond Road are strong and characterised by a surprising degree of involvement from parents in all aspects of school life. Parents feature prominently around the school and their involvement is not constrained to the usual role of sitting outside the principal's office. Parents contribute at times to the teaching within rōpū, particularly with regard to cultural matters. They are welcome to observe or participate in the rōpū at any time, and often do so. And they can be regularly seen at assemblies and other school functions. The strong links between the community run pre-schools and the school also help to foster close school and community relations. In Cazden's study, an American educator, Mary Snow, comments on her experience of this parental involvement when the visiting group she was in participated in a hangi (feast):

> At the end of a *long day*, parents began to drift in, and children who lived in the neighbourhood began to drift in; and it turned into a feast, and dancing. Parents were teaching American educators how to dance! It was very clear that they felt *very* much at home in that great room [SS3]. (cited in Cazden, 1989: 158)

As Cazden goes on to observe, this participation is the rule not the exception; 'the front door [of the school] is indeed always open' (ibid.). This degree of involvement would be unusual in most schools, but it is particularly unusual for ethnic minority parents, who often feel alienated by schooling. Again, this was something that Laughton was aware of, and wanted to change. He was concerned to make the school and its organisational processes more accessible and inclusive, particularly for minority parents. An example of this can be seen in his reorganisation of parent interviews:

> Jim was very keen to involve members of the community in the life of the school. Whenever there [are] functions...the Polynesian people just don't run up to the school and say 'how's my kid's reading', and 'how's this, and how's that...'—that's a very European, very middle-class European approach. But when things were required—social occasions or functions—our community was there *en masse*... One example, the parent interviews...our parents turned up in droves... If you go to some schools there are (pause) 'Dear Mr Smith, would you please say what time you would like to come for your five minute or ten minute interview'. Jim just wiped that. He said no, that's crap. Our people don't work like that. We just say between the hours of this and this come and talk to us about your children... It might seem a trivial kind of organisational thing but it's very important. (Frank Churchward: Interview, 28 May, 1991)

Parents at Richmond Road are required twice a year to come to an afternoon and evening set aside for the discussion of their child's report; the discussion is a requirement for receiving the report. Under normal circumstances minority parents could view this as an ordeal but, as Churchward observes, by attending to the cultural sensitivities involved in the process, the parental response has been overwhelming. A teacher in Cazden's study reiterates this: 'And the report system here, where parents have to come into the school to get the reports; it makes the parents feel involved, that their input is valuable [instead of] a them-and-us situation with the child in between' (cited in Cazden, 1989: 158). This familiarity and sense of partnership between parents and teachers was clearly evident in the parent interview process I observed in late 1992:

For parent interviews, the school remains open from 4.30–8.30 [pm]. Staff stay after school and have a meal together. Even non-teaching staff are available all evening. The librarian, for example, stays to show parents around the school. Teachers sit in their rōpū areas with displays of resources and samples of children's work prominent. Parents can come at any time and a steady stream of parents (often with other family members) arrive throughout the course of the evening. Children can also accompany their parents for the interview if the family wishes. The atmosphere is very informal, almost festive. Parents and children move freely throughout the school (children can also show parents through the school), refreshments are available in the staffroom for everyone, and children play freely in the school courtyard into the night... (Field Notes, 17 November, 1992)

Parents can also often be seen involved in the various rōpū. The long term relationships which the family groupings foster facilitate this familiarity between the school and parents. This is further supported by an open invitation to parents to observe and/or participate in the rōpū at any time:

On this particular Thursday afternoon, the afternoon programme is concluded by one of the children (an older child who has difficulties relating to other children) being given the opportunity to talk to the rest of the rōpū about the work he has been doing on caterpillars. He does so, along with his mother who has brought his work in (a pot plant) and who stays to support him in this activity. This appears to be a prior arrangement but is conducted as a natural part of the day's programme. On talking with the teachers at day's end, it transpires that the activity was previously arranged with the parent in order to give the child 'provisional authority' [see Chapter 7] within the group via the activity and to ensure full support was available to him during it. (Field Notes, 14 February, 1991)

The usual wariness with which teachers regard the intervention of parents in school life is not apparent at Richmond Road. Waller's (1965) long held thesis on the natural enmity between teachers and parents for once does not seem to apply. Rather, parental involvement is an accepted and prominent feature of the school. Shona Matthews, for example, is regularly involved in her children's rōpū, spending at least one afternoon a week in the family group. As she comments, 'I've wanted to be involved with my children's schooling, and that has been welcomed at this school, which is not necessarily the case in a lot of other schools...here you're very much welcomed at any time, when you have some spare time that you can come in' (Interview, 17 November, 1992). Matthews' contribution in class includes what one might possibly expect a parent to be involved in—reading with younger children, contributing to craft activities, and helping maintain resources. However, she also regularly takes whole-class activities in reading and has contributed in other areas where she has a particular interest or expertise. This is not uncommon at Richmond Road. As Matthews' concludes, 'you're treated very much as an equal' by teachers at the school, and you are encouraged to contribute when and where you can.

The weekly school assembly is another area where parents are prominently involved. Held every Friday morning, these assemblies are organised by individual rōpū on a rotating basis. The school's cultural group—which includes selected members from all rōpū—also contributes to the running of these assemblies. The task of each rōpū is to present cultural activities which are associated with their particular group membership, often in the form of music or dance. The school's cultural group presents a full range of cultural activities. Assemblies, as such, are always enjoyable spectacles and, along with special school functions, see parents and friends of the school regularly attend. This community involvement is also further strengthened by the participation of the pre-schools. As Luke Hiki, a teacher in the Māori bilingual unit, observes:

> When we put on assembly, ours is combined with the kōhanga reo [the Māori language pre-school]... Every Monday, for half an hour...we take our resources, our new songs, and they provide something, some new songs, and we work together. We learn the same songs so that when it comes to assembly we're able to perform together. And when SS3 perform they're with the A'oga [the Samoan language pre-school], because they've got the Samoan bilingual unit, so they do their assembly together. SS2, they've got...the Cook Islands unit and they do theirs with the Cook Islands pre-school. It's mostly a lot of parents come through then. (Interview, 13 August, 1991)

Richmond Road's association with its pre-schools, as Hiki's observation reveals, is not simply one of on-site accommodation. While the pre-schools are autonomous and community run, there are strong links between them and the school itself. These links benefit children by minimising the disruption of moving from a pre-school situation to primary school. As Graeme Page comments: 'the kids settle in so easily...it's not a fearsome place... They're already involved every Friday with the assembly so there's nothing intimidating about going to school. It's just moving from one classroom to another. And when you get there half the kids that are there, you've already been in the [pre-school] with anyway' (Interview, 14 August, 1991). They also provide continuity for language development as the bilingual units in the school tend to pick up the children from the associated language pre-schools: 'I think the transition...to school is easy... There's an interchange between the bilingual Māori and the Kōhanga Reo, and the bilingual Samoan and the A'oga...it works well' (ibid.)[14]

Direct links with ethnic groups within the community are also fostered via the pre-schools. The pre-schools have been established by these community groups to foster their respective minority languages and cultures through full-immersion teaching. The responsibility for developing and administering these initiatives is each group's ongoing responsibility, and they exercise complete administrative and financial control over the running of the pre-schools. However, the development process surrounding the pre-schools has also occurred in close consultation with Richmond Road, and in conjunction with the development of the school's own bilingual structures. The establishment of Ritimana Kōhanga Reo and the Māori bilingual unit clearly illustrate this reciprocal process.

In 1984–1985 the Samoan community were ready and willing to establish a Samoan language pre-school and brought this request to the then governing school committee of Richmond Road.[15] However, after considerable debate it was decided that this should be deferred until the kōhanga reo and Māori bilingual unit had first been established. The two prime movers for first establishing Māori bilingual structures within the school were Jim Laughton, and the chairperson of the committee, Pita Taouma—a local Samoan elder. John Matthews, the kaiārahi reo attached to the Māori bilingual unit, recalls this debate:

> The first group to want a bilingual unit were the Samoans. They wanted to have an *A'oga Fa'a Samoa* there. Jim wanted the Māori one. He'd been wanting a kōhanga as well about the same time. Pita Taouma was the chairman at that time, and he said 'no, we'll respect the tangata whenua [the indigenous people; see glossary] first'. So they did the kōhanga first...it was actually a Samoan who said 'put the Māori one up'. (Interview, 25 May, 1991)

While the Samoan community constitutes the largest ethnic group at Richmond Road, Taouma supported Laughton in advocating that a move towards multicultural and multilingual education must first recognise the particular responsibilities of New Zealand's bicultural heritage.[16] It was only from this basis that the Samoan—and later, Cook Islands—pre-schools and bilingual units were subsequently established. Taouma's role here is instructive. It reflects Laughton's influence on the wider school community, but also, as we shall see, the reciprocal influence of the community on the school.

Pita Taouma was chairperson of Richmond Road's management body for nearly a decade—from the early 1980s until he stood down in 1992. He is, and remains, one of the school's strongest advocates. Interestingly, though, Taouma was not initially supportive of what Laughton was trying to do at Richmond Road, particularly through the establishment of family groups:

he opposed family grouping, he opposed multi-levels [at first], and it was only when his own son went through, a boy who would have failed in most other schools because of a lack of patience which comes with most schooling... The thing about the family model is that it's very patient with kids, it just accepts that they might sit a long time before they start to [develop]. It's where they've moved to at the end from where they were at the beginning—that's the measuring point. So he learnt to read, slowly, he learnt to write, he became literate and over that period Pita Taouma understood what [Jim] was on about, and how successful they'd been with [his] son... And he was convinced by that. And of course he is now a very strong advocate of the school. (Eric McMillan: Interview, 26 February, 1991)

Taouma's son had come directly to Richmond Road from the Western Samoan school system and had found the adjustment hard to make. However, over time, he was able to prosper both academically and socially (he is currently pursuing a university degree in Film) and Taouma's initial scepticism turned to strong support. Taouma's case illustrates the growing influence within the community of the school's view of multicultural education. Just as Laughton was able to convince teachers of the merits of the educational changes he was implementing, so too was he able to influence community expectations. As Joy Glasson reflects, this occurred 'by making very small changes. That's why it took [so many] years. And, of course too, people during those years saw what was happening to the kids, actually saw that kids were achieving. Kids were succeeding, kids were doing really well' (Interview, 29 May, 1991).

However Taouma, and the community input he represents, has also significantly influenced the school, particularly in its management and decision-making processes. Since Taouma's appointment as chairperson, a number of significant changes have occurred to the school's management body. First, it has increasingly comprised Māori and Pacific Island representatives, reflecting the community it serves. Second, the management of the school has come to reflect more closely the style and concerns of the ethnic groups which make up the bulk of its clientele. An example may serve to illustrate this:

A special Board of Trustees meeting was called to discuss an incident of unacceptable behaviour by two Samoan boys (one in particular) towards a younger child. The main culprit was a difficult child, now in S4 (10 yrs), who had only arrived at the school the previous year. He had exhibited clearly aberrant behaviour since arriving at the school but he was also subject to strict physical discipline at home as a result. The discussion centred on the process and resolution of the incident. The younger child's parents were contacted and the suspension of the principal offender considered. However, suspension at the school appears to be a very rare event (only one in the last 10 years) and other solutions were also considered, particularly given the main offender's familiarity with punitive systems. An alternative which did not involve punishment was settled upon as an approach which might be sufficiently unfamiliar to break through to the child.

What was of particular interest in relation to this incident, however, was the process of consultation which ensued. The two sets of Samoan parents were called into the school to discuss the incident but were not directed to the principal's office. Instead, Pita Taouma...and Tuloto Mareko (a Samoan senior teacher) spoke with the parents (in Samoan) in the teacher resource room. They encouraged the parents—especially the parents of the difficult child—not to resort to physical punishment and also dealt with the issue of shame (*ma*) which has special cultural significance for Samoans. Only after these issues had been resolved did the parents talk with the principal, Lionel Pedersen. Thus hierarchical and intimidatory relationships between parents—particularly minority parents—and the school (seeing the principal in his office over a child's behaviour, when the principal is of a different ethnic origin) were avoided. Rather, non-hierarchical and culturally appropriate relationships were maintained and whānau principles were prominent. Accordingly, mana [influence; esteem] was maintained on all sides. (Field Notes, 22 February, 1991)

However, the process of change—which has seen cultural recognition and respect accorded to minority groups in the management of the school—has not been without its detractors; principally, those Pākehā who might otherwise have had an influence. As a former Pākehā teacher and parent at the school observes:

What community input we get to Board of Trustees meetings I'm not quite so sure about though... They have made it known that the community can go along [but] I've had some negative comments from some of the European parents about going to the Board of Trustees meetings... It may be a perception that's not true, *maybe they feel uncomfortable because it's not what they're used to*. I don't know. (my emphasis)

The ambivalence inherent in this comment highlights the difficulties which members of the majority group face when hegemony is contested; in this case, through a changed management structure more conversant with minority group values. Access to power for others is all very well until it actually impinges on your own! What this has seen at Richmond Road is the gradual loss of some of the initially enthusiastic white liberals from involvement in school management along with, at times, the development of conflict situations. Graeme Page—a current member and parent representative on the Board of Trustees—recalls one such occasion:

Interviewer: Have there ever been, to your knowledge, any conflicts of interest between parents and the school?

Page: Yes, there were big conflicts of interest over the [Māori] bilingual unit when it first started because the liberal [Pākehā] put all their kids in and wanted their kids to learn Māori. It was obviously an advantage [for them] *and it's an advantage on an advantage that the kid already has.* But the trouble with the parents is that they all decided that they would be like Māoris and they would start having huis [meetings] etc., and they would become a pressure group. And they did it in isolation from the committee. So that was a conflict, but it was really between the Pākehā parents and the school committee. Fortunately I was a parent then at the time, because they were basically speaking for me [as a Māori]—that was their attitude... They were parents who started at the same time as I did but have moved on...and they've done the same in other schools where they've gone—because they come from this very position of knowing everything you see. (Interview, 14 August, 1991; my emphasis)

Page is unapologetic about such conflict and the associated scepticism of some Pākehā towards the present Board of Trustees. Changing the rules of the game under Taouma's chairmanship, he argues, has affirmed minority groups within the school and has acted as an education for Pākehā of the processes to which minorities are usually subject. Having said that, access is never at any stage denied to Pākehā—this would contravene what the school stands for. Rather, what is asked of them is an accommodation to cultural norms which are not necessarily their own; a relinquishing of control that has been naturally assumed as of right. Page continues:

I think some [Pākehā] have moved on because they see it as a bit overpowering, probably how we feel in Pākehā situations. They feel intimidated by the...lack of form, because it isn't cut and dried. You don't have arguments...and things that end in debates. Ending a debate is sitting there and going the distance...

I've seen people for years come and go, but most of them were pushing something that dealt with them and them alone, and couldn't wait. So on that basis they didn't stay... But if you do and you join and you become part of it then it's time for you to say something. Really, I don't see anything wrong with being in the kitchen for a while, personally. I think that's where you start your apprenticeship, and so to come in and say 'well I've got no influence here so I won't come again' is bullshit. You haven't actually done the dishes yet... I think it's probably having some respect for the other point of view first. One of the problems is that people come in with this all knowing position, they know everything, so *you* listen. We've been here for years and we're still listening. (ibid.)

What comes through consistently in Page's observations, and what has been reflected elsewhere in the school's organisation through Laughton's influence, is that power comes through *knowledge*, not through position. As Eric McMillan, the former deputy principal, observes: 'you had to earn your right to speak at Richmond Road. If you went in there making noises that you couldn't support then you didn't survive' (Interview, 26 February, 1991). Those who were not willing to listen to other viewpoints soon became disillusioned. Those not willing to concede previously held positions of power met similar opposition. However, those who were able to make these accommodations have learnt to operate within more culturally pluralist forms of management and decision-making. As Shona Matthews, a Pākehā parent recently appointed to the Board of Trustees, argues:

I felt strongly from the beginning that it was important that I didn't want to see any of those [decision-making] systems change at all, because that obviously did work for the school, and it was important that anybody coming in—particularly from the Pākehā community—didn't try and change any of those things. It was important that they worked within that system and, OK, maybe added...particular skills that they had. And I think that those of us that are involved—that's what we've endeavoured to do. (Interview, 17 November, 1992)

The result is a communal and consensual approach to decision-making at Richmond Road. Matthews concludes that 'just through a process of talking they seem to come up with something that is appropriate for everybody' (ibid.) Steve Williams, another parent, reiterates this process:

The philosophy of the school—where decisions are made—is that the community—everybody that's involved with the school—makes a decision. It's the way it's always been as far back as I can remember. And it's not just a handful of people that say 'right we're going to do that'. I mean if the consensus is that we're not going to do it—this is from the community— well we won't do it. And that's it, and that's how it's always been. It seems to work well. Quite often it takes quite a long time to resolve things but that's the best way—don't rush into it, think about it. It might take a couple of months to resolve one particular thing but when it is resolved it's resolved well! (Interview, 17 November, 1992)

Holmes & Wynne, in a recent text on educational administration, argue: 'A successful school is likely to be one with strong consensual values shared by teachers, parents and students. If those values are lived on a daily basis in the community, so much the better' (1989: 143).[17] Richmond Road clearly demonstrates this kind of consensual interaction between school and community. As Graeme Page concludes, perhaps more as a parent than a board member in this particular case: 'I think the staff and the community are as one, and the community isn't in awe of the teaching profession here. I mean, I think you get a lot of situations where the teacher says "well *that's right*". I don't think it is here. I think that everybody's relaxed with everybody else'. (Interview, 14 August, 1991)

However, it is Luke Hiki, the Māori bilingual teacher, who perhaps identifies the key component of this school and community interrelationship:

Interviewer: ...And does that just happen because the school's kept talking to the community over the years and told them what they're doing and brought them on board?

Hiki: Yes, *and giving them the status*. They're giving the parents in the community the status to be able to come into the school and express what you want—your desires. I think that's what's kept the parents coming back again and again. (Interview, 13 August, 1991; my emphasis)

These participatory, reciprocal, and non-hierarchical relationships characterise Richmond Road's school organisation; in family grouping, staff development, collaborative management, and school and community relations. In the process, status is accorded to all participants. Children, parents, and teachers all have something to offer and it was Laughton's intention—supported by others both within the school and local community—that everyone's contribution would be valued. The specific pedagogic and relational principles underlying this process of inclusion and participation are what I want to look at in the next chapter.

Notes to Chapter 6

1. Laughton's background was Māori, McMillan's is Pākehā working-class.
2. Pedersen has a long-standing association with Richmond Road. He first came to the school as a teacher in 1973 and, after a period away teaching elsewhere, he returned again to the school in 1985 as an assistant principal. He was appointed principal in 1990.
3. Laughton took a year's leave in 1976 to do a Diploma in Teaching English as a Second Language from Victoria University in Wellington, New Zealand. His sophisticated knowledge of language issues dates from this time (Cazden, 1989).
4. Courtney Cazden from Harvard University is a notable example. She became involved with Richmond Road in the early 1980s and has developed a close relationship with the school since that time. Her regard for Jim Laughton as an educator has been central to that involvement (see Cazden, 1989).
5. While other schools in New Zealand have subsequently adopted these structures (popularly termed whānau groupings), Richmond Road was in the forefront of their development. Laughton was reticent, however, about using the term 'whānau' to describe the groups; preferring 'family grouping' or 'rōpū'. He wanted to avoid the

artificiality associated with the popularisation of the term and the consequent diminishing of its cultural significance. Whānau was used, though, to describe the school as a whole.

6. There is some degree of overlap in these levels to provide flexibility in the promotion of pupils.

7. Both Rōpū 2 and 3 also have English-speaking groups.

8. As I suggested in Chapter 5, the involvement of the two associate principals in shared teaching reflects the school's emphasis on non-hierarchical management structures. This is also reflected in the school's current unwillingness to distinguish between the two positions; the school has long since dispensed with the widely held distinction between deputy and assistant principal—both in title and practice. While Richmond Road, like other New Zealand primary schools, has to conform to the principalship structure, it has actively sought to reconstitute this along more egalitarian lines. I will also discuss further below the numerous other ways in which the school circumvents hierarchical management and teaching structures.

9. In addition to the four shared spaces, the Inner-City Language Unit and the various pre-schools are housed in prefabricated classrooms around the school. These have also been remodelled, where possible, to reflect a more interactive and open teaching and learning environment.

10. Except where she occasionally specifies a particular teacher, teachers' comments in Cazden's study are kept anonymous.

11. All that I have written on Richmond Road (including this present book) has been discussed and critiqued by the school. As part of this reciprocal process, I have been disabused of inadequate and/or outdated educational ideas, introduced to a great deal of educational theory with which I was previously unfamiliar (more than I care to admit in fact!), and constantly challenged to refine and support my own developing theoretical position(s) and arguments.

12. These documents provide a fascinating account of the development of Richmond Road's educational thinking. All the significant articles the school has examined are filed, and the content of the staff meeting discussions pertaining to them, readily available.

13. See May (1992a) for a fuller discussion of action research in the context of Richmond Road.

14. The Cook Islands bilingual unit has also now been established since the time of this interview, and the same sense of continuity can be said to apply to its relationship to *Te Apii Reo Kuki Airani*—the Cook Islands pre-school.

15. School committees comprised locally elected members but did not have the formal administrative responsibilities now bestowed upon Boards of Trustees (see Chapter 9).

16. New Zealand's bicultural heritage is based on the country's founding document, Te Tiriti o Waitangi (The Treaty of Waitangi). This reciprocal and binding agreement was signed in 1840 between the indigenous Māori and the British crown. It ensured Māori, as tangata whenua, legal right to their lands, language and other taonga (property; treasures) and allowed British immigrants to settle in the country. Treaty rights and responsibilities, however, were soon ignored and much of New Zealand's history since European settlement has followed a similar path to other colonial societies in the subjugation and marginalisation of its indigenous people (see Orange, 1987; Walker, 1990). It has only been in the last 20 years that the Treaty of Waitangi has been returned to centre stage in New Zealand. Māori has subsequently been recognised as an official language, along with English. Redress has been made retrospectively by New Zealand governments for misappropriation of lands. And

government policy-making now recognises the commitments and responsibilities of the Treaty of Waitangi as New Zealand moves again towards formalising a bilingual and bicultural society. Any move to multiculturalism in New Zealand, then, begins with the acknowledgement of bicultural responsibilities and the rights of Māori as tangata whenua, 'the people of the land'.

17. While Holmes & Wynne are drawn on here, their account—like many within the field of educational administration—is almost exclusively monocultural. For a critique of this approach in relation to Richmond Road, see May (1992b).

7 Pedagogy: Knowledge, Responsibility, and the Process of Learning

...for me it's about the only place I've ever seen where you've got both a structural change and a pedagogical change that link together. And that's, for me, what made it different. (Joy Glasson: Interview, 29 May, 1991)

Laughton believed that ascribing status to all participants in the process of learning necessarily involves both a recognition of, and a role for, the knowledge they bring with them. As Frank Churchward argues: 'that's another feature of Jim's approach, that everybody or anybody can be an expert, can have the knowledge' (Interview, 28 May, 1991). For Laughton, knowledge involved responsibility; a responsibility to share what knowledge you have with others. What he set out to achieve at Richmond Road—through the structural changes seen in family grouping, staff development and community involvement—were the opportunities for everyone to contribute to that process. Central to his endeavours was the distinction he drew from the work of R.S. Peters (1973) between *assigned* and *provisional authority*.

Provisional Authority: Whoever Has Knowledge Teaches

In Peters' definition, 'assigned authority' is authority which is ascribed or formalised through the role or position one fills. This is the teacher in the context of the classroom, and the senior teachers and administrators in the broader context of school administration. 'Provisional authority', however, is described by Peters as that held by the person 'who knows the most' in a given situation. People with personal knowledge and expertise in a given situation can be regarded as holders of provisional authority, irrespective of their assigned position within the school. It was Laughton's intention to promote this latter notion of provisional authority in order to include and empower those who would not otherwise have been given such responsibility. This included, in various contexts: children; teachers; and parents. As a teacher in Cazden's study observes:

Whoever has knowledge [at Richmond Road] teaches. Sometimes this would be a teacher; other times it can be a child; other times it can be a parent from the community. I particularly like that. Although we have a principal, assistant principal, senior teachers, and then we ordinary plebs, it has never really worked that way. It's always been a case of who has the greater knowledge... (cited in Cazden, 1989: 152)

In promoting the notion of provisional authority, Laughton's aim was to dismantle the hierarchical structures in schools which ascribe certain participants with status and exclude and disenfranchise others. For staff, this has led to the democratisation of school authority structures and the opportunity to participate actively in curriculum and policy development, irrespective of one's formal position within the school. For children, the rōpū structure has seen traditional teacher–pupil relationships redefined along more egalitarian lines to include pupils in the learning and teaching process.[1]

'If you had an ability you were recognised'

Skilbeck (1984) argues that school-based policy development must include the active participation of teachers if it is to be successfully implemented (see also, Corson, 1990; 1993). This requires, he suggests, a redefinition in schools of authority relationships because schools which are hierarchical and conservative in respect of decision-making can easily inhibit or frustrate curriculum policy and innovation. These concerns are echoed in recent multicultural education and antiracist education literature. Carrington & Short, for example, suggest that a 'collegial and democratic ethos' is necessary among both teaching and non-teaching staff if antiracist policy at the school level is to be effectively implemented, monitored and appraised (1989: 86). Likewise, Nieto, discussing whole school approaches to multicultural education, argues strongly for extending the decision-making role of teachers in the process of whole-school reform. As she candidly points out, 'disempowered teachers who show little thought can hardly be expected to help students become empowered and critical thinkers' (1992: 81). What is needed, in contrast, are 'new structures such as teacher-led schools, weekly released time, or job sharing [which] may help make teachers more active players in the schools...' (1992: 81). Richmond Road clearly demonstrates these characteristics of active and extended teacher participation. It was always Laughton's intention that his staff should be directly involved in developing the school's new educational directions and he specifically fostered this through the use of provisional authority among them. He may have been the catalyst—and in many ways he did direct the vision, particularly in the early years—but his aim was to equip teachers with all that was necessary for the school systems he set in place to be 'self-sustaining and self-generating' (Richmond Road School, 1983).

Laughton clearly had both assigned and provisional authority within the school, and initially at least he used this authority to establish the school's new organisational and curriculum directions. Eric McMillan recalls:

> [R.S.] Peters' ideas became incorporated in the place. The two levels of authority: the teachers' authority because they're in charge, they're responsible. But then it was a matter of finding out others' knowledge which gave *them* authority. And he lived that within the staff. He saw the principal's role initially as totally responsible for all scheme and curriculum development. He held that to himself because he discovered if he handed it over you've got varying points of view and you ended up with a curriculum that didn't match...and you shouldn't do that. There needs to be consistency across the curriculum. What applies here also applies there. And so people *earned* the right to become participants of curriculum development. And this was really when staff developed. That as people got to know that if they focused on a particular area and made it theirs that they then got status...
> (Interview, 26 February, 1990)

Laughton began the process of organisational and curriculum change but moved very quickly into a facilitative role; encouraging teachers to contribute their expertise in any area(s) in which they felt they had something to offer. This has seen, over time, the de-emphasis of traditional staff hierarchies within the school. Assigned authority still operates within the school—the associate principals, for example, have particular administrative responsibilities, and senior teachers organise and are accountable for rōpū teaching teams—but it does so *alongside* provisional authority. Where possible, emphasis is placed on non-hierarchical, collaborative staff relationships:

> it didn't matter whether you were a year two teacher, if you had an ability you were recognised, and I found that wonderful. We had senior teachers, but...just because you're a senior teacher doesn't mean you know everything. In some of our schools—say as a year two teacher you've got knowledge in a particular field—you daren't put yourself ahead of the senior teacher... Jim wiped all that aside. He said ...if you know, *you know*. (Frank Churchward: Interview, 28 May, 1991)

Judy Hucker recalls, for example, how as a Scale A [initial certification level] teacher she was made responsible for developing the Mathematics curriculum and its attendant resources (see Chapter 8); an area, in fact, in which she was not initially confident. 'We had a hard apprenticeship but it was very exciting...by that point I had never done anything really in mathematics, and now I'm on the National Curriculum writing committee for mathematic initiatives! Most of what I did, I began to develop at Richmond Road' (Interview, 15 August, 1991). Being given this level of responsibility was not uncommon at Richmond Road. The teacher who initially developed the social studies programme and its 'focus resources' (see below; also, Chapter 8) was only a first year teacher. Hucker again comments: 'she came as an older student, sure—she had been in pre-school education for quite some time—but she came as a year one teacher...she was the one that took over and really drove the social studies directions and that was as a year one teacher'. As Hucker concludes, 'most of the curriculum areas would not have been with people who were in the senior teacher hierarchy' (ibid.).

The composition of the staff at Richmond Road also demonstrates Laughton's attempt to attribute authority to teachers who might not otherwise have been recognised. John Matthews, the kaiārahi reo (see below), comments on the unusually high number of Māori and Pacific Island teachers at the school: 'he brought all these people in and gave them power. He made them normal teachers, whereas if they were at ordinary schools I think they wouldn't have made it, would have been the ones at the back... That was Jim Laughton. That's the school really' (Interview, 25 May, 1991). John Matthews is a case in point. Kaiārahi reo positions have been established since the mid 1980s in New Zealand primary schools, in lieu of formal teacher training qualifications, for fluent Māori speakers. While three year part-time training at a College of Education was subsequently incorporated into the positions in 1990, kaiārahi reo in most schools are not regarded as teachers. But not at Richmond Road. Matthews functions as a full teacher and has for some time now been regarded as the most senior and experienced teacher in the Māori bilingual unit. Right from the start of his time at Richmond Road (he came to the school in early 1986), Laughton insisted he take on a full teaching role, despite the fact that he had no prior teaching experience. As Cazden observes of this in her study:

> I asked him whether he was glad that Jim had insisted that he take on full teaching responsibilities. 'In the short term I was cursing. But in the long term, I'm glad. I know the stuff now. And it's helped make the rest of the staff accept me, I suppose'. As Jim had explained to him later, his insistence on a full teaching role was also based on the benefits of professional knowledge for a young Māori adult, should he want to require formal credentials. 'He was being mean to help me, really'. (1989: 152)

Matthews lack of professional background is not an issue at Richmond Road because the particular cultural and language skills he brings to the position are recognised as valued alternatives. Moreover, these particular skills see him take the lead in formal school occasions:

Graeme Page: Yes, well John Matthews speaks for the school, for example, when position wise, in terms of staff teaching status, his is the lowest I guess. But he is accorded the highest status [in this role] because of his knowledge, more than Lionel's [the principal],[2] that's what I mean.

Interviewer: And that's in any formal situation representing the school?

Graeme Page: Yes. And any [Māori] knowledge base as well. If you want to know, who do you ask? You don't ask anyone else. (Interview, 14 August, 1991)

In 1992, Matthews completed the formal training requirements established for kaiārahi reo and was awarded full teacher status within the New Zealand system. This, along with his experience at Richmond Road, has seen him subsequently win an appointment as head of department in Māori at a local secondary school. He is the first to admit that the opportunities he has had at Richmond Road—and particularly, Laughton's initial encouragement—are largely responsible for his ongoing professional recognition and development.

Tu Romia and Tiaki Katia, the school's caretaker (janitor) and cleaner, also clearly demonstrate the non-hierarchical nature of staff relationships at Richmond Road:

> In our staff we include the caretaker and the cleaners. A lot of other schools, they don't... With our's we've got Tu [who] is always with the kids at play time, and that's not because he has to—it's not part of his job—he's just that sort of a guy. That's why he's been here for so long. He's into it, just gets into it with the kids. And Tiaki, everyone knows Tiaki. She knows all the kids—all the kids know who Tiaki is, who Tu is. A lot of other schools, they wouldn't even know who their caretakers are—it would be 'Mr somebody'. Tiaki takes the Polynesian club [the school's cultural group] as well. She takes part in the assemblies, and anyone can have a go at that. (Luke Hiki: Interview, 13 August, 1991)

Tu and Tiaki, as Hiki suggests, are prominent members of the Richmond Road staff and no distinctions are made because of their non-teaching role. Tiaki, for example, is the elected staff representative on the Board of Trustees. Likewise, Tu's contribution to school life is significant and highly regarded. He can often be seen playing with children (he knows all the children by name) and particularly enjoys participating in Level 2 sports on Thursday afternoons. The children's regard and affection for him is also clearly evident. Tu attributes the opportunity he has had to develop these kinds of relationships with children, along with the role he has assumed as a full staff member, to Jim Laughton:

> I say Jim's like a father to me because there's a lot of things I learnt from Jim over the years I've been here. I miss him a lot. We talked, mainly when I'd go in the office, or sometimes he'd come out if there was something he wanted to talk about. He always talked about the school and the way the school used to run... He talked a lot about the kids. When I first came here I never had morning tea with the staff because we had our shed down the

bottom and we'd always have our morning tea [there]. One day he asked me if I wanted to join, sit with him. I said 'yeah, fair enough, why not'. I never [got] used to sitting with the teachers [until then]. (Interview, 27 May, 1991)

In Cazden's study, Romia elaborates on Laughton's encouragement:

When Jim was alive, we used to talk sometimes—about the school and the kids and the staff and everybody in the community. He always used to say, 'You don't have to feel low because you're only a caretaker. In a school like this, whether you're a caretaker or cleaner or staff or whatever, principal or deputy principal, you're all the same'. I think that's one of the most important things about Richmond Road; you don't just work *as* a caretaker; you have to get involved with the staff and kids. (cited in Cazden, 1989: 153)

The provisional authority accorded to Tu within the school is also demonstrated by his role, along with John Matthews, of speaking for the school on formal occasions: 'whatever [formal event] comes on in the school, I'll be one of the main speakers. It is good experience because I've never done any of this before, mostly to do with...welcoming visitors from other places. I really enjoy it [and] I can pass that on to the kids' (Interview, 27 May, 1991). At Jim's tangi (funeral) which was held at the school in September 1988, Tu was the one who gave the final farewell to Jim before his coffin was taken to the cemetery (Cazden, 1989). As he recalls:

Romia: ...it was a shock for [us] when he passed away. I did cry on the last day when they took him out to the cemetery. Our staff asked me to speak on behalf of the school. It's hard if you have to get up and you have to make a speech and it's somebody you really appreciated... I just couldn't help myself, yet when my grandmother died I didn't cry. It's really hard. I miss him a lot. A lot of people turned up...all the ex-pupils, they came, paid their respects on that day...the ex-staff—they all turned up.

Interviewer: And you ended up speaking on behalf of the school?

Romia: Yes. I was pleased that they asked me to speak for the school. Like I said, I never cried when my grandmother died but I cried when he died. I think it shows that bond between the caretaker and the principal. (Interview, 27 May, 1991)

Such relationships are unusual in schools, to say the least. Yet by recognising others, and according them with responsibility, Laughton was able to create a school culture which facilitated this kind of personal and interpersonal development among staff. However, this was not to be seen as an end in itself.

The learning and teaching opportunities afforded to the staff were also expected to be modelled with children in the family group.

'He recognised the potential within children to do things'

For children, the family group has been the key means by which the traditional hierarchical teacher–pupil relationship has been reconstituted. Within family groups, teachers are given the opportunity to learn and students the opportunity to teach:

> ...it's not only us adults who are the teachers, it's the children who teach as well. Of course, we worked a lot on those lines... I think if I came away with nothing else from Jim Laughton and his school, I came away recognising how dynamic a teaching force there is outside of adult teachers... I think this is one thing I respected in Jim, that he recognised the potential within children to do things, and as teachers we tend more to stifle rather than to liberate children. (Frank Churchward: Interview, 28 May, 1991)

Provisional authority is promoted in family grouping through the tuakana-teina (older-younger sibling) principle. Teachers need not be the only source of knowledge since the full range of ages within rōpū allows for significant peer interaction among the students. Older and/or more able children tutor the younger and/or less able and all children have the opportunity, where appropriate, to impart knowledge to the group as a whole. A description of a rōpū highlights this interaction:

> ...the children are involved in language activities; the older students are writing a story while the younger students are working on dictated texts. They move from these activities to paired reading. With minimal direction from the teacher, younger children find the books they want to read and locate their respective senior partners. The older child in the pair discusses with the younger child which book they want to read (and also, in some cases, assesses its appropriateness in terms of reading level—one younger child was asked to find another book because the one he had brought was deemed too easy) and then proceeds to help the younger child with his/her reading...
>
> I later asked two children, Naresh [S3; 9 yrs] and Dion [S4; 10 yrs], about this paired reading approach and how it worked. They confidently explained to me the procedures and responsibilities involved; that more able readers were matched with less able readers and that it was the responsibility of the former to tutor the latter with their reading during this time. They also elaborated on the specific strategies they employed to this end (in surprising detail). These included directing the younger child to words in the script, prompting rather than answering if a child was finding a particular word

difficult, and going over concepts and individual words to ensure the child was not simply memorising. Dion also explained that Pauli (his partner), who was just a beginning reader, was cued by pictures rather than by words at his stage of reading development. It was clear that both took their tutoring responsibilities very seriously and were confident and well informed concerning them. Other children around the room appeared to be similarly engaged... (Field Notes, 28 February, 1991)

When asked about the peer tutoring process at another time, Naresh explains it in the following way:

Well, in reading you get a book that they [the reading partner] choose, sit down with them, and then they read it to you. The words that they don't know you make them sound out and put them all together, and you make up the word with them...if they get stuck, we help them work out where they go and help them to get the answer. And if we get stuck we see the teacher or see Margaret who is 12 [years old]. (Interview, 20 November, 1992)

Peer interaction and instruction also provide a supportive social atmosphere. Shona Matthews comments as a parent on the benefits of such an approach for her children:

I think it's helped them more the fact that they do work with all the younger children and have to teach them and be considerate of them. I really like that, and the fact that the children of all different ages socialise...they all do socialise very well...whereas I think when you find them at a school where they are divided up into age groups that just doesn't happen to the same extent. (Interview, 13 November, 1992)

Likewise, ex-pupils at Richmond Road consistently mention the social and educational advantages associated with peer tutoring. Moana Saulala recalls: 'When I was learning [to read] it was sort of hard to understand, but my partner was really great because she would always read and she would always ask "do I understand or not?" and then she would help me out. And that's what I did when I was teaching' (Interview, 21 November, 1992). Folole Asaua comments more generally of her experience as a teina: 'You were well looked after. I mean you were looked after by those [older] students but it was like you were just the same age group. I felt like I was in the same age group with them whereas they were [actually] older than me' (Interview, 21 November, 1992).

While the tuakana is generally an older student, this is not necessarily so, and the tuakana-teina roles can be interchangeable for individual students. Luke Hiki describes the process working in the Māori bilingual unit:

Hiki: A tuakana's not necessarily an old kid... It's just a tuakana is
                       one who's a more able sort of person. In reading it's a more able
                       reader.

Interviewer: If they weren't so good at mathematics could they be a tuakana
                       in reading and a teina in [mathematics]?

Hiki: Yes, sure. It's just whatever subject we're working with. When
                       John [Matthews, the kaiārahi reo] comes in for Māori it's mostly
                       teina-tuakana too. He explains what the lesson is and then he
                       gives out the resources, gives them the work to do, and then
                       chooses the tuakana and...the teina. And he'll choose the good
                       ones that are usually quite reliable as a kaiwhakahaere [see
                       glossary] because they're the teachers in that time. They've got
                       the Māori [language] and so he gives the good Māori speak-
                       ing...kids the work to do... That's the philosophy of Jim
                       Laughton I reckon, that's what he wanted—to give the kids
                       access to power... [by] recognising them as a teacher, as a
                       tuakana. (Interview, 13 August, 1991)

Underlying these principles of participation, support, and the sharing of
knowledge is a recognition of their cultural appropriateness for many of the
ethnic minority children at Richmond Road. Ka'ai (1990) argues, for example,
in her research on Te Kōhanga Reo, that the tuakana-teina learning method is
culturally preferred by Māori. Likewise, Metge observes, in her discussion of
traditional Māori schooling, that 'in everyday contexts every person could
fulfil the interchangeable role of both teacher and learner' (1986: 2). This
emphasis on cooperative learning is also strongly supported as an effective
pedagogical strategy in multicultural and antiracist education literature (see
also Chapter 6). Nieto summarises this view: 'in investigating the characteristics of instructional features that have shown promise with language
minority students, [it has been] found that effective classrooms are characterized by, among other things, student collaboration in almost all academic
activity. That is, where students are involved in directing their own learning
in some way, they learn more effectively' (1992: 81; see also Cummins, 1986;
Fitz-Gibbon, 1983; Lynch, 1987; Troyna, 1993). By adopting this collaborative approach within the context of the extended family group, Māori and
Pacific Island children are acknowledged and affirmed by learning principles
with which they are familiar. Moreover, by spreading the dissemination of
knowledge, tuakana-teina relationships also allow for a more effective teaching and learning environment. Shared responsibility results in more effective
classroom interaction:

[The vertical grouping facilitated] a lot of peer interaction—teina-tuakana—
that relationship was just so easy. I suppose originally we enforced the

[learning concepts] we taught the children...but as time went by it just became a very natural part of the classroom process. It also allowed the teacher to have more in-depth time with individual children because there were more capable children in the room able to deal with the other petty problems that arose during that time. It gave you that wonderful spread of age and stage and ideas and expertise and your co-operative and collaborative groupings [see below]. It made us all more aware of the individual needs, personalities. Learning needs stuck out more, you could see them far more easily and deal with them far more easily than you can with a reasonably homogenous group of children, i.e. Standard 3, which makes all sorts of assumptions about age and stage that might not be realistic. (Helen Villers: Interview, 29 May, 1991)

The participation of children in tuakana-teina relationships is also demonstrated in other areas within the school. The function of the school's cultural group, for example, demonstrates the use of children as tuakana. Eight children from each rōpū are involved in the group for the year. They have a dual responsibility of representing the school on formal occasions and teaching what cultural activities they learn within the group back in their own rōpū (to both teachers and children). The tuakana-teina approach, then, recognises the limitations of teachers' knowledge and accords scope for the contribution of children to the teaching and learning process, both within and beyond the rōpū. As Lionel Pedersen, the current principal, argues:

I suppose...what people started realising is that *everybody* can learn. All you differ at is the rate that you work at—kids *and* teachers—and it's always a two way progression. The more the kids learn the more we learn and vice versa... What a teacher then has to realise is that they are a learner too... So not only do you have to know about it in the head and understand all the concepts, you've really got to believe that learning is an ongoing process and that the more knowledge or the more you learn, the more responsibility you have to teach other people. From there we've devised a system that keeps growing. There's no end product. (Interview, 26 February, 1990)

A teacher in Cazden's study echoes Pedersen's observation:

For me, the *most* important thing is that [Richmond Road] really is a place for (pause) all sorts of people. I'm not just talking about children. I'm talking about people in teaching; I'm talking about community. But along with that goes a real responsibility to learn. And when I say *learn*, I mean step back and not always want control, not want to be the powerful one. What happens with teachers—we've been trained to think that we're knowledgeable people, that we should control situations and always contribute and always participate and take the lead. There are people who may *lead* things who may not have the qualifications that we have as teachers. But to *learn*, there are times when you can't contribute, when you can't participate—because listening to other people and having their experience *first* is more of a learning situation. (cited in Cazden, 1989: 149)

The use of provisional authority through tuakana-teina teaching promotes learning because sources of knowledge are diversified. Within this, the relationship between knowledge and responsibility is fore-grounded; both for teachers and children. As Helen Villers comments, this was one of Jim Laughton's main concerns:

he talked constantly to us about rights and responsibilities, and...privilege and responsibility specifically... We [as teachers] were privileged to have the attributes, I suppose, to work with those children. Therefore it was our responsibility to do what we could, as much as we could, more than we possibly were able to do! (laughs) But the same thing worked with the children in the classroom. It was a privilege for some children to be older or more gifted or more skilled, therefore they had to share that knowledge, that ability, those skills, with others who were less privileged in that circumstance...we operated from this notion of the authentic source and getting into Stenhouse's notions too—relinquishing of power if it doesn't properly belong to you and looking at all of us as resources and to the appropriate time to use those resources at hand... I saw that I suppose as our responsibility [as teachers] to do that, and our privilege to be able to do it, and hopefully they [the children] saw that reciprocally as such as well. (Interview, 29 May, 1991)

Reciprocity is the key to the success of such teaching and learning arrangements. For children, there is a reciprocal obligation to respond with and be responsible for knowledge already held. For teachers, there is a responsibility to apply these principles in classroom teaching and also, as I outlined in the previous section, in school organisation and curriculum development.

Child-Centred and Process Learning

'The Kids Always Come First'

The nature of the staff and teacher–pupil relationships established at Richmond Road through the use of provisional authority are consistently commented upon by those who know the school. Every pupil or ex-pupil I talked with mentioned the positive relationships they had with teachers. For most, it was actually the main feature of the school. When I asked Naresh Patel, who was 10 years old at the time, what he most liked about Richmond Road, he replied without hesitation: 'the relationships with the children and the teachers' (Interview, 20 November, 1992). Other pupils, ex-pupils, and parents I have talked with provide a remarkably similar account. Quite simply, the children at Richmond Road *enjoy* the place and the reason for this is that children always come first at Richmond Road. This might seem self-evident but it is not always the case in schools. Colleen Belsham—a long-standing teacher at the school—comments along these lines: 'From talking to other teachers and principals, I think children are often the last things thought about. I really do. Yet that's what schools are all about. That's the main thing that has struck me always about [this] school, that the children *are* the focal point' (Interview, 25 May, 1991). Belsham goes on to observe:

> I think the thing that strikes me most is that the children turn up every day. Children don't just turn up to school every day in places probably like this, unless they have got something to come for... I think's that's what has made [Richmond Road]—[Jim's] honesty and his commitment to wanting us to become a place for children, and nurture all the things that are important to children like who they are, their individuality, their uniqueness. That is what is nurtured here. They keep their identity and that is celebrated; it is respected; it is important to everyone so that it becomes important to them... That's what we strive for...*as a place for children to feel secure, respected, what they are.* (Interview, 25 May, 1991; my emphasis)

A teacher in Cazden's study echoes these sentiments:

> The thing that's special about Richmond Road is that it's a school for children. It's something that I always wished was around me when I was a child, because it's a place where children are made to feel—not *overly* important—but important. They've got a place there. (cited in Cazden, 1989: 145)

Frank Churchward describes how Jim conveyed to staff his concern to make children a priority at Richmond Road:

> Jim always said he was the children's advocate. He did care about his staff, but he stood between the children and the teachers. He said 'who else have the kids got to be their advocate, but me?' So he would take their side. Not only to just sort out anything like that, but in terms of how a school should be run. He argued for them, not for us. It wasn't cut and dried like that, it just meant that if something came up, say in a staff meeting and we said 'look, let's organise ourselves and do this and this', Jim would say 'how's it going to benefit the children?' That was always the direction from which he came—how will the children benefit, how will they improve their learning, how will conditions work to make sure that they get the best out of everything? (Interview, 28 May, 1991)

It was from this concern that the learning needs of children at Richmond Road were prioritised. The use of provisional authority facilitated this approach but it was underpinned by a recognition of the need for a *process* approach to learning. Along with the work of R.S. Peters then, Lawrence Stenhouse's ideas on curriculum development feature prominently in the pedagogical ethos of the school.

'The process was underlined all the time'

Tied in with Peters' notion of provisional authority at Richmond Road is an understanding of the *developmental* nature of learning, and the appropriate *resourcing* of learning. Laughton came to the view that if children are to achieve control over their own learning, and if learning is to be a dynamic and creative process for them, then the learning model adopted needs to be both child-centred and resource-based. That is, the pedagogical approach must be both responsive to children's learning needs and supported by flexible, culturally appropriate, interactive and extending educational materials (Richmond Road School, 1983). Stenhouse's (1975) curriculum process model was to provide this combination:

> Stenhouse was where the process model came from... [Jim] wasn't comfortable with the behaviourist model which was so popular at the time...it didn't seem to have much relevance to kids, it seemed to him—and I'm paraphrasing him here—that kids copped it for whatever went wrong. And...when he got a hold of Stenhouse's stuff that really rang some bells because it said forget about objectives and concentrate on resources, that's the part of the teaching model, the teaching model he ended up with... If you get kids rich and diverse resources and give them some control over their use, that's a far more productive way of operating than being constrained by a series of objectives. (Eric McMillan: Interview, 26 February, 1991)

As two collectively written school documents (Richmond Road School, 1983; 1985) outline, a resource-based programme can allow for different ways of learning and different outcomes. Resource materials can activate children's initial competencies and serve as a guide or framework for the learner's communicative knowledge and abilities. Children at different ages and levels of abilities need not be constrained, therefore, by predictive materials and can work with resources either independently or collaboratively. For this to occur, however, resources need to be both differentiated and problem-posing. Resources must be open enough to allow for alternative means and modes of learning, and should be concerned with genuine questions, not with providing answers. The development of such resources began in the early 1980s at Richmond Road, just as Eric McMillan was leaving the school:

> I just wish that Stenhouse could have gone and seen what [Jim] had done because *he made that theoretical model which Stenhouse proposed—the*

process model—actually operate, and developed a school around resources that they made. And I think they still do that. That was just beginning when I left, this idea of teachers producing wide ranging resources—involved in specific resources...resources that could be used by a wide range of ability levels. (Eric McMillan: Interview, 26 February, 1991; my emphasis)

The decision to develop cooperatively made resources arose from the perceived need in the Social Studies curriculum area to provide more culturally relevant material for children. The process began by providing 'focus resources' for specific topic areas within Social Studies. From there, teacher-made resources have been developed by curriculum teams for other curriculum areas within the school.[3] There are ready-made resources available in the form of 'boxed books' and 'fluency kits', which will be discussed further below in the section on language experience activities, but for the most part resources at Richmond Road are developed by teachers. These resources become part of integrated resource kits which are rotated through the school, staying in each rōpū area for four-five weeks. Teachers prepare resources at ten levels of reading independence and in four learning contexts. The reading levels match the material to the pupils while the learning contexts facilitate their wide-ranging, interactive and open ended use:

> [Resource kits] are housed in plastic bags and identified in the rōpū by curriculum area, description of activity, learning context... and reading level. Children appear quite conversant with these various designations and choose appropriate resources for their reading age and the activity being undertaken, with a minimum of teacher direction. One younger child explains to me what the activities in her resource kit involve. Even the very young know exactly what the resources require of them and what reading level they are meant to be working at in the use of these resources (Field Notes, 19 August, 1990).

The learning arrangements which underpin the resources used at Richmond Road were developed by Laughton, in conjunction with Stenhouse's notions, from a paper by Breen, Candlin & Waters (1979) and from Fillion's (1983) 'Let Me See You Learn'. Breen *et al.* advocate a differentiated approach to learning materials, while Fillion argues that children develop their understanding of the learning process by seeing each other learn. The four learning contexts which Laughton was subsequently to establish within the school from these readings were: superior/inferior; cooperative; collaborative; and independent.

Storytelling and Superior/inferior arrangements. This is material suitable for sharing with a whole (family) group and usually involves one, or a number participants taking a lead role. This need not be the teacher(s), however, and thus these arrangements allow all children to be involved and to participate as they choose, and when they feel comfortable and/or confident. It also allows children (along with parents) to exercise provisional authority in areas in which they have expertise and skills.

Cooperative arrangements put children into shared situations where they support each other while completing a task. These groups are usually self-chosen and encompass a wide range of skills and ability. They foster the notion of cooperation rather than competition and aim to reduce children's fear of failure through active participation in a supportive system which demands corporate rather than individual accountability.

Collaborative arrangements bring children together in situations which require shared understanding because those involved have different information that they are required to put together to complete a task. This involves children in the sharing of information, the negotiation of meaning, and debate, until consensus is reached. Children are free to express a wide range of their own ideas, beliefs, values and attitudes in order to produce a shared conclusion, although it is the process of negotiation rather than the eventual outcome which is emphasised.

Independent arrangements allow every child the opportunity to operate individually at her or his own speed and level, with materials suited to individual needs and interests. In this way, independence is developed and the child is encouraged to take responsibility for his or her own learning. This learning is still, however, tied to the underlying principle of cooperation because it aims to encourage the acceptance of responsibility for knowledge already held, rather than independent learning at the expense of others.

Encompassing all the various learning strategies are resource materials designed to introduce concepts, theme approaches and base stories to the whole group. This gives the coherence and continuity necessary for drawing together the variety of activities in which children can be involved (Richmond Road School, 1983; 1985; 1986). Laughton's intention, via these learning arrangements, was to provide children with different opportunities and responsibilities in the learning process:

> ...he saw those [learning contexts] as skills which maintained a cultural thread because they were consistent with the sorts of things that children would be doing in their homes, and be familiar with from their ethnic backgrounds, and yet they also honed the skills that were required to have children function adequately in the mainstream. And this goes back to the notion of [provisional] authority, the authentic source, who owns the knowledge. And that was a real display of equity and learning in process because *every child had the opportunity to hold the power, if you like, be the knowledge giver.* Groups were largely mixed...so children got used to

reciprocal learning, guided learning, supportive learning. (Helen Villers: Interview, 29 May, 1991; my emphasis)

The result for teachers has also been a different approach to learning and teaching:

those learning arrangements were different...they carry different expectations of kids, and different expectations of you, and...they provided different opportunities for kids too. The hope, of course, was that while they were formalised for the resource making they were actually the way that [teachers] should have been operating throughout the day. So there was actually to be a spin-off, and I think in a large sense there was. It got rid of whole-class teaching, almost got rid of whole-group teaching, almost, never quite. It certainly made people recognise and address kids much more as individuals and again, this comes back to knowing where kids are, what kids liked, what kids were interested in, what they chose to do, all of those kinds of things. (Joy Glasson: Interview, 29 May, 1991)

The benefits for both children and teachers of these varied learning contexts are strongly advocated by the school but the cost of developing the necessary resources has also been high: 'the resources that [Jim] provided were very very rich, very powerful. And good teachers can probably do them better than anybody else. That's what he proved there... [but] at some cost. I've not known teachers who have worked harder than there, especially in the years that followed me... [when] resource development reached a very high level' (Eric McMillan: Interview, 26 February, 1991). The demands associated with resource making were also mentioned by a number of teachers as the principal cause of the extra time required of them at the school. However, despite these reservations (and remembering that 'schools are for kids'), the resource-based pedagogy employed at Richmond Road has led to the achievement of Laughton's principal educational intentions. As Helen Villers summarises it:

...there are two major strands to the way the school operates and one is cultural maintenance, being proud of who you are and developing a notion of that further, and the other of access to power, functioning adequately in the mainstream, and *the resource system, the child-centred resource-based system that we established addressed both those needs*. (Interview, 29 May, 1991; my emphasis)

Moreover, by concentrating on the process of learning at Richmond Road the 'product', so elusive to ethnic minority children in the normal circumstances of schooling, is also being achieved. Joy Glasson argues:

There was often an interpretation that it was process as *opposed* to product. It wasn't. But it was a belief that if you think about process and you concentrate on that, on creating a learning environment for kids, and on getting kids involved in learning and engaging in learning then the product comes out of it... But if you concentrate on learning and on finding things that are actually going to make kids *choose* to learn—because no-one else can make the choice for them—the learning does take place and the product is of high quality. And then you help the kids, of course, keep on increasing the level of the product. Of course you do. But it comes out of the process, rather than the other way round. (Interview, 29 May, 1991)

The resource-based process model provides a means for fostering the independence of learners. It also allows for the inclusion and affirmation of cultural and language differences in the learning process, and it is to this latter dimension that I now want to turn.

A Multilingual Environment: The Role of Language and Culture [4]

Fostering Home Languages

Laughton, in a 1985 position paper on the Māori bilingual option at Richmond Road, clearly articulates his conception of the role of languages within the school:

There are many children at Richmond Road School whose mother tongue is not English. Submerged unavoidably in a strange language from school entry these children are particularly vulnerable. It is the school's task to ameliorate that condition—to show them respect, to encourage pride in their identity by including their languages and cultures to a significant degree, to lessen in as many ways as possible the potential indignity and counter-productivity of mandatory bilingualism (through monolingual schooling in another's language). In short, to facilitate educational advancement from a solid platform of self-knowledge, self-assurance and an acknowledged first language competence. (1985a: 1)

Laughton saw bilingualism as a cognitive and educational advantage. In this, as in other areas, his educational thinking was ahead of his time. While the 1970s saw his contemporaries ascribing the educational underachievement of minority children to the deficit theory—and, in so doing, strenuously attempting to exclude and/or 'correct' home language influences—Laughton specifically set out to affirm and incorporate the languages and cultures of his students within the school. This proactive approach to cultural and language maintenance, which has seen the development of the dual-medium bilingual units and the associated language pre-schools, began with the establishment of the Inner-City Language Unit at the school in 1976. At that time, Laughton encouraged Joy Glasson to develop a new approach to second language teaching methodology within the unit:

> ...it started because of the language unit...and right from the beginning at that time it was something relatively new...because we adopted a pedagogy and a methodology and techniques with kids that were different to the climate of the times. Remember, in the [1970s] in New Zealand you still had the deficit theory operating and you had a lot of behaviourist teaching going on... We started from cognitive theory which actually says that you have to allow kids opportunities to learn. You also then, of course, have to allow them opportunities to process language and it has to be real...it was always based in a theory of language acquisition and in a learning theory generally. I linked that particularly to a lot of the Labov material about factors that affect learning. So what I actually did was combine a Chomsky base in language acquisition here with a Labov difference base and attitudes to learning and language, and what affects it. (Joy Glasson: Interview, 29 May, 1991)[5]

Again, a theoretical basis underpinned the approach adopted at Richmond Road and the methodology begun in the language unit was soon to permeate throughout the school. The language unit was set up at Richmond Road to cater for recent arrivals to New Zealand who had little knowledge of English, and served the inner-city Auckland area at the primary school level. For these children the emphasis has been on developing oral and literacy skills in English through the use, where possible, of their home language(s), and by a contextualised and integrative approach to language acquisition which concentrates on meaning. Within this, the role of the teacher in recognising children's expertise in the language(s) and culture(s) they bring with them is emphasised. The importance of home language maintenance features prominently in the language ethos adopted by the unit (as it does elsewhere in the school) and is supported by the cooperative arrangements which the vertical groups facilitate. Language and culture are regarded as an area of strength and competency for all children and teachers recognise and acknowledge Ken Goodman's view that if, as teachers, they undermine a child's language they also undermine that child's ability to learn (Richmond Road School, 1983).

The centrality of language and culture in the teaching methodology of the language unit is a pedagogical feature which has come to characterise the school as a whole. The children's use of their home language is encouraged wherever possible within the school and, in the case of the Māori, Samoan and Cook Islands bilingual rōpū, is formalised in a bilingual curriculum. The bilingual rōpū are based on a dual-medium approach to language. During half of each morning and every other afternoon, the teachers speak only the home language to the children and the children are encouraged to respond in the same language. At other times, English is spoken. When the home language is in use, however, pupils are not required to speak the language prescribed if they do not wish to. As Cazden (1989) observes, this might be a weakness of the programmes since low-status languages such as these need as much support as possible within the school to avoid being swamped beyond it. The school's approach is consistent though with its broader conception of the role of language(s) in the fostering of cultural identity. Teachers within the school would argue that the fostering of language(s) cannot be separated from the cultural context from which it springs nor from the type of society one would wish to see result (Richmond Road School, 1983). Richmond Road locates its view of the role of languages in the school within a wider frame of reference; that of recognising and affirming cultural respect, autonomy and difference through the structures of the school. As Lionel Pedersen argues, 'the school is about a way of living rather than just language. It is no use knowing the language at the expense of cultural tradition—all it becomes then is a translation, however fluent, of Pākehā culture' (Field Notes, 22 August, 1990). Fostering language is important but the cultural context which it represents, and from which it comes, should never be lost from sight.

The broader cultural context which the school has adopted in relation to the promotion of home languages again stems directly from Jim Laughton's educational thinking. His obvious endorsement of a maintenance rather than a transitional view of bilingual education (see Baker, 1993; Romaine, 1989) can be seen when he argues: 'bilingual education...wisely conceived... [can] make a difference—as an act of respect and humility by the powerful, as an expression of confidence and determination by the powerless, [and] as an exercise in genuine communication among all' (1985a: 1). But, as Cazden's earlier observation reveals, he was also clearly ambivalent about full-immersion programmes or any notion of language coercion which such programmes might involve for children. He argued that there were educational reasons for his reservations which were reflected in the bilingual debate itself:

> You will be aware that bilingual education is a complex, contentious issue, particularly where it bears on the language revival of indigenous minorities. Even at the level of methodology there is bitter dispute. Some advocate bilingualism as a goal with total immersion in the target language the means. Others (our programmes included) regard bilingualism as both a process and a goal in the belief that the context of learning is a major part of the learning... For us bilingualism in its most embracing sense must be part of the process or it won't be part of the outcome. (Principal's Report, 8 March, 1988)

He also believed strongly in the importance of English literature. As Lionel Pedersen comments, 'it was quite simple with Jim, the wealth of English literature would never be replaced' (Field Notes, 11 February, 1991). Another teacher, in Cazden's study, describes the confluence of both of these elements in Laughton's thinking:

> I actually thought it was very difficult to teach Māori in a dual immersion [approach], because you can't do justice to the one that you wanted them to learn *most*, which for me was Māori. So I went to see Jim. I said, 'I can't see the point of this dual immersion'. He said, 'The point of dual immersion [is] that if you put children into just one area, one language, then you forget about all the good things that other [language] has to offer'. He said to me, 'How many books are written for children in Māori that are as rich as the literature in English? Sure, they might read those afterwards, after school. But this is the point of school: to offer that variety'. (cited in Cazden, 1989: 157)

The notion of variety is also reflected in Laughton's insistence on *choice* in relation to bilingualism. Parents, on bringing their children to the school for example, are given the choice of which rōpū they wish their children to enter. This overcomes the significant problem of ambivalence or confusion for parents as to the role of home languages in the school (Corson, 1990). Parents are able to clearly identify what the school offers in comparison to others and can then make their choice within the variety of language structures the school itself offers. The identification of choice as a crucial variable in the success of bilingual programmes (particularly in relation to community support; see Cummins, 1983; Holmes, 1984) supports this position. However, Laughton took this a step further by extending the notion of choice to include children as well as parents and the wider community. As a Samoan bilingual unit teacher comments in Cazden's study:

> The bilingual unit works on a *choice* basis. Parents have the option of putting their children into the bilingual unit. In the morning I speak only Samoan, and the children have the choice. They're encouraged to speak Samoan. The fluent ones do, and the little ones sort of copy. When I first came in, Jim said, 'The parents do not have to put the children in, and the children do not have to try and make a sentence in Samoan'. He said, '*You* have that responsibility, because you have that expertise, but the children don't. The most *important* idea is their identity, and to value what they've got'. (cited in Cazden, 1989: 156)

Laughton reiterates this in his position paper when he states: 'although the teacher is prescribed as to when she may speak English, the pupil always has a choice. In the search for new understandings, linguistic imperialism finds no place' (1985a: 1). In this context, emphasis is placed on the development of a child's *identity* (which includes acknowledging their home language(s)) rather than on the development of language *per se*. For Laughton, the fostering of bilingualism needed always to be tempered by a recognition of the child's ability to opt out of speaking the home language if she or he so chose. The educational reasons he argued for this position have been outlined, but notwithstanding these, Laughton's expressed reticence towards a full-immersion approach to bilingualism may also have been for personal reasons—particularly, his own lack of fluency in Māori.

Laughton's father, John G. Laughton, was a prominent missionary and later moderator of the Presbyterian church in New Zealand. A Scot, he had been a fluent Māori speaker (he chaired the committee which undertook the last Māori translation of the bible in the 1950s). His mother, Horiana Tekauru, was Māori. Despite this background, Jim Laughton's parents consciously decided to bring him up speaking English. Assimilation was the dominant ideology in New Zealand education at the time and the Māori language was not highly regarded and, indeed, actively repressed (see Chapter 3). The result of that decision was to have significant effects:

> Now Jim, I think, was one of the youngest. It was a large family. And he was taught no Māori. His...father was (pause) John Laughton, the Scotsman...a scholar in the Māori language [and] a fluent speaker, and yet they made the conscious decision not to teach young Jimmy the language because they figured he would do better with English. And the irony is that in the finish that is probably what killed him. That was what he became more passionate about than anything, the Māori language, and an ability with it. And all from a decision made all those years ago. (Eric McMillan: Interview, 26 February, 1991)

Wally Penetito expands on the consequences of this personal history in the context of the school:

Penetito: He and I had some differences of opinion from time to time but nothing really marked that I can think of.

Interviewer: What about his ambivalence about immersion [issues]?

Penetito: Yes, that was kind of one of them I think...Jim knew that he couldn't speak Māori [and] he believed that a principal has to know everything that's going on in the school...he believed that as the principal...it was part of his responsibility to be everywhere in the school, know what's going on. And if he allowed an immersion Māori language class that would be one area that he couldn't actually be part of because of his own inadequacies. (Interview, 14 October, 1991)

The experience of his own language background contributed to Laughton's advocacy for bilingualism, and he was more aware than most, at both a personal and professional level, of the difficulties associated with such an enterprise. Ironically, however, his personal experiences were also to see him draw back from the full implications of fostering bilingualism within Richmond Road. His insistence on a dual-medium approach to language within the school rather than full-immersion was not made, it seems, for educational reasons alone. The results of Laughton's ambivalence can still be seen within the school today, with teachers holding various conceptions of the role of bilingual teaching. In 1991, for example, the Māori bilingual unit had three out of four teachers who spoke Māori fluently, and was consequently moving towards more of an immersion approach to language:

> Each morning in SS4 [the Māori bilingual unit] John Matthews, the kaiārahi reo, takes 'topic maths'[6] for 45 minutes—rotating throughout the course of the morning between the three home groups in the rōpū. In each home group's allocated time for topic maths he speaks only Māori to the children and they are encouraged to do likewise. Older children act as tuakana in the language to the younger children to facilitate this process. At other times children speak in both English and Māori within the rōpū. While Luke [Hiki] tends to respond in the language used by the children his instructions are almost entirely in Māori. Horo [Karauti] tends to speak in Māori and translate into English when necessary... (Field Notes, 22 February, 1991)

As Luke Hiki elaborates:

Hiki: we're just speaking Māori all the time...the kids are always hearing it... Some of them aren't shy to use it all the time when they're speaking to each other. The ones that are just coming in at five [yrs] ...it takes them a few weeks to get used to hearing it all the time. They understand...the language, we just have to give them encouragement to use the spoken Māori more often'. So when John [Matthews] comes in he doesn't ask questions in English. All his questions are done in Māori, so they've got to fend for themselves in that context.

Interviewer: And the kids know that?

Hiki: Yes. They know that it's Māori time...if the teachers aren't speaking Māori to each other it doesn't work either. So we've jumped on that more...we speak Māori more often to each other, and speak Māori directly to the kids in that time. (Interview, 13 August, 1991)

Yet in other areas of the schools, some teachers have expressed reservations about these developments. One in particular comments:

> I think it's very good for children to have their own strong language base [but] I feel sorry when—well I think it's happening in the Māori bilingual [unit]—I think they're missing out on the English side of it. Bilingualism

does mean two languages, not just a strong [one] ...if you can get somebody strong in both, and that's the idea isn't it, if you're only going to end up speaking one well and the other in a mediocre way then I don't think you've achieved a tremendous amount particularly. I think it's great that children speak Māori, and well, but I think you do them a great disservice if you don't check that their English is good too. After all it is English that most of them are going to have to use... Actually there are other teachers on the staff who wonder the same. It may not really be a problem, I don't know, it just seems important that you do give them strengths in all areas and you don't just forget about one at the expense of the others.

Some of the concerns expressed here as to the possible disadvantages of focusing on one language (particularly a non-dominant language) are not supported by current bilingual research (see Appel & Muysken, 1987; Baker, 1988; 1993; Cummins & Swain, 1986; Hakuta, 1986; Romaine, 1989) although they are views often held in the wider community. It may be useful for the school, as such, to specifically address the theoretical issues underlying approaches to bilingual teaching as part of their ongoing staff development programme, in order to clarify these points of concern. However, while the school's further exploration of these issues may prove useful, it needs to be reiterated that Richmond Road under Laughton's influence has been at the forefront of bilingual education initiatives in New Zealand. Given the relative recency of these initiatives and the school's leading role within them, Richmond Road can be expected to have encountered some difficulties along the way. As Margaret Leaming comments:

Nobody ever taught people how to teach in bilingual schools, so these teachers went in there and literally had to do an extremely difficult job. Not in one language but in two, if you were doing bi-modal, which Richmond Road was. Bi-modal meaning both English and Māori, not immersion... To me it's not an issue, bi-modal or immersion, I could never get excited about it, you learn this way or you learn that way. But what was difficult for people was—here they were *starting* bilingual education...and I mean, it had its ups and downs, there's no two ways about that, but it was something that you focused on and you looked at where you could go, so it would get better in terms of empowering children. (Interview, 28 May, 1991)

There were also difficulties encountered in staffing bilingual units. Laughton may have been more successful than most in attracting teaching staff with those particular attributes to his school but the limited number of bilingual teachers in New Zealand from which he could draw was a constant cause for concern: 'bilingual initiatives may provide the greatest agents of change both for those directly involved and those indirectly affected. The problem is that...even the current sparse initiatives may founder for want of bilingual teaching personnel' (Principal's Report, 2 June, 1987). Lionel Pedersen argues, along similar lines, that full-immersion is not a goal for the school simply because it cannot guarantee the personnel required from year to year (Field Notes, 11 February, 1991). The Māori bilingual unit bears out this point clearly. In 1991 it had three fluent speakers (at the start of that year it had four) and was moving more to an immersion approach. In 1992 and 1993 it has had only two Māori speakers. For much of 1992 a non-Māori speaker was employed as a relief teacher to replace Luke Hiki who had left to take up another appointment. And in 1993, while the school has a new kaiārahi reo, it now has to look for a replacement for John Matthews. These staffing difficulties remain a cause for concern in the development of bilingual education at the school, as they do in other New Zealand schools. However, as Eric McMillan points out, these difficulties should not cause us to lose sight of the broader agenda of educational innovation which Laughton was able to set in place at Richmond Road:

Interviewer: ...before Jim moved into the whānau [family group] concept there were no inner-city schools in New Zealand that operated in that way?

McMillan: Yes, at that time. Jim [showed] them it could work...well I wouldn't say the bilingual unit worked particularly well...In talking with him about [how hard] it was to keep the thing going—desperately trying to get staff organised... And that's the problem all over, we are desperate to incorporate a level of bilingual awareness but you cannot get a [fluent Māori-speaking] teacher, you can't even start... So I don't see that as the big contribution from Richmond Road. *I see it more as an educational institution in which Māori and Pacific Island children succeeded beyond any other place,* that there was a place where they were comfortable, where they learned, where they read and wrote to a superior level...that's the important contribution. The other struggle will go on, the bilingual one... (Interview, 26 February, 1991; my emphasis)

McMillan's observations highlight that bilingualism, for all its importance, was for Laughton only one strand in promoting an educational environment which benefited minority children. It was not to be seen as an end in itself. In this light, it is worth briefly discussing other key aspects in the language pedagogy adopted at Richmond Road which bear on Laughton's broader educational intentions. I will discuss more fully in Chapter 8 the ten reading levels employed within the school, and the close monitoring involved in matching resources at these various reading levels to children. The 'language experience' approach to language and reading within the school, however, can be further explored here. This approach, as evidenced earlier by the activities of the Inner-City Language Unit, aims to contextualise and integrate language activities, and emphasises meaning rather than form.

Language experience: 'We are concerned that children express their ideas in real situations'

'Language experience' involves children in developing and expanding language in the context of experiences, books and/or events. For example, children discuss an event or experience which is recorded in written form by the teacher (a chart or wall story is often used) and then the children read back what has been written. In a family group, which encompasses a range of backgrounds and experiences, this process provides a common experience with which children can identify. Reading the material back to the teacher is facilitated by a written form of language familiar to the children and the difficulties associated with using school texts, which tend to exclude minority cultures, are consequently obviated. A 'shared book' offers a similar familiarity. It provides reading for all children in the family group, regardless of instructional level, principally through the use of paired reading activities. Paired reading, as we have seen, is based on tuakana-teina relationships. Children are listed in terms of their level of individual reading independence and the information is displayed on charts within the rōpū—not, as in many cases, as a means of ranking, but rather, as a means of identifying for children whom they can go to for support and whom they can assist. Levels of reading independence are also used as the basis for 'sustained silent reading' which complements shared book activities.

Shared book and silent reading methods were introduced at Richmond Road as a result of Warwick Elley's and Francis Mangubhai's comparison of both approaches with the use of traditional school texts. Elley & Mangubhai (1983) found that shared book and silent reading, particularly the former, accelerated and maintained children's reading development. What was required, however, to sustain these activities was the availability of a sufficient number of books at a wide range of reading levels; a 'book flood'. As a result, Laughton set up the 'boxed book' system and 'extended fluency' kits within the school. The boxed book system consists of sets of graded reading material from 5–11 years which are issued to rōpū on a fortnightly basis. Those with reading ages above 11 years are expected to use other sources such as the school library or public library for their reading. Fluency kits are boxes of books which are designed for beginning readers who are experiencing difficulties at their assigned reading level. The kits provide a range of reading formats and are designed to be used in silent reading at approximately two levels below the child's instructional level.

Richmond Road's approach to written language incorporates similar ideals and strategies to those adopted in reading. The school specifically avoids what Koch (1982) has described as the 'learned terror' of writing for many children—

where the avoidance of errors in work invigilated by teachers becomes the children's primary focus. Emphasis is placed, instead, on making writing fun. Writing is de-emphasised as a separate activity and encouraged as a necessary part of other curriculum activities in accordance with the principle of language experience. Closely allied to this is the recognition of children as experts in the writing process. The different cultural, linguistic and personal responses children incorporate into learning to write—and the experimentation necessarily involved in such a process—are encouraged. Concomitantly, the notion of teaching a 'correct' writing model is discounted. As a result, a variety of writing activities are employed: private writing; supported writing; and cooperative writing.

> *Private writing* is characterised by little, if any, teacher correction. Children are encouraged to express themselves freely in writing and to view writing, accordingly, as an effective means of personal communication. A time is set aside each day for writing of this kind which is not corrected and is only shared at the child's discretion. Private writing can also include pre-writing or rehearsal which emphasises for children the developmental nature of the writing process.

> *Supported writing* involves providing a framework for writing such as the retelling of favourite stories, the completion of stories or the writing of stories from a different point of view. Whatever framework is adopted, however, support is always available to the children when required.

> *Cooperative writing* sees children working together in accomplishing a task which includes written work.

In all of these language activities, the experiences of the children constitute their starting point. The aim is to adopt a pedagogy based on developmental learning where language acquisition grows within a setting of meaningful, active, and real learning contexts. An integrated approach to the curriculum is also adopted using these language experience techniques. Language is not demarcated as a separate area of study but is incorporated into all curriculum areas (see also May, 1991; 1994).

Richmond Road demonstrates an integrated approach to curriculum and a child-centred pedagogy which clearly facilitates children's learning and, particularly, that of minority children. However, an integrated and child-centred curriculum, as Bernstein (1971; 1990) has observed, does not *necessarily* work to the advantage of ethnic minority children, based as it is on self-directed learning techniques and expectations with which majority group children are often more familiar.[7] Accordingly, the school has recognised the disadvantages minority children may face with these learning strategies and has attempted to counter any possible unfamiliarity by an emphasis on the place of routines in learning.

Timetabling Children's Learning

Routines feature prominently in the learning activities conducted at Richmond Road. The use of routines provides a structure for the team teaching approach demanded by family group organisation and ensures that children are familiar with the particular learning arrangements conducted within rōpū. The timetable, as such, is highly structured. Individual rōpū have some autonomy in deciding the composition of their weekly programme—depending on their particular clientele—but the programmes must operate within the learning arrangements described above. Given this, rōpū programmes can only be set in place when they have been presented to and approved by the staff as a whole. Approval must also be sought for any changes in rōpū organisation that occur during the course of the year. Any relevant theoretical justifications must also be outlined by the teachers involved to support these changes. Once rōpū timetables have been established, children in particular rōpū will know that at certain times each day they carry out particular activities. Each day may vary in what it offers, depending on the overall balance of the weekly programme, but children are always aware of what any given day holds for them.

The advantage of this highly structured approach to timetabling is that children gain security from knowing what comes next. Hodson (1986) argues that children learn best in this type of secure environment where they can explore, test, share, communicate and develop their ideas in an atmosphere of trusted confidence. At Richmond Road strict timetabling 'ensures predictability of organisation, programme and social milieu' (Staff Meeting Agenda, 24 November, 1987; 17 October, 1989; 27 November, 1990).[8] As John Matthews observes: 'I suppose that's why we don't have so many disciplinary problems. It's routines. *The kids are used to the routines, like we are...* Once the routine's broken, that's when you get your problems. The kids don't know what they're doing, and neither do I' (Interview, 25 May, 1991). The use of routines to provide familiarity for children is particularly evident in the organisation of rōpū from year to year. Rather than reconstitute groups at the start of each new year the school programme begins in the last two weeks of the previous year. This minimises the disruption associated with beginning a new year's programme since children are already familiar with the nature of the programme, their teachers, and their classroom environment.

The organisation of the timetable along these highly structured lines is not without its difficulties. When it was initially introduced by Laughton it met with some opposition. Helen Villers recalls:

I was very angry that was handed down to us at a time when I felt that we were developing something that was more flexible. But I had to concede after using it for a period of time that it was very effective, very effective in terms of children's learning. We probably lost a bit of the nice time you have with children if you've got the time to take your breath, sit around and talk things out a little bit further. But in terms of pumping in what's required academically, yes it worked. (Interview, 29 May, 1991)

While set in place by Laughton to aid children's learning, the consequent loss of flexibility in timetabling is often mentioned as a point of concern by staff. As a teacher in Cazden's study comments:

I do feel the timetable has become too rigid. If you're really into a piece of work involving drama, or expression with poetry or prose writing, it's always breaking, and putting away, and coming back to. The afternoon's are freer, but the morning programmes are very compartmentalised. I think the *main* reason is that we've put such things as sustained silent reading, paired reading, paired writing, topic maths, number maths—all have to be scheduled. And although these things are very admirable, I think the adverse effect is that they've made the timetable very rigid. (cited in Cazden, 1989: 161)

Flexibility can be accommodated within rōpū timetables but the constraints are significant. Still, as Cazden observes, the benefits of such an approach would seem to significantly outweigh its disadvantages:

Consider, just as an illuminating contrast, a possible alternative: each home group could operate as a single-cell class—retaining the vertical grouping but allowing each teacher more flexibility in planning the day. Although this would indeed give more flexibility in planning, the costs would escalate: decreasing the opportunities for children to learn from a larger group of their peers and from a more diverse group of teachers; and eliminating some of the need for teachers to work together and learn from each other. (1989: 162)

Obviously, all teaching and learning arrangements have their limitations, and issues pertaining to immersion and the flexibility of timetables are, perhaps, Richmond Road's. However, what distinguishes this school's approach to pedagogy from the majority of schools is its intrinsic connection with changes in school organisation and its coordinated and theoretically conversant approach to meeting the learning needs of its predominantly minority students. As Joy Glasson concludes:

Interviewer: So what were the key components of the pedagogical change then?

Glasson: I actually do think that probably one of them was bringing together the vertical kind of grouping, the actual bringing together of a wide age range. One of them was the acceptance of responsibility. One of them was allowing children to learn instead of blocking it, not trying to predetermine in fact what they will learn, but going with them and providing them ways of learning, and then helping them actually see what they've learnt and how they've learnt it. And then, of course, helping kids *become*—not tying, not binding them to the systems in school. And underpinning that, I suppose, a respect of difference... While that's not pedagogy in one sense of the word that certainly *is* pedagogy. It's the systems that go into place to allow that to happen (Interview, 29 May, 1991).

I have already discussed the systems set in place for family group organisation, but those which pertain to the use of resources and the development of curriculum content can now be explored.

Notes to Chapter 7

1. As I have already discussed in Chapter 6, parents are also actively involved in both of these areas; contributing to school management and policy decisions, and teaching within rōpū.
2. Like Laughton, Lionel Pedersen is Māori, but is not a fluent speaker.
3. See Chapter 8 for an extended discussion of how teachers focus resources within curriculum teams.
4. For a discussion of this dimension of the school in particular relation to 'language policies across the curriculum', see May (1991; 1994).
5. Joy Glasson is now regarded in New Zealand educational circles as an authority on second language development. Like Judy Hucker's nationally recognised expertise in mathematics (see above), Glasson owes her development in this area to Laughton's initial encouragement and support.
6. For a discussion of specific curriculum areas (including topic maths), see Chapter 8.
7. Bernstein argues, in fact, that an integrated curriculum, while it may be more attractive than the clear subject demarcation and didactic teaching associated with traditional approaches to curriculum, is nevertheless still weighted in favour of the dominant group. He suggests that the distinctions between traditional and integrated approaches to curriculum reflect a struggle between the new and old middle-classes (the new middle-class preferring the latter) rather than any attempt to ameliorate the educational disadvantages of minority groups (see also Chapter 2).
8. Key tenets of the school's organisation and pedagogy are often revisited in staff meeting discussions in order that new teachers are introduced to them and older staff continue to remain conversant with them (see also Chapter 6).

8 Curriculum and Assessment: Resourcing and Monitoring Children's Learning

As I argued in Chapter 3, there are definite limitations to many of the more popular approaches to multicultural education adopted in schools. These approaches—which I have described as 'benevolent multiculturalism'—tend to merely 'insert' minorities into the curriculum, most often in the form of subject content. The resulting emphasis is on the *lifestyles* rather than the *life chances* of ethnic minority groups. As Hulmes (1989) has argued, the voices of minority cultures are effectively ignored, except when they speak at the levels of cultural activity such as music, dance, cuisine and social customs.

In terms of curriculum development, this expressive conception of culture and cultural difference(s) usually sees the addition of an 'ethnic' component to an already prefigured and monocultural curriculum. Multicultural education as ordinarily practised is transmitted within dominant cultural forms and 'leave[s] obscured and intact existing cultural hierarchies and criteria of stratification' (Olneck, 1990: 163). The 'selection' of cultural differences continues to be mediated by the dominant group and existing power relations are consequently little affected. The study of minority cultures, in fact, may actually serve to reinforce dominant power relations by acting as a benefit to children of the majority culture rather than to minority children themselves. As Graeme Page observed of this process in Chapter 6, 'it's an advantage on an advantage that the [Pākehā] kid already has'.

The inherent paternalism associated with the 'selection' of cultures within benevolent multiculturalism is specifically rejected by teachers at Richmond Road. Maggie Wood, a teacher in SS2, argues:

> That's another thing actually that I've learnt [at Richmond Road], that you don't intrude on someone else's culture like a tourist because it's very easy to go bungling in, and it's also a very colonial thing to assume that you're doing a culture a great favour by picking up bits of it that appeal to you and using it. In actual fact that's someone's identity you're mucking around

with. It isn't always [appropriate] for the white man to come and do this sort of magnanimous—'this little piece of your culture interests me therefore I will pick it up and use it when I feel like it'. It isn't actually showing any real respect, it's just toying with something or trifling with it. I think a lot of New Zealanders have a nasty habit of collecting cultures. And I've learnt not to do that. (Interview, 12 August, 1991)

Wally Penetito argues, along similar lines, that paternalism is avoided at Richmond Road because the responsibility for cultural selection rests where it belongs—with the members of the cultural groups themselves:

I think that's built into the way their school runs too [and it] follows from that then that people in the school have access to some knowledge which belongs to their cultural group. And they're the ones who are the first repositories of it...they should now be given opportunities to share it if that's what they want to do with it, and which parts of it, and how, and who, are the questions they've got to answer for themselves. And I think Richmond Road started establishing ways of allowing that to happen—of facilitating that. (Interview, 14 October, 1991)

Both Wood's and Penetito's comments highlight a process which has been identified in multicultural and bilingual education literature as 'mutual accommodation' (see Nieto, 1992; Tharp, 1989). In most schooling, the process of accommodation is usually one way—that is, minority students (and the ethnic communities they represent) accommodate to the dominant culture of the school. Mutual accommodation, however, suggests that schools, and teachers, can also do some accommodating by drawing on the social and linguistic resources of their students as part of the teaching and learning process. The result sees both teachers and students modifying their behaviours in the direction of a common goal—'academic success with cultural integrity' (Nieto, 1992: 258). This process of mutual accommodation is clearly evident at Richmond Road and has had much to do with the reciprocal learning relationships the school has established (see Chapter 7). However, another key facet to the fostering of mutual accommodation within the school has been the school's resource-based curriculum development programme. As Maggie Wood goes on to observe:

The resources help a lot because you get such a diverse pack of things that you are always working with some other culture and you have children there of that culture, therefore you pay a lot of respect to it. It's also the fact that *each culture, I think, is still seen as a living thing*. The children there often live a [Pacific] Island life in the middle of Auckland, therefore you have to tune in very quickly to what is important in their lives, how things are done... It's not just a matter of saying 'that kid's a Samoan', you have to know things about Samoans, and the more you discover the more you take it into yourself so the more you feel comfortable with each culture—the more you see the differences and see the similarities. You almost end up feeling as if you're a multicultural person rather than just a Pākehā with an overlay of a few cultures...they become part of you, not in a superficial way, not just...picking them up like tokens but because you suddenly realise that you actually do and can feel similar things. (Interview, 12 August, 1991)

Resourcing Children's Learning

At Richmond Road the additive curriculum approach indicative of benevolent multiculturalism is replaced by the *incorporation*[1] of other cultures *into* the curriculum and their integration across the curriculum. Joan Metge, writing on New Zealand education, argues that incorporating the study of minority cultures across the curriculum is a promising strategy for multicultural education, but is not without its difficulties. For it to be successful, she concludes, 'it requires a broadening of the base of education, and this must begin with teachers and the provision of good resource material' (1990: 48). This is exactly what Richmond Road has sought to achieve.

The approach to curriculum development which the school has adopted began with the decision by Laughton in the early 1980s to resource certain topics in social studies. Recognising that the necessary first step to establishing a multicultural curriculum in New Zealand was the inclusion of its bicultural heritage, he began by establishing the study of a major Māori theme each year. From this followed the development of themes relating to the various Pacific Island groups within the school, and subsequently, to all other ethnic groups represented at Richmond Road. The collaboratively made resources, outlined in the previous chapter, were to result from these curriculum initiatives. Their development was facilitated by Laughton's establishment of curriculum teams which deliberately cut across the rōpū teaching teams. These teams, still in operation today, are responsible for developing the curriculum resources during the course of the year, supervising these materials, and providing support for staff working in other areas. As I indicated in Chapter 5, the involvement of all staff in this process leads to a significant coherence and consistency across the curriculum and a great deal of mutual support among teachers (Cazden, 1989). The discussion of curriculum issues within the school is also, consequently, well established, wide-ranging and inclusive.

'Most of our curriculum is based on our children'

Given that the process model adopted at Richmond Road accords priority to the use of quality resources, teachers are expected to spend a high proportion of their time on resource preparation. The curriculum teams form the basis for this development and use of resources within the school. They have varied in number over the years but presently there are four teams in the areas of Science, Music & Expressive Arts, Health & Physical Education, and Art. The teams comprise staff members from across the school and aim for a diversity of expertise and background experience. Māori and Samoan teachers, for example, are spread throughout the teams to facilitate the development of Māori and Samoan resources in all curriculum areas. Staff with strengths in certain curriculum areas are often associated with particular curriculum teams. Curriculum teams are also, however, regularly reconstituted to ensure teachers gain experience in curriculum areas in which they may be less familiar. The composition of curriculum teams along these lines enables teachers to interact with others beyond their own rōpū, thus avoiding any possible isolationism that might occur between family groups. At a more pragmatic level, it also ensures that there is at least one teacher who is familiar with the particular resources developed in a team and who is able to take the lead in its introduction to the teachers and children within a family group.

The task of each curriculum team is to plan and produce 'focus resources'. These are a set of social studies and associated curriculum resources developed around a variety of school-wide topics and 'focused' by the exploration of a particular concept. School-wide topics are studied each year in a two semester system and are part of an integrated three year cycle. Māori themes are given priority in this process—they run over both semester programmes in any given year—but over the course of the three years other ethnic groups represented within the school are also incorporated. 1991 was the first year of the latest cycle and the current three year plan can be seen in Table 8.1.

Table 8.1 Three year focus plan (adapted from Staff Meeting Agenda, 24 July, 1990)

| | Semester 1 | | Semester 2 | |
	Team 1 & 2	Team 3 & 4	Team 1 & 2	Team 3 & 4
Year 1 (1991)	Māori	Samoa	India	Māori
Year 2 (1992)	Māori	Tonga	Europe	Māori
Year 3 (1993)	Māori	Cook Islands	Niue	Māori

Team 1: Science Team, Team 2: Health Team, Team 3: Music and Expressive Arts, Team 4: Art

The three year focus plan for Māori can be described as an example. In 1991 the emphasis was on the study of Māori Gods. The Māori focus topic was 'creation and origins through mythology', and the particular concept explored was mauri (life force). Given this, the science team developed its curriculum resources by exploring science as the realm of Tāwhirimatea, the god of the winds and the storms. Specific curriculum aspects explored were earth science, water, air and weather. In 1992 the emphasis moved to a study of Māori history and, in 1993, on Māori today. Concepts explored in these last two years by the various curriculum teams have been mana (influence; esteem), tapu (sacredness) and te ihi me te wehi (power and importance). Areas of study in which these concepts have been framed have included Māori tribes, Māori genealogy and Māori leaders. Thus in 1993, for example, the science curriculum team has developed social studies material on particular rural tribal communities in contemporary New Zealand, using the concept of mana to gauge the effects of their economic and social development. The science curriculum content has been provided through an examination of the growing influence of technology on these communities. Other topic areas follow a similar pattern. In studying Samoa in 1991, for example, the art team developed resources around the particular concept of *Fa'a Samoa* (the Samoan way). Their exploration of the social studies element concentrated on the historical and contemporary aspects of *Fa'a Samoa* and their curriculum area was incorporated by looking at carving, patterning and printmaking in relation to Samoan tattooing.[2]

In planning the activities for use in each kit, each staff member in a curriculum team is responsible for developing a certain number of specific resources.[3] This is where the demands of resource making, discussed in the previous chapter, become apparent. In 1990, for example, every staff member had to prepare two activities per reading level, per week (incorporating the variety of learning contexts already outlined), and present them to staff meeting. In 1991 the requirements were changed to re-emphasise the need for open-ended activities. Teams were allowed to present activities at three weekly intervals, at a number of reading levels, but covering only one learning arrangement. This also was subsequently changed when the school won a national contract later in the year to develop a consumer studies package for New Zealand primary schools. What followed was an intensive programme of resource preparation—using the curriculum teams, and the processes already established—to complete the package. Richmond Road, as is its way, also bought the necessary computer software to develop the material to desktop presentation level. In 1992 the final product was formally launched by New Zealand's Education Department and has subsequently received considerable acclaim for the depth and variety of its activities and the strength of its thematic concerns.

The accommodation of the consumer package demonstrates that the organisation of resource making in curriculum teams is both flexible and effective. However, it is also clear that the pressures on staff to prepare and present resources, in whatever form, are considerable. This concern surfaces on a number of occasions in interviews and informal discussions with staff (see also Chapter 7), as do questions on the nature of the resources themselves.

Lyn Malaugh, a teacher who had just left Richmond Road at the time of this interview, argues:

Interviewer: You mentioned time a lot—about the time it took to make all those resources. Would that have been the major detrimental aspect of all the things that went on at Richmond Road?

Malaugh: It was very stressful to do those—particularly with this deadline hanging over your head, and particularly when...you had to do this bulk of resources each term—it was very stressful. Unfortunately some of [these resources] seemed to be rushed out because you had to meet a quantity deadline not a quality deadline. They overcame that a little bit last year [1990], but you still had to produce two per week and show the lot that you were doing in staff meetings. It did overcome the quality thing because you had to show everything. Before that you had to show six, so you're only going to show your six best aren't you...so that got over it. It also got over the fact that not everybody completed the requirement, and that was happening... (Interview, 27 May, 1991)

A number of teachers in Cazden's study, when asked what needs rethinking at Richmond Road, express a similar concern over resources. One comments:

Personally, the thing that comes to mind is the resources. It's very time consuming for teachers. We've done it long enough along the same sort of lines, and now we've got to the stage where we're just doing the same resources with different content. There's so much stuff there that the kids don't get full use of it. The kids are tired too, tired of the same activities being reproduced. I'd be more willing to carry on the way things are if I felt that the time I put in, and the understanding that I wanted the kids to get—not only through the resources but from the whole study—that they would be getting that. But I'm not sure that they are. (cited in Cazden, 1989: 162–163)

However, these reservations notwithstanding, it is interesting to return to Malaugh and her response when asked what she most missed about Richmond Road at her new school:

I did miss all the resources that are there. I did. I've gone looking for reading things and there's nothing, apart from being told. So I miss the 'book flood' [see Chapter 7] and I miss all those reasonings that were behind that. I miss that because it makes it very easy in lots of ways. I haven't found my way around all the other things that are [at this school], but I did say to the [deputy principal] there—who's in the junior school—what reading programmes operate here? What are the books I use? And she took me out into a little storeroom and said 'I think there are these', but she couldn't tell me.

And then I went to her today and said—because I've started off in maths...looking at time, I've got a whole lot of resources that I've got myself—I went to her and said what has the infant department got for time? Have you got clock faces? Have you got this? Have you got that? 'No'. So those are the things that I miss—those very organised set-ups. (Interview, 27 May, 1991)

The curriculum resources, whatever their limitations might be, do provide a rich base for children's learning at Richmond Road. They are also, as Malaugh reveals, not limited to just focus resources. However, before moving on to a discussion of the mathematics curriculum to which she refers, we need to briefly examine the significance of the various literacy levels underpinning the development of focus resources.

'You had to tie it to developmental age, as well as concept, as well as your curriculum area'

While the development and use of focus resources now constitute the majority of work conducted in curriculum development at Richmond Road, it was not the first curriculum consideration given attention by Laughton. His initial concern, on which focus resources were to be based, was literacy and the accurate matching of children to their levels of reading ability. As he argued, primacy needed to be given to the development of reading proficiency because it 'gives students independence within the school system more than do other proficiencies (getting the cap out of the hand)... [and] indicate[s] more than most things the culturally different student's acceptance of and ability to profit from the school experience' (Staff Meeting Agenda, 30 March, 1982). The ten reading levels that were subsequently established within the school to monitor this proficiency determine the nature and demands of the various resource activities produced by teachers. When in use, they also allow all children in a family group the opportunity to work on a focus topic with material that is appropriate to their levels of reading independence.

The literacy levels, and the activities conducted within them, have emerged from the school's exploration over the years of issues pertaining to literacy development. Some influences, such as Elley & Mangubhai's 'book flood', and the development of various approaches to reading and writing, have already been discussed. Other influences include the work of Marie Clay, Ken Goodman, Courtney Cazden and Frank Smith on the development of early reading and writing, and the work of Brian Cambourne on naturalised learning (Richmond Road School, 1983; 1985; 1986). Laughton's own background and knowledge of language issues were also to provide a significant impetus to these developments. The resulting literacy levels see closely monitored activities that range from the use of dictated text—allowing children to master early reading strategies such as left to right, return sweep and 1:1—through to fully independent reading activities. In writing, a similar range is demonstrated. Children begin with the use of shared books for familiarisation with book language and story structure and end up conversant with, an able to write independently in, a full range of writing styles. Teachers, on producing focus resources, are aware of the specific demands of each level and gauge their resources appropriately. As Helen Villers comments, on being asked how focus resources were monitored:

> By I think a unilateral understanding of what was required at each level... Because we all dealt so extensively with the boxed book system, we knew what each level was like. Because of our monitoring and evaluation we were very tuned in to the expectations of each level, and we did our combined resource presentations [at staff meetings] and got a very good sense of what was appropriate. And because we evaluated as we went. Resources that shot too high were always shiny and pristine by the time the boxes came back to you. (Interview, 29 May, 1991)

Along with focus resources, the mathematics curriculum also reflects a concern with matching resources to levels of ability and parallels many of the learning activities discussed above. Mathematics programming is divided into two daily sessions. One session (Number Maths) deals with the number system and number operations. The second session (Topic Maths) focuses on measurement, geometry and logic. The two sessions, in terms of timetabling, are kept separate in order to maximise interest and learning in mathematics for children. 'Topic Maths' kits, which are allocated to rōpū in a two weekly cycle, are organised by an additional mathematics curriculum team. These kits include redistributed material from the national mathematics curriculum and are undifferentiated by level.[4] 'Number Maths' kits have been developed by staff at ten levels of competency and stay in rōpū areas. The ten levels established for 'number maths' parallel the literacy levels used for reading and focus resources. These range from 'undirected maths experiences', which involve children in initial self-exploration of number concepts, through to 'extended operations' which deal with multiplication and division.

The mathematics curriculum also parallels learning arrangements that are found elsewhere in the school curriculum. Sustained silent mathematics (SSM) and paired mathematics apply the same principles as their counterparts in reading and writing. In SSM children choose from the resources and work with them as they wish; experimenting, in so doing, with the processes involved in mathematics. Likewise, paired mathematics sees more able children tutoring the less able in paired activities. Another feature, this time specific to the curriculum area, is the use of elicitation procedures. Based on John Gay's (1974; cited in Richmond Road School, n.d.) work on mathematics literacy, a distinction is drawn between 'elicitation'—activities designed to develop and reinforce understanding of a mathematics concept—and 'maintenance'. Elicitation procedures emerge from three principles identified by Gay in relation to mathematics learning: (i) mathematics knowledge is implicit in the structural elements of language; (ii) mathematics is present in essentially the same ways in every language; (iii) recognition, use and description of a concept precedes naming it as an abstract entity. Teachers employ these principles by encouraging children to experiment and explore with mathematics concepts and to express in their own language what they are doing and why. Concepts which are initially established by children in this way are consolidated and extended by a spiral curriculum approach.

The approach to reading and mathematics at Richmond Road that I have just outlined clearly illustrates the importance the school places on linking closely monitored assessment procedures with the process model of learning. Children only have the scope to learn in the ways they do at Richmond Road because they have the use of resources which arc matched to their levels of ability. This accurate matching occurs because of the detailed and rigorous monitoring system employed in reading and mathematics in conjunction with these various resources and learning arrangements.

Assessment: Monitoring Children's Progress

The individual monitoring of children underpins the pedagogical, curriculum and organisational initiatives undertaken at Richmond Road. In line with his notion of access to power, Laughton eschewed testing children and argued instead for a regular and reflective approach to the monitoring of children's academic progress:

> our system is to *monitor* progress rather than to test attainment. Monitoring entails observation of behaviour in familiar contexts using familiar processes, often focused on unfamiliar content at judiciously increasing levels of difficulty. The purpose is to find out how the student operates, what she knows and the priorities in what she needs to know. The function of familiarity is to facilitate access to underlying competence, imperfectly reflected at best in the student's performance. (1985b: 1)

In relation to testing, Laughton goes on to suggest that

> the concept of testing carries rather more arbitrary connotations with an undue emphasis, it appears, on finding out what the student *doesn't* know. Such procedures are likely to inhibit her ability to give an adequate indication of her true levels of competence... Therefore, when deliberating what techniques to use in assessing children's progress the need for paradigms

that promote learning as well as the need for a more reliable indication of competence should prevail. (1985b: 1)

Laughton's scepticism towards testing was based on its effects on children, particularly ethnic minority children, in the educational process since, historically, assessment based on testing has played the role of legitimising the disabling of minority students in classrooms (Cummins, 1986). As John Matthews observes: '[Jim] used to say kids have already been tested, and they've already failed. What's the point in testing them? That's all they were. Tests were to make you fail' (Interview, 25 May, 1991). A teacher in Cazden's study elaborates on this observation:

Jim believed all people can go *somewhere*. When children leave this school, he hasn't put expectations on them that they would disappoint him with. The only time Jim says you will ever *fail* is somebody saying, 'This is the benchmark that makes you a success or failure'. And you have to have failure as soon as you say, 'Well at age 7, you've got to be here; at age 10 you've got to be here'. We don't do that. And it doesn't happen. (cited in Cazden, 1989: 155)

Laughton's reservations were also based, pragmatically, on the limited amount of information testing could provide:

He had an aversion to the sort of standardised, non-[child] based testing that the P.A.T.s [standardised New Zealand achievement tests] represented—and I would believe rightly, because what does it tell you? That a kid's on a certain percentile? The sort of testing and evaluation that he wanted was the sort of thing that would show us what a kid could do *and where next*. (Judy Hucker: Interview, 15 August, 1991; my emphasis)

For Laughton, individual monitoring was to provide this kind of developmental rather than prescriptive information on children. By this, the developmental learning emphasised in the organisation of family groups and the curriculum process model was reinforced. As Frank Churchward comments:

Churchward: Learning is a developmental task and kids have various rates of learning. Some learn quickly, some learn slowly. So you accommodate to the child's pace of learning. Because a kid's 10 [yrs] it doesn't mean he will be able to do everything that other ten-year-olds can do. He may do a lot more and you accommodate to where the kid is.

Interviewer: This is really individual monitoring?

Churchward: Yes, and that was very good. Otherwise how can I as a teacher say that John can recognise 56 letters...if I haven't monitored the kid carefully. We did that in maths and reading. Like, for example, one parent came to an interview a bit anxious about their child and I explained, and I used the running records as an example, and she said 'oh, can't do this, can't do that'. I said 'no, but *can* do this, *can* do that'. I think one of the strengths for us as teachers was that we had to know, really know, where a kid was up to, say in their reading and in their maths development... So if a kid was 10 and could only read at a 7 [year old] level—so what? That's where he's at. So work with him, or work with her at the level at which he or she is because the better you work at that level, the more rapid will be the progress they make. The kids benefited from that point of view. (Interview, 28 May, 1991)

Running records in reading and mathematics are kept on all children and teachers are required to individually monitor at least three children every week to ensure that records are kept current. These records include not only the children's levels but also specific information concerning the skills or cues used, needed or misused by individual children.[5] Movement from one level to the next requires children to meet stringent criteria. In reading, for example, a child needs to read fluently, independently and with understanding at her or his current instructional level, with 95% accuracy and at least a 1:3 self-correction rate, before being able to move to the next reading level. The easy reading level (for library and taking home) requires 98–100% accuracy. The school argues that these requirements are deliberately conservative so as to ensure confidence and success for the child.

As mentioned in Chapter 7, these records are also used as resources by both children and teachers in the family group context. The competitive intentions most often associated with such listings in other schools are not apparent at Richmond Road. Through the records each child knows their own level of reading and mathematics independence and those of others within the rōpū. They are thus able to choose for themselves resources appropriate to their level and if they want to work with more difficult resources they know whom they can go to for support. Likewise, children know whom they are able to assist in any given activity.

Along with children and teachers, parents are also included in the monitoring process; facilitating their involvement and support in their children's education:

Interviewer: Why is monitoring so important? Would it not work without all the systems?

Lyn Malaugh: No. But it's also part of...being accountable, and being accountable to parents. Parents can come into [the rōpū] and you can tell them exactly where their child's at, at a given point in time, in reading and in maths. I haven't got a clue where these kids are that I've got [at my present school]. (Interview, 27 May, 1991)

While monitoring is conducted informally in other curriculum areas as well (keeping files of children's work, for example), the formal monitoring procedures adopted for reading and mathematics accord priority to these particular areas within the school. Both were seen by Laughton as necessary core skills for children, and the emphasis he placed upon them ensured that the systems which fostered cultural maintenance within the school (such as family groupings and focus resources development) were coupled with systems which facilitated access to power. As a school document summarises it:

> Maintenance of programme development in Social Studies, Literacy and Mathematics and of the existing monitoring systems in Reading and Mathematics is essential to meeting the on-going needs of the pupils. The Social Studies programme encompasses the belief structure of the school emphasising family values and the search for a harmonious multicultural society. Its requirement on teachers is for cooperation within a pluralistic context and its teacher-product a vast array of resources. Literacy and mathematical competence have a direct bearing on life chances and in a family grouped school such as Richmond Road, accurate knowledge of the competence of individual children is a prerequisite to effective matching of pupil, task and resources. (Principal's Report, 2 August, 1989)

Richmond Road staff have a remarkably detailed knowledge of each student's level of learning at any given time and also, perhaps more significantly, what is required for each child to progress to higher levels of learning. This concern with detailed and accurate monitoring of individual children is encapsulated in a comment which Jim Laughton often made. As one staff member paraphrased it (numerous others mentioned this observation when discussing monitoring): 'Jim said, don't ask "can a child read?" Ask *how are they reading?*"' (Field Notes, 25 February, 1991). As Margaret Leaming concludes, in her role as staffing inspector to the school, and specifically in relation to literacy:

Interviewer: ...that's why I was so interested in Richmond Road because it seemed to me to be a school that actually was aware of the position of minority students—it seemed to be very theoretically conversant with [that] ...but actually then took the theory and put it into practice.

Leaming: *And of course turned out students who were literate.* They were much into the monitoring of children's progress although never very much into the business of publishing you know, how many were here and how many were there. But...if you like to look, as I did, at the achievement in terms of literacy, and I'm talking about children's ability to read and handle language, I'm talking about children who came out of Standard 4, because these [teachers] were never hung-up on whether someone couldn't do something at 7 [yrs]—they simply kept working with them... So a child who couldn't do things at 7 was not a cause for the roof to be lowered, [rather] it was a cause for teachers continually looking at where they were taking the child and the kinds of experiences in terms of language that they were getting. Because they thought they had different times of learning and different spurts of learning—so you didn't ignore them—they kept on having learning chances and learning experiences. [And] the results to my mind were phenomenal compared with other [schools]. (Interview, 28 May, 1991)

Analysing Outcomes

Margaret Leaming's comment above, as well as many of those associated with Richmond Road, suggest strong anecdotal evidence for the academic skills its students acquire while at the school. Assessing such evidence, however, is notoriously difficult. As such, I had initially wanted to avoid any analysis of educational outcomes in my research on Richmond Road. This was mainly due to my concern at the way educational statistics have been used against ethnic minority children, and schools with large multicultural populations. In New Zealand, as elsewhere, statistics of children's educational attainment levels, particularly when used to rank schools, invariably posit multicultural schools at or near the bottom of the educational heap. This analysis, of course, completely fails to take account of how far children have come in reaching those educational end points. An affluent school with a narrow range of pupils (socially, culturally, and academically) may achieve higher educational outcomes but it is highly likely to have had a considerable head start to begin with (see Chapter 2). A multicultural school with a wide range of ethnic groups, high numbers of second language speakers of English, and children with widely differing academic abilities, may not fare so well in an 'outcomes' analysis. However, it may well have brought children a long way further from the educational points at which they began their schooling.

The other difficulty with assessing the educational activities of a primary school is the number of intervening variables that might affect a child's subsequent secondary school career. Thus, tracking the academic 'success' of ex-Richmond Road pupils in secondary school is also fraught with difficulty. Even the notion of what constitutes success is problematic here since Richmond Road would adopt a broader definition of what this means (including home language maintenance, cultural identity and personal autonomy) than, perhaps, would others.[6] In this light, Richmond Road's response to the inevitable question of 'outcomes' is simply to argue that this is not something the school can determine once the children leave at age 13 years. Rather, they are interested in the process—equipping children, particularly minority children, with cultural recognition (cultural maintenance) *and* academic skills (access to power), something usually denied them by schooling. By such a process, they argue, the opportunity for such children to succeed in a society which invariably undermines them is much greater than it might otherwise have been.

However, at least some analysis of outcomes is required to give credence to Richmond Road's educational activities. Accordingly, it seemed to me that the best avenue to pursue in assessing the educational outcomes of Richmond Road was to conduct a cohort study. What I have attempted to do, therefore, is provide a brief analysis below of the reading development of a cohort of children at Richmond Road over the period 1986–1992. In effect, I have taken the Form 1 (11 yrs) group in 1992 and traced their reading development back to the time they entered the school. The advantage of a cohort study such as this is that it is able to assess the *progress* children make in reading while at Richmond Road; i.e. both educational starting and end points are taken into account. By limiting the analysis to an internal investigation, the difficulties of determining and isolating factors associated with long term academic success are also avoided. Finally, the results of the study can be compared with age norms to give it a wider application.

Before examining this though,'I want to briefly consider a similar assessment made by Jim Laughton in 1983. This is presented in summary form in Table 8.2. Here Laughton has attempted to analyse the whole of the school population at a given point in time with regard to reading level. While his analysis is not a sophisticated one statistically[7] it does nevertheless reveal a clear pattern. The majority of the children at entry to school (72%) are below the national reading norm for their age. On leaving the school, however, 65% are above their expected reading level.[8] Laughton argues in an associated paper that these initial reading levels are to be expected, given that 90% of the school population at this time comprised non-Pākehā children, and 10% of these had been in New Zealand less than three years:

> Comparison of the reading data with ethnic composition displays the typical relationship between English language fluency and reading attainment, particularly in a child's first years in the New Zealand school system. The mismatch between the child's cultural and linguistic entering behaviours and the school's immediate, pedagogical capabilities is revealed clearly in the distribution of competence levels in the first few years. (Principal's Report, 5 July, 1983)

Table 8.2 Richmond Road reading data, June 1983.[9]

Book Level age-range groupings:

- 1–2: Pre-reading
- 3–5: 5–5.5 years
- 6–10: 5.5–6 years
- 11–15: 6–6.5 years
- 16–20: 6.5–7 years
- 21–22: 7–7.5 years
- 23–24: 7.5–8 years
- 25–28: 8–9 years
- 29: 9–10 yrs
- 30: 10–11 yrs
- 31: 11–12 yrs
- 32: 12–13 yrs
- 33: 13–14 yrs
- 34: 14+ yrs

Rdg age	1	2	3	4	5	6	7	8	9	10	11	12	13	14	15	16	17	18	19	20	21	22	23	24	25	26	27	28	29	30	31	32	33	34	Total
NE	14	5	1			1																													21
J1	14	14	17	9	10	1																											1	1	67
J2	4		3	15	10	5	3	2	1	1	3	1	1	2	3	2							1						2					1	60
J3/S1	2		2	5	3	3	5	4	3	2	4	1	4		1		1			1	2	3	2	3	2	1	1	3	3						61
S2	3	2		1	1	1	1	1	2		2		2				2			3	1		3	3	2	4		3	6	3				9	55
S3		2			1		1				1	1					2	1			4	1	2	5	3	4		3	5	5	8	4	1	7	61
S4	1						1							1			2			1	1	1	1		1	4	1	3	3	5	14	12	1	9	62
Total	38	23	23	30	25	11	11	7	6	3	10	3	7	3	4	2	7	1		5	8	5	9	11	8	13	2	12	19	13	22	16	3	27	

Source: Adapted from Principal's Report, 5 July, 1983.

Summary of data: Class Expectancy

Class	% below	% at	% above
J2	72	20	8
J3/S1	67	12	21
S2	58	16	26
S3	52	8	40
S4	29	6	65

Richmond Road, like many other multicultural schools in New Zealand, draws on a predominantly lower socio-economic population and has a majority of Māori and Pacific Island children. The ethnic population of the school has not changed in this regard in the intervening ten years since Laughton's analysis. In June 1992, 65% of the school's students came from homes where the main income earner was dependent on a state benefit, had no fixed income, or was employed as a manual worker (Richmond Road School, 1992). 80.7% of the school's students at that time also identified as Māori, Pacific Island, or as being from another minority ethnic group (Richmond Road School, 1992; see also Chapter 5). Educational achievement patterns in New Zealand for such groups have also remained similar over the last decade with Māori and Pacific Island children, particularly, continuing to be over-represented in the educational failure statistics. In 1988, for example, 41 out of 100 Māori students would have left school by Form 6 (16 yrs) compared with 29 Pākehā (Hirsh, 1990: 73). In 1989, 36.8% of those who left school with no formal qualifications were Māori compared with 12.5% Pākehā. (Manatū Māori, 1991: 18) And, in an eleven year longitudinal study, Fegusson, Lloyd & Harwood found that in 'nearly all comparisons [with Pākehā], children of Māori or Pacific Island ethnicity had lower verbal IQ scores, poorer word recognition rates, lower reading comprehension and mathematics ability scores, and were rated by teachers as having poorer performance in reading, written expression, spelling and mathematics' (1991: 54).

In the recent IEA study[10] of reading literacy, New Zealand children at 9 years fared well above expectation in all three domains used in the test—narrative prose, expository prose and use of documents—and ranked 6th out of 31 countries. At age 14 years a similar pattern emerges with New Zealand children ranked 4th overall (Elley, 1992). However, New Zealand also demonstrated the greatest gap in achievement levels—at both age levels—between first and second language speakers of English. This 'home language achievement gap' was gauged by the size of the achievement discrepancy between the average scores (combined across domains) for those learning in their home language and for those who were not. As Elley observes, this saw in New Zealand,

> non-English speaking children score 70 points below the mainstream English-speaking students at the 9-year-old level and 81 points at age fourteen. The minorities in this case were made up predominantly of Pacific Island students... These students are clearly experiencing difficulties with reading requirements in the official language. (1992: 60)

Clearly then, Māori and Pacific Island children continue to be academically disadvantaged in New Zealand schools. Given Laughton's previous analysis, I expected to find a similar pattern of lower-level reading ability in the early years of their schooling. I also expected to find—as did Laughton—this pattern reversed over the course of time at Richmond Road. In both instances, this proved to be the case.

A Reading Cohort Study

The cohort which I examined comprised 35 children, 18 of whom were female and 17 male. At the end of 1992, when this analysis was undertaken, the group was completing Form 1 (F1; 11 yrs) and had one more year at Richmond Road ahead of them before they entered secondary school. Using the Statistical Package for Social Sciences (SPSS), the analysis traces their reading development retrospectively from this point; a period of seven years for some children. Children within the group had entered the school at various stages in the preceding years but apart from two children who left at the end of Standard 4 (in 1991), the bulk of the cohort had remained at Richmond Road to complete their primary schooling. Years of entry are detailed as follows: 1986 (NE/J1) 5; 1987 (J2) 11; 1988 (J3/S1) 5; 1989 (S2) 1; 1990 (S3) 5; 1991 (S4) 3; 1992 (F1) 5.

The ethnic composition of the group was ascertained from school records and comprises: 3 Pākehā; 9 Maori; 8 Samoan; 7 Cook Islands; 5 Tongan; and 3 Other (1 Niuean; 1 Indian; 1 Dutch). In terms of language, I have divided the group—both from school records and teacher assessment—into monolingual English, bilingual, and English second language (ESL) speakers. Bilingual children, in this context, are those who on entry to school spoke both a home language and English. ESL speakers are identified as those who spoke a home language but had limited or no language facility in English on school entry. The following break down occurs here: 13 Monolingual English; 9 Bilingual; 13 ESL. One other sub-group of significance in the following analysis comprises 11 'late' children. These are children who came to Richmond Road after 1987 and were, at their time of entry to the school, either ESL or two or more years behind their chronological age in reading.

Children in the cohort were born between the years of 1979 and 1982: 1 in 1979; 13 in 1980; 18 in 1981; and 3 in 1982. This is an unusually wide range for a group at the same level at school. However, it may be due to those children who have come to New Zealand directly from the Pacific Islands as they tend to be somewhat older in comparison to the others in the group. Notwithstanding this, I have taken each child's chronological age as a broad measure of comparison with reading age level. This actually weights the odds against my analysis but it seems a fair measure by which the effectiveness of Richmond Road's reading programme can be judged. What I expected to find was that children's reading age would be below their chronological age in the first few years of schooling; given the ethnic composition of the cohort and the number of ESL speakers. In light of Richmond Road's claims, however, this should have been largely reversed by the later years of schooling.

The following analysis of reading age level is based on the school's requirement that a child needs to read fluently, independently and with understanding at any given level, with 95% accuracy and at least a 1:3 self-correction rate. As such, the designation of reading ages, as outlined below, can be regarded as deliberately conservative. Reading ages for each child over the course of their time at the school were ascertained from running records. These records designate the exact book levels at which children are reading fluently and independently. From this, I have extrapolated reading age (see also Laughton's analysis in Table 8.2). Entry and exit reading ages are compared and children's reading progress through the years charted via their first and last running record assessment for each year.[11] The following is a summary of the analysis with much of the detail, necessarily, excluded.

Achieving Success in Reading

The first comparison examined is that between the chronological age and the reading age of each child at their time of entry to the school. When the entry age (ENTAGE) is compared with the reading age (ENTRA) at time of entry (given that children in the cohort entered the school throughout the seven year period; see above), the following occurs:

WILCOXON MATCHED-PAIRS SIGNED-RANKS TEST ENTRA WITH ENTAGE

MEAN RANK	CASES
6.33	3 - RANKS (ENTAGE LT ENTRA)
19.09	32 + RANKS (ENTAGE GT ENTRA)
	0 TIES (ENTAGE EQ ENTRA)
	–
	35 TOTAL
$Z = -4.8482$	2-TAILED P = 0.0000

In other words, on entry to Richmond Road only three of the cohort had a reading age greater than their chronological age. Of these three, none were more than a year ahead in reading. In contrast, 18 were over a year behind in reading and three of these were over three years behind. Admittedly, this comparison is limited by the difficulties of establishing accurate differences between reading and chronological age for those 16 children in the cohort who started school at age 5. Accordingly, it may be useful to examine individual years to see how these two variables compare. By 1987 (Year 3) for example,

21 out of 35 of the cohort had entered the school. The comparison between their reading age (RDGAGE) and chronological age (AGE) at the time of the first reading assessment in this year is as follows:

WILCOXON MATCHED-PAIRS SIGNED-RANKS TEST RDGAGE WITH AGE 1987 1ST ASSESSMENT

MEAN RANK	CASES
10.50	2 - RANKS (AGE LT RDGAGE)
11.05	19 + RANKS (AGE GT RDGAGE)
	0 TIES (AGE EQ RDGAGE)
	—
	21 TOTAL
$Z = -3.2846$	2-TAILED P = 0.0010

By the second assessment of that year, the following pattern had emerged:

WILCOXON MATCHED-PAIRS SIGNED-RANKS TEST RDGAGE WITH AGE 1987 2ND ASSESSMENT

MEAN RANK	CASES
11.75	6 - RANKS (AGE LT RDGAGE)
10.70	15 + RANKS (AGE GT RDGAGE)
	0 TIES (AGE EQ RDGAGE)
	—
	21 TOTAL
$Z = -1.5641$	2-TAILED P = 0.1178

Even though some of the cohort are now in their 3rd year of schooling, the majority remain below their chronological age in reading level. This reflects the cultural and language discontinuities faced by many of the ethnic minority children in the cohort (see above) and is consistent with Laughton's prior analysis.

By the 2nd assessment in Year 5 (1990), with the cohort now in Standard 3, the pattern is beginning to change:

WILCOXON MATCHED-PAIRS SIGNED-RANKS TEST RDGAGE WITH AGE 1990 2ND ASSESSMENT

MEAN RANK	CASES
12.00	17 - RANKS (AGE LT RDGAGE)

16.33   9 + RANKS (AGE GT RDGAGE)

                               1 TIES (AGE EQ RDGAGE)

                               –

                               27 TOTAL

Z = –0.7238   2-TAILED P = 0.4692

However, by the time of the 2nd reading assessment in 1992—the last assessment analysed here—a somewhat different picture had emerged:

WILCOXON MATCHED-PAIRS SIGNED-RANKS TEST RDGAGE WITH AGE 1992 2ND ASSESSMENT

MEAN RANK   CASES

15.52   25 - RANKS (AGE LT RDGAGE)

20.00   7 + RANKS (AGE GT RDGAGE)

                               1 TIES (AGE EQ RDGAGE)

                               –

                               33 TOTAL

Z = –2.3187   2-TAILED P = 0.0204

Adjusting for the two pupils who left in 1991, the exit reading ages (EXITRA) of the cohort can now be examined in comparison to chronological age. As seen in Table 8.3, 26 of the cohort are now reading at or above their chronological age. Of these, 20 (57.1%) are reading at the top two reading levels of 14 and 14+. There are, however, nine children whose EXITRA is still below their chronological age (these include the two who left in 1991) and this does present some cause for concern. It is interesting to note though that seven of these nine children come from the 'late' category sub-group. That is, they entered Richmond Road after 1987 and were either ESL or already over two years behind in their reading on entry to the school. Table 8.4 details the EXITRA of the 'late' group.

Table 8.3 Exit reading ages (EXITRA) of cohort

EXITRA Value label	Value	Frequency	Percent	Cum Percent
	7	1	2.9	2.9
	7.5	2	5.7	8.6
	8	1	2.9	11.4
	9	4	11.4	22.9
	10	1	2.9	25.7
	12	2	5.7	31.4
	13	4	11.4	42.9
	14	4	11.4	54.3
	14+	16	45.7	100.0
	Total		100.0	
Valid cases	35	Missing cases	0	

Table 8.4 Exit reading age (EXITRA) of late group

EXITRA Value label	Value	Frequency	Percent	Cum Percent
	7	1	9.1	9.1
	7.5	2	18.2	27.3
	8	1	9.1	36.4
	9	3	27.3	63.6
	12	2	18.2	81.8
	13	1	9.1	90.9
	14	1	9.1	100.0
	Total		100.0	
Valid cases	11	Missing cases	0	

The 'home language achievement gap' for ESL students (see above) still appears to have some influence at Richmond Road for those children in the 'late' sub-group. The school would argue, however, that its approach to reading is the best means by which this gap can be closed. Indeed, for the majority of the cohort this has already been achieved; a remarkable achievement given the disadvantaged starting points at which some of these children began their schooling. For the remainder, the close individual attention that the monitoring process affords, the conservative nature of the school's reading level assessment, and the fact that the cohort still has one year left at the school, augurs well for their continued improvement in reading. As Margaret Learning has observed above, the strength of Richmond Road's approach is that children keep 'on having learning chances and learning experiences' at *all* levels of reading attainment.

Notes to Chapter 8

1. As I outlined in Chapter 3, incorporation means more than simply inclusion—it suggests organic rather than incremental change within schools (Hulmes, 1989).
2. The social studies and curriculum aspects of a curriculum team's resources can either be integrated as one set of resources or used, in conjunction, as two sets.
3. These can be based on a variety of starting points—journals, picture books, legends etc.—depending on the particular context and/or level.
4. Topic Maths kits, like focus resources, take a theme or topic. Examples of particular topics are: for geometry—shape, lines, planes, movement & position, and symmetry; for measurement—length & weight, time, money, capacity, and volume area; and for logic—sets, patterning, classification, and graphing (Staff Meeting Agenda, 9 December, 1986).
5. Teachers undergo regular training and retraining in the use of running records as part of the staff development process to ensure that these aspects are accurately identified.
6. Having said that, there is again strong anecdotal evidence that ex-Richmond Road children continue to succeed in the education system. Of the Form 6 (16 yrs) group of ex-pupils I talked with—six at one local secondary school and three at another— three had received A passes in the previous year's national external examination and all had been promoted to Form 6 as a result of these examination results. Given that only one of this group was Pākehā, this compares favourably with national norms which see Māori and Pacific Island pupils disproportionately failing in schools, usually prior to this level (see also below).
7. Laughton has simply collated the reading records of each year group (NE-S4) and listed individual children within these by reading level. He has then compared reading attainment with national expectations and assessed this in light of the school's ethnic population. Two points should be noted here. First, New Zealand children begin school immediately after their fifth birthday and thus enter at variable times in the first two years of school. Second, Richmond Road was still a contributing primary school at this time (see Chapter 5) and the top level of the school was subsequently Standard 4 (10 yrs). By the time of my analysis, however (see below), the school had extended to Form 2 level.
8. Most students are grouped at either end of the spectrum because learning to read is not a linear activity. Once certain keys have been unlocked in the reading process, particularly the ability to decode, children who might have been at one level for some time can make sudden and rapid progress. The school argues that this is the principal advantage of their approach to reading. They are willing to wait with a child until they make this kind of breakthrough.
9. The book levels here refer to the graded readers that are used within the school. These readers begin at Level 3. The first two book levels are 'pre-dictated text' and 'dictated text' and I have assigned these as pre-reading levels. I have also included the reading ages to which the book levels correspond. As can be seen, the number of graded readers varies within each reading age.

10. The International Association for the Evaluation of Educational Achievement (IEA) conducts regular comparisons of reading literacy among children in OECD countries. The levels at which children are assessed are 9 and 14 years.

11. The exact times of these assessments obviously vary for each child, and from year to year. However, given the school's rigorous monitoring policy, all initial and end of year running records employed here occurred within respective six week periods in any given year.

9 New Directions

Smith & Keith (1971), in their watershed ethnographic study on innovation in schooling, examined the first year of Kensington school, a progressive experimental school with a radical child-centred pedagogy. Their description of Kensington in those early days bears a remarkable similarity to Richmond Road as a school which 'represented a special and unique blend of architecture, people, ideas, and pedagogy to all who knew the school and its purposes' (Smith *et al.*, 1987: 174). However, in their follow up study of Kensington School 15 years on, Smith *et al.* found it to be just another 'average school, only one of many in the...district' (1987: 186). One of the significant factors they attributed to this metamorphosis of a once radical school was the influence of the principal. Kensington had had four principals over the intervening fifteen year period and the change in school direction could be significantly attributed to their differing educational philosophies: 'Perhaps more than anyone the principal has the opportunity to shape the school's identity. Shelby, Edwards, Hawkins, and Wales, professional educators all, were very different in vision, goals, beliefs and actions' (1987: 195). As the authors conclude, Kensington is as it is now because the traditional educational approach of its present principal, Wales, stands in almost complete opposition to that of its founding principal, Shelby.

In contrast to Kensington, Richmond Road twenty years on is still remarkably similar in purpose and practice to the radical vision Jim Laughton had for the school in the early 1970s; proving, at least, that an emancipatory educational approach can survive over time. However, while the histories of these two schools may be opposed, the influence of the principal remains, perhaps, the key factor behind each. In the case of Richmond Road, the dominating influence of Laughton cannot be avoided (as indeed I quickly found out in the course of my research on the school). As Judy Hucker comments in Chapter 6, 'you cannot talk about Richmond Road without talking about Jim Laughton'. How then, one might reasonably ask, can Richmond Road cope without him? The answer lies in a principal's report he wrote two months prior to his death:

> The objective of an administrator, it is said, should be self-redundancy. The evidence of the past three months, during my extended illness suggests that that objective has been attained. It is clear that the school not only can, but

has become self-sustaining under the guidance of Joy and Lionel[1] and with the support of the staff and the School Council. I acknowledge the professionalism of the staff with gratitude. (Principal's Report, 19 July, 1988)

While Laughton's vision was the catalyst for the educational innovations that were undertaken at Richmond Road, it was never his intention that those developments be dependent upon him. In fact, as I have tried to show in Chapter 6, the opposite could be said to be true. Laughton specifically set about establishing systems within the school which enabled his staff, both individually and collectively, to take increasing responsibility for the school's educational directions. As Wally Penetito argues:

> I've heard people saying, and other principals saying, with some jealousy I think, the reason Richmond Road works is because of Jim Laughton. Take Jim Laughton out and what will it be? It's a kind of stupid statement to make to begin with, of course it is, but...he's not the only person that's there. I mean what he was always working on too was trying to make the place self-sufficient...he had absolute confidence in the people who were there, in the leadership that was there in his school...he had actually made that leadership anyway, facilitated *it* the same way that he did so many other things like that. He kind of covered all those bases. (Interview, 14 October, 1991)

Inevitably, Langton's death has been a huge loss to Richmond Road and the school cannot be the same without him, but nor, by all accounts, would he have wanted it to be. Laughton was always interested in creating 'self-sustaining and self-generating systems' (see Chapter 5) within the school and those processes have continued to characterise Richmond Road's development since his death. At first, more emphasis was placed on consolidation—on sustaining the systems already established. When Courtney Cazden conducted the research for her article on the school in May/June of 1989, for example, staff at Richmond Road were still coming to terms with Jim's death and only one staff member had left the school in the intervening nine month period. One teacher's reply to Cazden's question about the future of the school reflects this period of transition: 'Everything's going really well. We just lost Jim, that's all. The thing is—Jim's still here, because of the way things are being maintained and moving on' (cited in Cazden, 1989: 161). At the end of 1989, however, a number of staff left the school and took with them their personal histories of Richmond Road under Laughton. The subsequent influx of new teachers in 1990, the appointment of Lionel Pedersen as the new principal, and the major educational reforms which also occurred in New Zealand at that time,[2] posed significant challenges for those who remained at the school. But as another teacher in Cazden's study observed, prior to these developments occurring: 'One thing I'm sure is that everybody has got this aim: to not let it have been something for nothing. We're about change remember? But *our* change. We'll change, but [it will be] *our* change' (cited in Cazden, 1989: 161).

And so it has been. The changes which Richmond Road has subsequently undertaken, in line with Laughton's philosophy, have been carefully introduced and closely monitored. In 1990, for example, the consolidation process was continued. A core of staff under Pedersen remained at the school and new staff were introduced to Laughton's educational philosophies via the staff development process. For the year, staff development concentrated almost solely on revisiting current school systems, the educational rationales underlying them, and the developmental histories surrounding them. As Pedersen observes, this developmental process was necessary in order to give new staff a personal involvement in and understanding of the systems Laughton had established within the school:

Pedersen: [1990] was a learning environment in a tremendous context for people like me. It was a learning context to every new teacher here, but it was a very prescribed learning context in a way. We set out to introduce them into our maths programmes, into our reading programmes and all of those programmes that we've got running... Of course, most things should change every year...but the learning context was a much more prescribed one [in 1990] so that we had everyone knowing the systems...

Interviewer: You would have needed that year to keep the systems going?

Pedersen: I believe we couldn't have done without it, like all learning, it was a progression... Last year I suppose the best purpose for prescribed learning was because we needed it. This year...it hasn't got that specific aim of introducing everybody into systems. Now it's looking at the systems themselves. (Interview, 11 February, 1991)

If Luke Hiki, a first year teacher in 1990, is anything to go by, the process outlined by Pedersen has been remarkably successful:

Interviewer: You've [only] been here since Jim died... What's it been like coming in, not knowing him? How has his influence been shown to you in the school?

Hiki: You feel like you really do know him because you come in and you have a look at those personal folders, and all of his writings and his philosophies are written in there... Like paired reading, the teina-tuakana and the whānau grouping. If you have a look at the whānau grouping...you participate in the whānau grouping and then you're actually told why that was implemented...so it seems to be like you really get to know what Jim wanted. He must have been a pretty freaky dude, but I never met him. And he must have had a lot of influence on people too because they're still here, just taking over from where he left off. (Interview, 13 August, 1991)

However, with the systems established among the newcomers, the process of change was to begin again. Pedersen comments, along these lines: 'This year [1991] the real learning is—do they [the systems] need changing? Everybody can be part of that, just because we've experienced it and done it... They're starting to be able to make their own decisions about what will work or not within the parameters of what...operated before' (Field Notes, 18 February, 1991). As he goes on to observe, the principle of owning any changes by prior involvement and commitment to them (see Chapter 6) remains central to the school's philosophy: 'It's the basis that we believe in learning. If you're part of a process then that's it. If you're not part of a process it's difficult to actually *know*... Now we've set a base [again] we're not scared any more, we're not scared to drop things, we're not scared to look at it and really re-evaluate it and say forget it' (ibid.).

In moving forward without Laughton, other personalities have begun to exert themselves. As John Matthews comments, 'people had to get stronger, and that's what happened. People did get stronger—about everything. *So his passing away gave room for other people to grow*' (Interview, 25 May, 1991; my emphasis). Maggie Wood, who came to teach at the school only subsequently to Jim's death, similarly comments and expands on the nature of this changing dynamic:

[I came to the school in] '89 and he died the previous September so his ghost was still stalking around the school making its presence very strongly felt... It was really quite interesting because at the beginning it was virtually as if he was just in the next room because everybody spoke about him as if he was going to come in and start going on where he left off before...all his writings were still quoted, the things he said, [people] were still saying 'as Jim would say', and gradually this has petered out. Other people's identities have started to impose themselves...gradually it's come to a stage where people are no longer afraid to even disagree with things that he said, because of course times change and something that was relevant [then] may not be relevant now. (Interview, 12 August, 1991)

Wood's comment is reiterated by Shona Matthews, a parent and current Board of Trustees member: 'Obviously the school seems to have been through...a period of change and transition... I guess earlier on it was Jim Laughton's influence that was the uniting force, and I think that after his death that perhaps was lost to some extent. But I feel quite strongly that they've very much got back on top of that and that they're taking a new direction' (Interview, 17 November, 1992). Matthews' comment also suggests, however, that while the school has successfully survived this period of transition, the process has not always been an easy one.

New Challenges

One example of the demands of this transition period can be seen in the particular responsibilities and challenges Lionel Pedersen has had to face since becoming principal in 1990. Laughton died in September 1988 and the school deliberately did not choose a new principal until after the national educational reforms of 1988–1989 allowed them to do so.[3] Since his appointment, Pedersen—who has been associated with the school since the early 1970s—has had to adjust not only to the professional demands of the position but to other factors as well. As one teacher observed:

> ...it's also been a grieving process [for Pedersen]. Most new principals to a school don't have to contend with the past to that extent. Mostly you take up the reins and it's your baby and you just go ahead the way you want to. He's had to cope with everything that went before as well as being personally involved with what was before... It's quite complex...and related to Jim as well, so he had personal grieving on various levels.

The Board of Trustees, in its newly appointed role of administering the school, has been undergoing a similar learning curve. Soon after assuming responsibility for the school in 1989, the Board of Trustees decided to proceed with recapitation to Form 2 level. However, because it was still unclear at that time nationally as to whether the Board was legally entitled to, the decision was delayed. Consequently, the local community, which had been involved in and supportive of the move, lost some faith in the school. It led Pedersen and the Board to reevaluate the school's relationship with the community and attempt to strengthen it. The subsequent setting up of ethnic associations to represent individual group interests to the school has been one example of this new approach. Another has been the school's attempt to extend the relationships already established with the pre-schools. A Tongan pre-school, for example, has been seen for some time as the next language pre-school that should be set in place. Priority is being accorded to this development because of the Tongan community's presence within the school population. More Tongan teachers are also being actively sought for the school itself.

Discussions on recapitation have also led the school to closely examine the reasons for the continued loss of student numbers. How can the inner-city's decline and the attendant process of 'white flight' (see Chapter 5) be redressed, and why can a school with an international reputation not attract more local pupils? A number of strategies have been implemented to address this dilemma. The school's eventual recapitation in 1992 has extended its pupil range from 5–13 years. While this is congruent with the school's emphasis on long term relationships, it should also, more pragmatically, increase or at least hold student numbers. Richmond Road's participation in the national three year trial for local funding of schools (see Chapter 6) has also brought direct benefits. In addition to increasing the school's autonomy within the educational system, the controversial nature of the scheme has generated considerable media interest and has allowed the school to articulate its educational approach through local and national media channels. The pilot funding scheme has also released additional finance which is being used to implement a major school building programme aimed at enhancing the school's buildings and grounds, and thus its profile in the local community. The production of a national consumer education package resource for use in all primary schools in the country (see Chapter 8) has also focused interest on the school's innovative and integrative curriculum, and its resource and staff development processes.

In using all of these strategies Richmond Road still recognises the odds stacked against them. The wider inequalities operating within education and society—of which racism and 'white flight' are two obvious, and related, examples—are not easily circumscribed. However, in adopting a realist position, the school attempts to employ whatever resistance strategies are available in order to safeguard the emancipatory educational agenda it has established over the years. In many ways, the school's recent educational history has been about just such resistance. Laughton knew what he was up against and those who remain at Richmond Road continue to also. This ongoing oppositional mode is clearly demonstrated in the school's response in 1991 to an unsympathetic report from the newly constituted Education Review Office.

New Contests

At the end of the 1990 school year the Education Review Office (ERO) conducted a three day school audit; one of the first to be undertaken by the new organisation. The ensuing report was critical of the school. The review team asserted:

> The report commends the school philosophy expounded by the previous principal, Jim Laughton, the school policies, systems and many other aspects of school life. However, the reviewers closely examined the quality of the learning opportunities provided and the standards of educational achievement. The reviewers found that, in a number of dimensions of the curriculum, standards of achievement were low and improvements to teaching programmes should be made to increase learning opportunities and standards. (Education Review Office, 1991: 16)

In support of this claim, the particular concerns outlined by the team were:

Individual instruction has value but *there is a need to group children with similar learning needs* for instruction...

Small group teaching needs to be a more regular feature of the programme to ensure that children develop real understanding of mathematical concepts. In some classrooms, *children's work needs to be marked more regularly.* Generally speaking, *there needs to be a higher expectation from teachers that children will produce tidy work.*

The standard of written language was generally low...most of the written language time [observed by the team] was devoted to children's private writing...the narrow range of writing opportunities *limited teacher intervention and restricted the teaching of* written language skills...peer modelling did not appear effective in teaching writing...handwriting and spelling were not generally viewed as an important part of written language.

The school attempts to integrate the teaching of social studies, art, health, science and music. Reviewers question whether *the integrity of these disciplines* is being maintained.

In curriculum delivery, some timetables appear to hinder learning...in many instances, reviewers saw learning arrested when children were just warming to the task at hand. Flexibility should be allowed in programmes to let teachers capitalise on 'teachable moments'. This flexibility can be gained by allowing longer periods of *uninterrupted time in subject areas.* School policy is to integrate learning. (Education Review Office, 1991: 6–8; my emphasis)

As Lionel Pedersen acknowledged at the time of the report, there is always room for criticism since, at any given time, the school is likely to be falling short in some aspect of its educational intentions. This is even more likely to occur in a period of transition. The review team has also highlighted the reservations, already discussed in Chapter 7, concerning the lack of flexibility in timetabling (although I would not endorse the ERO team's underlying educational rationale; see below). But the school has, in turn, been extremely critical of the review. These criticisms, and the way the school formulated them, are particularly instructive here.

The school's concerns about the ERO review centre on: the nature of the review process itself; the educational paradigms employed; and the superficiality of the conclusions reached by the review team. These concerns are outlined in their own document; a formal response to, and critique of, the ERO report. As with most activities at Richmond Road, the school's response was a collaborative enterprise. It included extensive discussion at staff meetings and considerable and wide ranging involvement from staff and other interested parties (including myself). The school also involved me in the development and revision of the final written report. The central conclusions of the school's rejoinder are outlined below:

> The school's principal impression of the [ERO] report is one of incoherence. The report is badly constructed, fragmented, at times contradictory and, overall, of little practical relevance and/or use to the school. In terms of educational theory the report is weak but its behavioural objectives for curriculum suggest that an endorsement of a transmission approach to education is implicit throughout. The philosophy of education which Richmond Road School has developed over the last fifteen years concerning the effect of such education on minority children stands in clear contrast to this perspective. Although platitudes to the school's educational approach are stated in the report, no real cognisance seems to have been taken of them.

> If there is an overall thrust to the [ERO] Report, it might appear to be the intimation that Richmond [Road]…says a lot but does not put into practice much of what it espouses… This statement presents no problem for the school and school community, since constant evaluation is intrinsic to the generative model of education that the school espouses ('self-sustaining and self-generating systems'). A process model, after all, means constant evaluation and examination of *all facets of political, managerial, organisational and curriculum implementation*. What is contested is the educational validity of the subsequent recommendations in the report. It does not context the school in relation to the changes that have both occurred internally and externally in this and the wider community and so has no reference points. It merely list superficial items, most of which are, and have been, ongoing areas of evolutionary development subject to the priority goals of the whole… (Richmond Road School, 1991: 4–5; my emphasis)

The school goes on to argue specific points of concern arising from the ERO Review Report and its preoccupations:

> There is no demonstration that the review team recognised or understood school systems that arise from [the multiethnic nature of the school] or that they elicited such information from the school. Neither does it establish or define what the school's view of learning is. The report does not demonstrate *an understanding of the link between the philosophical base and ethos of the school and its organisation and structure*.

> There is no real reference to 'family' concepts and the underpinning nature of these, nor are there references to the complementary nature of individuals, groups and organisations where this is being attempted or has been achieved.

> [There] is no explanation or acknowledgement of cognitive learning theory, knowledge as used here…how it is incorporated into the school, or process-based education in operational terms. There are, however, several attempts

to match the school to a behavioural base reflecting, it appears, the personal, educational and cultural biases of the reviewers.

There is no acknowledgement of how [the promotion of cultural difference] is inherent within the whole-school context, nor recognition of how the curriculum deals with this, linked to the key ideas of inclusiveness/ distinctiveness. Nor is there recognition of the variety of learning contexts offered to children or the pivotal role of the negotiation process built into operations. The structures that are successfully operating to promote this are ignored.

The report fails to define how the operation, management and structures of both staff and community organisations operate. It does not consider the empowerment of people by the recognition of authentic knowledge [provisional authority] in pursuing alternatives in management, organisation and learning. (Richmond Road School, 1991: 5–6; my emphasis)

The principal conclusions drawn by the school on the ERO report concern its inherent superficiality, its functionalist and behaviourist underpinnings, and its essentially unhelpful (and non-reciprocal) nature. Concerning the review process itself, many staff and community members saw the review team's approach as hierarchical, non-consultative and culturally inappropriate. The school had initially negotiated the parameters of the review with ERO but subsequently had little, if any, input into the review. Staff and community disillusionment concerning this lack of participation was clearly apparent when the draft report was presented by the review team at an open meeting on 13 November, 1990 at which I was present; (the team had initially only wanted to present the report to the principal). The report was read out by the review team and no response was offered by those in attendance, the view being, it seemed, that a rejoinder at that point would give status to the report that the school believed it did not warrant. In cultural terms, such silence emphasised rather than deflected the school's rejection of the report. As John Matthews comments, on behalf of many others who expressed similar sentiments:

They came in for a few days, had a quick look …that was a rip off and it didn't stop there… The document itself, there were a lot of points there that they came up with which were true. But they were points that we already knew, and they were points that were written in the [school] documents anyway, in our folders…what we need to do, what we have to do. It was pretty clear. Handwriting…we already know that we're pretty slack on handwriting. How we deal with it, our assessment…that was another thing. They didn't even look at that… Well they touched on it, a typical report, it was just bad things, that's all they wanted to look at. And there were no offerings to us on how to make it better *within our system.* (Interview, 25 May, 1991; my emphasis)

The school's response to the superficiality of the review process is reminiscent of Laughton's dismissal of those who were only interested in a summary assessment of the school (see Chapter 6). Likewise, Richmond Road continues to treat its detractors dismissively, as Laughton did, when it judges the criteria used to be invalid and/or inapplicable. As Wally Penetito concludes concerning the position of the school in relation to the review: 'Even on that...very small thing Richmond Road is in the same position it always was—fighting the battle' (Interview, 14 October, 1991).

The result of this particular battle was a standoff, with neither party willing to accede. As such, the ERO report stood virtually unchanged but the school's subsequent response was also formally acknowledged. The controversy surrounding the school's assessment did cause some embarrassment to the Review Office though; embarrassment they could ill afford as a fledgling organisation in the new educational structure (see above). The school's engagement with ERO was not to end here, however, as another review process was conducted in February, 1993 as a follow-up to the 1990 review. The school's response to ERO on this occasion illustrates another dimension of the school's resistance within the system.

By the time of this subsequent review, political developments in New Zealand education had seen ERO assume more of an audit function in their examination of schools. With individual school's responsible for their own management practices, ERO teams were now asked to simply assess whether schools were meeting the objectives outlined in their school charters. These objectives included a legislative requirement to provide written policies on key aspects of the school's curriculum and organisation.[4] When Richmond Road heard towards the end of 1992 of this impending ERO audit, the school's response was to employ me as an educational consultant. My job description was to formalise a number of key school policies in accordance with statutory requirements since, at the time, the necessary information pertaining to these policies was still dispersed throughout various school documents. I was to consult as required and complete the written policies in time for the review process. It was clearly apparent that Richmond Road viewed my conversancy with the school's ethos and operation, my familiarity with writing the necessary policy documents and, perhaps most crucially, my support of the school's educational endeavours, as the necessary prerequisites for such a task.

Without ascribing too much to my involvement (other policies and review requirements were provided by the school), the subsequent ERO review was uneventful. In their report, the review team state: 'There are high levels of compliance in governance and management systems and practice and [sic] curriculum management and implementation' (Education Review Office, 1993: 2). What is of most interest here though is the school's continued use and knowledge of educational legislation to ensure its safety within the system (see also Chapter 6). If certain expertise (provisional authority) is needed from elsewhere, it is employed to this end. My involvement in this instance, though a willing one, can be seen in this light. My participation also highlights, however, the reciprocal obligation required of me by the school. As a researcher, I have benefited from my association with Richmond Road; most obviously, perhaps, in my publications on the school. Likewise, where I can, I am expected to contribute in return. As I discussed in Chapter 7, all the school's teaching and learning arrangements are based on this underlying principle of cooperation. Even in independent learning at the school (of which I have considerable experience!) the aim is to encourage the acceptance of responsibility for knowledge already held, rather than independent learning at the expense of others. This was, for me, a particular case in point.

Whole-School Policies

Barry Troyna in Racism and Education (1993) observes that if one thing can be agreed on in the literature on multicultural and antiracist education it is the need for whole-school change. This is a position I have also outlined in the preceding chapters (although I differ with Troyna's dismissal of multicultural education; see Chapter 3). Troyna goes on to argue, however, that the implementation of whole-school antiracist policies has as yet had limited impact because of the inherent difficulties associated with gaining the consistent support of staff for such policies. There is, he suggests, a gap between the recognition of the need for whole-school policies on antiracist education and their actual implementation. (See Troyna, 1993: Chap. 4) This theory/practice dilemma is also recognised by North American commentators on multicultural education (see my discussion of Grant, 1992; Nieto, 1992 in Chapter 3) and is a central theme running throughout this book. However, unlike previous studies which have specifically explored these connections at the school level (and there have been relatively few), this account provides a positive example of what can be achieved when cultural and structural pluralism, in the form of whole-school change, are combined. I acknowledge that such organisational change is extremely demanding, and is further exacerbated at the secondary level where subject demarcation and didactic teaching tend to dominate.[5] Nevertheless, Richmond Road demonstrates the possibilities inherent in this kind of structural reorganisation.

With this aim, I have included below the policy drafts (collated from other school documents) which I wrote for the 1993 ERO review. These summarise the key characteristics of the school's educational approach to multiculturalism that have been discussed in the preceding chapters. They also provide a working model of whole-school policy development in multicultural education for schools wishing to pursue a similar agenda. It should be noted, however, that the policies as presented here are simply indicative of Richmond Road's educational approach and should not be seen as formal school policy,[6] nor should the particulars be seen as appropriate for all schools (see Laughton's reservations on this in Chapter 6). Also, if these policies are to be of most use to schools they should be read in conjunction with wider school-based policy development texts. David Corson's *Language Policy Across the Curriculum* (1990) is particularly useful in this regard as it directly addresses the questions that schools first need to consider in developing whole-school policies (see especially Chapter 10). The following policies are a response to the framework provided by Corson[7] (see also, Corson, 1993; Skilbeck, 1984).

Richmond Road School Policy on Policy Development

Rationale

The following policy outlines the current position of Richmond Road School in relation to school-based policy development. Policy documents, while attempting to accurately reflect the school's ethos and operations, are seen as dynamic. They are evaluated against the real world of the school and adjusted accordingly. This 'critically informed action' (Carr & Kemmis, 1983; Kemmis & McTaggart, 1988) also accords with the school's aim to create 'self-sustaining self-generating systems' and to place more importance on process than on product (Richmond Road School, 1983).

Purposes

1. To establish a process through which the Board of Trustees (BOT) can fulfil its Governance role in the school, as required under *Tomorrow's Schools* (1988).
2. To facilitate the school's own move towards increasing self-determination.
3. To establish guidelines which will ensure that charter objectives are realised in the organisational and curricular practices of the school.
4. To ensure, given the above, that the school remains committed to fostering cultural and language pluralism; both within the curriculum, and in the life of the school generally.
5. To ensure that policy development continues to be based on a process of collaborative and informed decision-making by BOT, staff, and management, in consultation with the community.

Guidelines

1. The focus of policy development is to provide equitable practices and outcomes for all children within the school.

2. The Treaty of Waitangi[8] and other issues relating to equity will frame the development of policy along these lines.

3. Written policies are provided for the following:

    (a) policy development

    (b) school organisation

    (c) community involvement

    (d) curriculum delivery

    (e) language across the curriculum

    (f) assessment

    (g) equity

4. All staff are required to know and act on written policy requirements. Action in accordance with these requirements provides for consistency and for use of appropriate services where relevant.

5. All policies are subject to BOT, staff, and management review, in consultation with the community.

6. Final approval of all policy is subject to the ratification of the Board of Trustees.

Conclusion

School-based policy development at Richmond Road is underpinned by the school's philosophy of, and commitment to, a culturally pluralist, integrative, and process approach to education. Within this, certain values are considered prerequisite: difference is never equated with deficiency; co-operation is fostered not competition; cultural respect is seen as essential to developing a pluralistic society; and the school's function is directed towards increasing a child's options rather than changing them.

References

Carr, W., and Kemmis, S. (1983) *Becoming Critical: Knowing Through Action Research.* Victoria: Deakin University Press.

Kemmis, S., and McTaggart, R. (eds.) (1988) *The Action Research Planner* (3rd edn). Geelong: Deakin University.

Lange, D. (1988) *Tomorrow's Schools.* Wellington: Government Printer.

Richmond Road School (1983), Learning and teaching in multi-cultural settings. Seminar given at Auckland Teachers' College by Principal and Staff.

Richmond Road School Policy on School Organisation

Rationale

Richmond Road School aims to foster the full potential of each child, and to reflect and encourage the ethnic diversity of the community it serves, by establishing inclusive, vertically-based organisational systems (rōpū). These derive from the model of the extended family group and comprise the entire range of pupils at the school. Rōpū aim to provide educational, cultural, and social learning opportunities within a supportive, cooperative learning environment which is consistent with the values of the minority cultures of many of the students, and with the ethos of the school. Rōpū also provide the basis for the various language programmes that operate within the school.

Purposes

1. To provide a culturally appropriate organisational framework which encourages and facilitates the full learning potential of all students, and which reflects the inclusive, integrative and process approach to learning adopted by the school.

2. To increase the age and ability range of organised groups of students.

3. To encourage teacher commitment to individual students by increasing length of association.

4. To provide for greater common purpose among teachers by reducing the classification categories of the school.

5. To institute a pattern of delegation which emphasises responsibility for individual students throughout their schooling.

The rōpū structure aims to:

6. Increase the age and ability range with which children are in contact.

7. Provide children with opportunities to experience a variety of learning roles and to develop an appropriate range of educational, cultural and social skills.

8. Allow children to develop and be responsible for their own learning, at their own pace, by dispensing with artificial expectations relating to class grouping by age.

9. Foster the parallel expectation that individual learning requires the acceptance of responsibility for knowledge already held, rather than independent learning at the expense of others.

10. Facilitate the child-centred, process approach to learning and the individual monitoring of children's progress arising from this.

11. Assist the growth of self-respect through the recognition of ethnic diversity and the wide range of skills, interests and cultural perspectives children bring to the group as a whole.

12. Allow parents, on bringing their children to the school, to choose the rōpū (and its associated language programme(s)) in which they wish their children to participate.

Guidelines

1. Rōpū, where possible, are to be taught in open plan 'shared spaces' with at least two teachers in every room. This allows the rōpū to be further divided into 'home groups' which are the responsibility of each individual teacher. Home groups are the basic teaching groups and it is the pupils in them that are monitored and reported on to parents by individual teachers.

2. Close liaison is to be maintained with the pre-schools on site at Richmond Road (Ritimana Kōhanga Reo; *A'oga Fa'a Samoa*; and *Apii Reo Kuki Airani*): to ensure the promotion of a wider school community ethos; and to facilitate the smooth transition of pre-school pupils into the school programmes.

Conclusion

The family organisational structure at Richmond Road is based on inclusive and cooperative learning systems. These aim to provide as full a range of learning opportunities for pupils as is possible, and to foster both individual and corporate responsibility among pupils (and teachers). The school desires that all children reach their full potential, and that they be actively involved in encouraging the learning potential of others:

> Family grouping...rests on the idea of integration of differences—differences of ethnicity, age, ability, gender, interest and knowledge. These factors are brought together so children may grow in knowledge, appreciation and respect for themselves and others...they are encouraged to take responsibility for their own learning and [to] support the learning process of those around them. (Richmond Road School, 1986:4)

References

Richmond Road School (1986), Cultural diversity: Challenge and response. Richmond Road School Working Paper.

Richmond Road School Policy on Community Involvement

Rationale

Richmond Road School views the education of its pupils as a shared responsibility between the school and its local school community. As such, the school is committed to ensuring a reciprocal, collaborative, and consultative relationship with its community.

Purposes

1. To acknowledge the important position of the tangata whenua in the school community and the reciprocal relationship between the school and the local community.

2. To ensure all school and curriculum policy decisions are developed in consultation with the school community.

3. To ensure that the management practices of the school are sensitive to the cultural practices of the local community.

4. To ensure that the involvement of parents in the life of the school, either formally or informally, is a continuing priority.

5. To utilise the expertise of parents, and people within the wider community, to enhance the learning and teaching programmes within the school.

6. To create a close association between students, parents, and teachers.

7. To promote and enhance close, effective communication channels between parents and the school.

8. To encourage continuing community and staff commitment to the school.

9. To continue to build links with the pre-schools on site in order to enhance the wider school community ethos of the school.

Guidelines

1. The composition of the Board of Trustees should reflect the cultural diversity of the school community it serves. If necessary, this can be achieved by co-option.

2. Board of Trustees meetings are to be held regularly and all community members can attend and participate. All decisions are to be arrived at by consensus by those in attendance, as this constitutes the major forum for official community consultation. These meetings should also include representation from the local pre-schools.

3. Other school forums and means of communication should be culturally sensitive and inclusive in order to reflect the cultural diversity of the local

community and to encourage parental involvement and commitment to the school.

4. The school should remain accessible to parents and the wider school community at all times and should encourage their direct involvement wherever possible.

5. Family grouping organisation should continue to encourage long term relationships between the school and parents.

6. Weekly school assemblies—in association with the various pre-schools—should continue to provide a focus for school and community participation, and should provide continuing opportunities for children to perform a range of cultural activities.

7. The school should encourage parental initiatives in relation to school programmes, activities, and/or concerns.

8. Teachers are required to participate in school/community forums and should be encouraged to participate in other local community activities where they can.

Conclusion

The development of a strong and active school/community relationship is a continuing priority of the school. Long term and reciprocal associations are encouraged wherever possible and the school aims to reflect and cater for the interests and concerns of parents and local community groups. The definition of the school community is broadly defined and includes the active involvement of the pre-schools in the life of the school.

Richmond Road School Policy on Curriculum Delivery

Rationale

The delivery of curriculum programmes within the school adheres to the requirements of the New Zealand Primary Curriculum in all respects. Local curriculum goals and objectives reflect the child-centred, process, and bilingual approach to education developed by the school since the 1970s for meeting the educational needs of its culturally diverse school community. These local goals and objectives are grounded in current educational theory, and are supported by appropriate resources and ongoing resource development. Programmes and resources are intrinsically allied with the organisational changes undertaken by the school.

Purposes

1. To provide approaches to teaching and learning which: effectively deliver the national curriculum; recognise the primary place of Māori within the curriculum and; recognise and respond to the multicultural nature of our society.

2. To provide approaches to teaching and learning that are educationally sound, theoretically based, and culturally appropriate, and which encourage and facilitate the full learning potential of all children in the school community.

3. To provide a staff development plan which equips staff professionally and which meets the needs of the school and the requirements of the national curriculum.

4. To provide an integrated and holistic approach to learning which is not circumscribed by hard subject boundaries nor by artificial grouping by age. Increasing the age and ability range of organised groups of students within the school, through family grouping, facilitates this process.

5. To provide dual-medium bilingual curricula where possible. These presently include Māori, Samoan and Cook Islands Māori options.

6. To foster the notion of 'provisional authority' as opposed to 'assigned authority' (Peters, 1973) in learning and teaching arrangements. This conception facilitates the sharing of teaching and learning roles between children and teachers—and also, where appropriate, with parents—particularly through the use of tuakana–teina roles.

7. Given the above, to develop teachers as facilitators of children's learning, and as learners themselves. This includes continual reflection on educational theory and teaching practice.

8. To develop resources, in addition to those used nationally, which support these learning and language approaches and which reflect the cultural diversity and interests of the school community.

Guidelines

1. Staff development is closely allied with curriculum development and includes both internal and external in-service input. Internally, staff spend at least two hours per week on curriculum development in staff, focus resource, and team meetings. External courses comprise a variety of short-term in-service training options.

2. The goals of staff development remain the furthering of staff knowledge in the curriculum, management and organisation of the school, the sharing of this with the wider community, and the engendering, through this process, of the key components of cultural maintenance and access to power in a learning environment for adults and children.

3. The Associate Principals are responsible for coordinating and promoting the professional development of staff. This includes releasing teachers for specific curriculum purposes, and providing induction/extension programmes for beginning teachers.

4. The involvement in curriculum development by staff is also supported through the organisation of staff into curriculum teams. Curriculum teams develop resources for the curriculum during the course of the year, supervise these materials, and provide support for staff working in other areas.

5. Curriculum teams comprise staff members from across the school and aim for a diversity of expertise and background experience. They may be reconstituted, at the discretion of the principal, to ensure that teachers gain experience in a variety of curriculum areas.

6. Curriculum team leaders are responsible for keeping up to date with new curriculum developments in their area, and for coordinating and disseminating this information as appropriate.

7. Each year the school will highlight particular curriculum areas for extension and development through the staff development process.

8. Focus resource teams also operate to resource the social studies programme. The task of each team is to plan and produce a set of social studies and associated curriculum resources on a given 'focus' topic. While these topics may be wide ranging, they are 'focused' by the exploration of a particular concept. These school-wide topics are studied each year in a two semester system and are part of an integrated three year cycle.

9. Resources developed by focus resource teams must reflect the multiethnic nature of the school and support and extend children's experiences, knowledge, imagination, language, and reading.

10. Focus resources are to be prepared for independent and guided programmes, and at ten levels of reading independence so that individual children can be carefully matched to appropriate resource levels.

11. A variety of learning contexts can be employed in the development of focus resources. These include: superior/inferior; cooperative; collaborative and; independent.

12. Other resources developed within the school must also be designated by appropriate level and learning context.

Conclusion

Involvement of all staff members in curriculum development, and in the provision of curriculum resources, results in conversancy with ongoing curriculum developments at a national level and with the holistic and culturally diverse delivery of curriculum within the school. This furthers the growth of individual teachers' professional development and responsibility. It will also lead to all pupils needs being better met, and to successful school self-management.

References

Peters, R. (ed.) (1973), *The Philosophy of Education*. London: Oxford University Press.

Richmond Road School Language Policy across the Curriculum (LPAC)

Rationale

In line with the school's emphasis on an integrative and process approach to learning, Richmond Road endorses the use of 'language across the curriculum' and the promotion of a maintenance view of bilingualism. The use of home languages within the school is encouraged wherever possible and formalised in bilingual curricula. Reading and writing activities are integrated across the curriculum and children's reading and writing is closely monitored.

Purposes

1. To maintain and enrich the home language(s) of minority children in the school by establishing and maintaining dual-medium bilingual rōpū.

2. To extend bilingual curriculum options where possible. In 1991, for example, a Cook Islands dual-medium bilingual unit was established in addition to the Māori and Samoan units.

3. To promote parental choice concerning the involvement of children in these programmes and to extend this notion of choice to the pupils within these programmes who may be encouraged, but should not be coerced, into speaking the language prescribed.

4. To foster the principle in the school reading/language programme of 'language experience', where children are encouraged to develop and expand language in the context of experiences, books or events.

5. To encourage peer support in reading—particularly through tuakana–teina roles in paired reading—to complement the support given by the teacher.

6. To encourage writing (including spelling and handwriting) as a necessary part of other curriculum activities as well as an activity in itself.

7. To encourage communicative modalities which, while including reading and writing, are not limited to them.

8. To regularly monitor individual children's language progress, including the use of running records for reading and the collection of samples of children's written work (see also, Assessment Policy).

9. To combine accurate matching, careful monitoring, and teacher and peer support to develop confident and competent speakers, readers, and writers.

Guidelines

1. Children should be encouraged to speak in the language(s) of their choice at any given time, including, but not limited to, English.

2. Children should be matched at their reading levels not their age level.

3. Regular oversight of individual reading needs to be maintained, at least once a term with all children and more often for lower levels. Running records on all children are to be kept.

4. Reading recovery trained teachers should work with children identified from the programme, and act as resources for other teachers.

5. Reading materials (boxed books and fluency kits) are to be available for children with reading ages under 11 years. The school library is available for children with reading ages over 11 years.

6. A variety of writing activities are to be encouraged: private writing; supported writing; and cooperative writing.

7. Children are to be regarded as experts in the writing process. The notion of teaching a 'correct' model of writing is discounted and experimentation in children's writing is to be encouraged.

8. Spelling and handwriting are to form an integral part of all written language programmes and are to be taught within an integrated and process context.

Conclusion

The school believes in a developmental approach to language learning; language as a process rather than a product. This is supported by theoretical developments in language and reading and accords with the school's pedagogical emphases. The rigorous monitoring processes adopted by the school underpin these approaches to language and reading and seek to provide all children at the school with the literacy skills necessary to function fully in society, as well as recognising that bilingual skills are an additional advantage.

Richmond Road School Policy on Assessment

Rationale

The individual monitoring of children underpins the pedagogical, curriculum and organisational initiatives undertaken at Richmond Road School and is consistent in all respects with the demands of the New Zealand Curriculum. Individual monitoring within the school emphasises developmental rather than prescriptive assessment and includes regular diagnostic assessment based on observation of learning behaviour over an extended period.

Purposes

1. To provide, through individual monitoring, developmental rather than prescriptive information on children. This reinforces the developmental learning emphasised in the organisation of family groups and the curriculum process model.
2. To ensure regular and consistent reporting of student progress in all areas; both within family groups and to parents/caregivers.
3. To avoid counterproductive comparisons and competitiveness and to maintain a positive learning environment.
4. To place priority on the development of basic skills, leading to independence in learning at all levels.
5. To allow for a range of communicative modalities including, but not limited to, reading and writing.
6. To recognise and include assessment procedures, where possible, in languages other than English.
7. To allow children to respond to the meaning conveyed, rather than to form, in communicating and relating.

Guidelines

1. Teachers are required to individually monitor at least three children every week within their rōpū and to discuss and document these observations. Documentation should include: running records on reading and mathematics; samples of written language, mathematics, art, and book work; and observations on social factors (relationships, and ability to interact with others) and work habits.
2. All observations should accumulate in personal folders for each child. Samples of work should accumulate in work files that can be used as a resource, and for presentation to families on parent conference night. Both personal and work folders are to be regularly updated.

3. Running records in reading and mathematics are to be kept on all children. These records include not only the children's levels but also specific information concerning the skills or cues used, needed, or misused by individual children.

4. Movement from one level to the next requires children to meet stringent criteria. In reading, for example, a child needs to read fluently, independently and with understanding at her or his current instructional level—with 95% accuracy and at least a 1:3 self-correction rate—before being able to move to the next reading level.

5. Running records may be used as resources by both children and teachers in the family group context.

6. As part of the staff development process, teachers will undergo regular training and retraining in the use of running records and observation techniques to ensure familiarity with requirements.

7. Rōpū leaders are responsible for maintaining the assessment requirements, as outlined, for their respective groups.

Conclusion

The individual monitoring and the diagnostic assessment undertaken at Richmond Road School recognise the importance of obtaining developmental rather than prescriptive information on children. This arises from the developmental learning emphases embodied in the school's family group organisation and curriculum process model, and accords with national developments in assessment. This approach also avoids the normative model associated with testing which has historically played the role of legitimising the disabling of students (particularly minority students) in classrooms (Cummins, 1986).

References

Cummins, J. (1986), Empowering minority students: A framework for intervention. *Harvard Educational Review* 56, 18–36.

Richmond Road School Policy on Equity

Rationale

All educational activities undertaken at Richmond Road School are framed by equity objectives in order that equitable outcomes might be achieved for every child at the school, irrespective of cultural, ethnic, social, class, gender or religious background, and irrespective of their ability or disability. Equity considerations also underpin family organisation and process curriculum rationales. Within these equity objectives special recognition is accorded to the obligations pursuant to The Treaty of Waitangi.

Purposes

1. To accord recognition of Māori as tangata whenua, and to provide a curriculum which: reflects Māori perspectives; makes equitable provision in the curriculum for the instructional needs of Māori children; provides opportunities for students to be educated through the Māori language; and recognises Māori values in the provision of resources and facilities within the school.

2. To provide alternatives in school organisation, curriculum delivery, and in the language of instruction employed in classrooms, which recognise and foster the multiethnic nature of the school community.

3. To model in staff composition, and in the delegation of staff responsibilities, positive cultural and gender roles to which children can aspire.

4. To provide an education which enhances all children's learning; building on their needs and respecting their dignity.

5. To demonstrate through teacher behaviour a respect for all children's cultural identity, an acceptance of diversity, and the avoidance of selective practices that lead to stereotyping.

6. To select (and create) learning materials that are non racist and non sexist and which provide a range of positive role models.

7. To support children who have particular learning difficulties and to seek, where necessary, support from appropriate agencies.

Guidelines

1. The democratic and reciprocal nature of the rōpū (vertical family grouping) framework will facilitate equitable outcomes for both children and staff, and provide a variety of positive and inclusive role models.

2. The opportunity within family group organisation to adopt a range of teaching and learning roles is conversant with the cultural backgrounds of Māori and Pacific Island students, and is a powerful framework for learning for both Māori and non-Māori alike.

3. The organisational and learning programmes adopted within rōpū will allow for children's individual learning needs to be catered for at all levels, irrespective of age and class related constraints.

4. Children who are experiencing difficulties can be readily identified and supported by the monitoring and assessment policies which operate within rōpū and throughout the school.

5. Bilingual curricula will cater for languages of instruction other than English within the school, and will link in closely with pre-school language programmes on site.

6. The appointment of Māori and Pacific Island language speakers to the staff will facilitate the delivery of bilingual curricula.

7. The appointment, and promotion, of Māori, Pacific Islands, and women staff members will provide positive role models for children.

8. Resources will be provided which have positive role models, and content and/or language which is representative of the many cultures in the school.

9. Knowledge and experiences from members of the school community—parents, teachers and children—will be valued as an authentic knowledge base for resource development.

Conclusion

The school actively promotes diversity as an important factor in its role as an institute of learning. As such, school organisation and curricula aim to provide an educational approach which both celebrates difference and actively promotes it, while also promoting commonalities of experience. This cultivation of a respect for difference, along with the reciprocal responsibilities required of all school participants to make intercultural relationships work, characterise the school's view of equity:

> this school's educational provisions arise [from] the perceived need to recognise and celebrate difference and to try and weave from the many cultural threads a fabric, a unity that retains the colour and texture of each. (Principal's Report, 9 February, 1988)

Richmond Road Without Laughton

These policy documents reflect both the ongoing nature of Richmond Road's educational enterprise and the history of Jim Laughton's influence that underpins them. This twofold dimension is nicely captured by Cazden, in the conclusion to her article on the school. There she talks of the oak tree that Laughton had planted some years ago at the school and which has subsequently had the deck to the Kōhanga Reo built around it. He had loved that tree and at his tangi one of the tree's first spring shoots had been placed on his coffin. As she goes on to observe:

More than one staff member thought of that tree as Jim. 'Now he can look down and see all the roots growing and spreading'. 'The roots growing and spreading' are Richmond Road's children. They can be Jim's ideas too: spreading by being taken by former Richmond Road teachers to other schools, and to other areas of New Zealand life...; and growing deeper in the understanding of those who now can't rely on Jim but have to act and understand for themselves. (1989: 165)

Richmond Road may no longer have Jim Laughton to lead it and the school has certainly been, as a consequence, through a difficult transition period. But those who remain *are* learning to act and understand for themselves and have no intentions, just yet it seems, of renouncing the educational commitments and innovations he established along with them at Richmond Road. Those particular commitments and innovations are ably summarised by Wally Penetito:

Richmond Road is in my opinion (and in the opinion of a considerable number of others) one of the best attempts anywhere in the world to create a school community where structural alternatives exist for both learning and delivery, where hierarchy is deliberately played down in all relationships, where cultural diversity is enhanced through practice, where monitoring [the] progress of children is never subordinated to the results from test attainments... Richmond Road School operates within an explicit theory of schooling which has been a theory-in-the-making consciously, since 1972. The school works in my terms according to a 'socially critical pedagogy'. It is an attempt to integrate a humanistic education with a political education by ensuring that the child (not the teacher, not the programme, not the school, nor even the parent and the community) is always at the centre. How successful the school is in practising its philosophy at any one moment is problematic but I do know that critical dialogue and intellectual rigour have always been cornerstones of the way the school [operates]. (Personal Communication, 26 April, 1991)

Moreover, as the recent changes within the school indicate, Richmond Road continues to take cognisance of the changing context of the times (and continues to use that knowledge to its best advantage) in realising an approach to multicultural education which makes a difference for minority children. Fittingly, then, it is a relative newcomer to the school who, perhaps, best outlines the school's current state:

There's something alive at Richmond Road, there's something organic that just keeps growing and whether it is due to Jim Laughton because...you would think that his influence would have (pause) something would have diluted it by now. Because after all there are children there who've never heard of him. There's teachers there who could hardly avoid actually hearing

of him, but who have no real knowledge of him at all. So there's something…there that keeps the school…there is definitely something that over-
rides, that makes multiculturalism there work on a different level to
[elsewhere]. (Maggie Wood: Interview, 12 August, 1991)

Notes to Chapter 9

1. Joy Glasson and Lionel Pedersen ran the school collaboratively on an associate
   principalship basis during the time of Jim's illness. This arrangement continued until
   Glasson left to take up a position elsewhere and Pedersen was subsequently appointed
   as Jim's successor.
2. These reforms, instituted in 1988–1989, saw the complete administrative reorganisation of New Zealand education. The previous Department of Education—which had
   been concerned with policy, school provision, curriculum, and professional development—was dissolved. In its place was established a new Ministry of Education,
   concerned solely with policy. The school review functions of the previous department
   were taken up by the newly constituted Education Review Office (ERO). Administrative responsibilities were 'decentralised' to local school level. Local education
   boards (equivalent to Local Education Authorities) were abolished and replaced with
   individual school Boards of Trustees. These Boards of Trustees have assumed legal
   and financial responsibility for the running of schools although the curriculum is still
   centrally controlled. For discussions on the nature of these reforms and the 'new right'
   agenda which has driven them, see Codd *et al.* (1990); Lauder & Wylie (1990); and
   Middleton *et al.* (1990).
3. The administrative reforms were initially advocated in the policy document *Tomorrow's Schools* (Lange, 1988). However, implementation of these reforms did not occur
   until October, 1989. Accordingly, Richmond Road delayed appointing a new principal
   until after this time so that its Board of Trustees could appoint a principal whom they
   felt would continue what Laughton had established. (Previously, the local education
   board would have been responsible for appointing a new principal).
4. In a similar way to the centralising tendencies of the Educational Reform Act (1988)
   in England and Wales (see Troyna, 1993, Chap. 3, for a useful discussion here), there
   is a discrepancy between the emphasis on parental choice, devolution, and local school
   management in the New Zealand reforms, and the actual centralising of state control
   over curriculum and organisational issues. The latter tendency is seen in New Zealand
   in the use of institutional school charters to bind elected Boards of Trustees to the
   state. Although the Board of Trustees and state relationship was initially advocated in
   the reforms as a partnership model, its subsequent development was to see a more
   unequal model emerge. As it now stands, the school charter (which is largely
   prescribed) is an undertaking by Boards *to* the Minister of Education. It requires
   schools to provide certain educational services—the effectiveness of which, can be
   judged by the state (see Codd & Gordon, 1991; Gordon, 1993). These services include
   the satisfactory delivery of the core curriculum, efficient financial and organisational
   management and, as I have already discussed, written school policies in accordance
   with established requirements.
5. Both Troyna (1993) and Bagley (1992) provide interesting recent accounts of the
   attendant difficulties in secondary schools of adopting whole-school policies.
6. These documents have subsequently been modified by Richmond Road as part of the
   ongoing staff development process in 1993.

7. Corson outlines a broad framework for whole-school policy development, the principles of which I have applied in developing the policies below. He does not provide actual policies as is the case here.

8. As I outlined in Chapter 6, the Treaty of Waitangi, signed in 1840 by Māori and Pākehā, is New Zealand's foundational document. After over one hundred years of neglect by Pākehā, the last twenty years has seen it reaffirmed as the legal basis of New Zealand's bicultural and bilingual heritage. Its partnership model, and its recognition of indigenous Māori rights, is seen as the basis for any subsequent move to multiculturalism; hence the school's attendant emphasis on Māori. Multiculturalism in New Zealand cannot occur without first addressing our bicultural commitments.

10 A Critical Pedagogy at Work

In Chapter 4, I outlined the critical ethnographic nature of this account of Richmond Road. Critical ethnography, as a research process, is both critical and transformative (Lather, 1986a). It recognises that structural forces are at work within schooling but also allows for the possibilities which inhere in human agency. Put another way, critical ethnography combines a conception of macro-sociological forces operating within education with their *mediation* in the everyday lived experiences of human actors in a particular institution. As Angus has argued, this mediation can lead to contradiction and resistance:

> Such mediation, given the essential human agency of school participants, will never be simple, enabling the automatic reproduction of prior arrange-ments, but will instead allow for *moments of contradiction* which will signal new social or institutional forces, or *the beginnings of new organisational forms*. (1986b: 75; my emphasis)

These 'moments of contradiction' from the ordinary practices of schooling, and the subsequent 'beginnings of new organisational forms', are clearly apparent at Richmond Road. The result is a critical and transformative approach to multicultural education; an approach which finally bridges the gap between emancipatory theory and practice. Richmond Road's educational approach is multifaceted, reflective and reflexive. More remarkably though, it is also coherent, integrated and holistic. What follows is an attempt to highlight the key moments of contradiction involved here and the new organisational forms which have been their result.

Richmond Road School: A Critical Pedagogy at Work

Christine Brown, writing on the classification of educational ideologies, argues that past attempts to describe ideologies of education which differ from dominant conceptions of schooling have been limited to simple dichotomies—for example, teacher-centred/child-centred, traditional/progressive, and in relation to ethnic minority education, assimilationist/pluralist. These dichoto-mies, she suggests, are limiting and conceal the variations apparent in real situations; one might even argue that they fail at times to address real situations at all.[1] The complexities of Richmond Road's educational approach, and the ideologies of education underpinning it, clearly attest to Brown's concern. The framework of analysis she subsequently advocates as a means of highlighting these complexities will be used to structure the ensuing discussion:

> What may be required is the kind of analysis which attempts to account for the element of complexity in educational ideologies... The form of analysis used by Meighan & Roberts (1979) and extended by Meighan & Brown (1980) is suggested here. It consists of the following features of an educational ideology:
>
> (a) a view (or theory) of knowledge, its content and structure;
>
> (b) a view of learning and the learner's role;
>
> (c) a view of resources appropriate for learning;
>
> (e) a view of the organisation of learning situations;
>
> (f) a view of assessment that learning has taken place;
>
> (g) a view of aims, objectives and outcomes;
>
> (h) a view of the location of learning;
>
> (i) a view of language and its educational use.
>
> In the special case of curriculum responses to ethnic minority groups, it will also be worth considering something like:
>
> (j) a view of racial integration... (Brown, 1988: 56)[2]

A view (or theory) of knowledge...

The basis of Jim Laughton's conception of educational theory is clear. As Eric McMillan comments: 'I think...conflict theory was what interested him... He had read widely of educational theorists' (Interview, 26 February, 1991). Perhaps this was the first, and underlying 'moment of contradiction' in what was subsequently to develop at Richmond Road. Laughton knew that traditional forms of schooling perpetuated inequalities for minority children. As he said of them: 'I don't know what's right in education, but over the years, these things have proved to me that at least for minority people, they haven't been successful. So what is the point of pursuing those same things?' (cited in Cazden, 1989: 145). And as he has elsewhere argued, on the nature of assigned authority and its realisation in institutionalised power:

> The exercise of assigned authority [in traditional conceptions of schooling] has great influence on the educational opportunities and subsequent life chances of pupils. Boguslaw (1971) has defined this authority as 'institutionalised power' and power 'as the ability to apply force'. He says that force in this context refers to the reduction, limitation, closure or total

elimination of alternatives to the social action of one person or group by another person or group. Children from groups with little access to 'institutionalised' power in New Zealand society may be, more than most, victims of such force. *It is the school's task to increase their alternatives.* (Richmond Road School, 1986: 1; my emphasis)

Laughton's pursuit of wider alternatives for minority children in education led him in new educational directions; directions which were to both obviate and challenge the hegemonic processes to which minority children are normally subject in and through schooling. The educational theories upon which he drew for this task were eclectic, arising both from his own extensive reading and his ability to incorporate the knowledge of others. However, the principal influences on his thinking were, perhaps, the work of R.S. Peters and Lawrence Stenhouse; the former for his distinction between assigned and provisional authority, and the latter for his advocacy of a resource-based process approach to learning. The two central tenets of Laughton's educational philosophy were his concern for *cultural maintenance*—the fostering of identity and self esteem through the affirmation of cultural difference, and *access to power*—equipping minority children with the skills necessary to live in mainstream society:

The first principle...cultural maintenance...is the right of every child to know and be proud of who she/he is. If a child is strong and proud in self-knowledge, this results in respect for other people's differences; differences are no longer a threat. At Richmond Road we promote difference and actively celebrate it. The second principle, access to power, deals with the teacher's responsibility to help children acquire the skills they may need to function in the wider context of the power society, as it exists at present. It is each child's choice whether these skills are used. (Richmond Road School, 1985: 2)

Laughton believed that both principles are necessary if dominant power relations in society are to be effectively contested. In implementing these ideas, he saw certain values as prerequisite: difference is never equated with deficiency; co-operation is fostered not competition; cultural respect is seen as essential to developing a pluralistic society; and the school's function is directed towards increasing a child's options rather than changing them. These parameters accord with the concept of the 'socially critical school'; a concept with which Laughton was familiar from the work of Stephen Kemmis (1983; see Chapter 6). A similar concept argued for more recently by Morrison (1989)—the 'socially critical primary school'—also bears a remarkable resemblance to what has resulted at Richmond Road. Morrison's discussion centres on progressive education. He argues, in this context, that teachers need to re-examine their principles and practices so that the developing autonomy of the child becomes and remains a central concern of the school. He suggests that schooling and teaching must also allow pupils more curricular choice; 'Teachers must be prepared for children to move out of their given frameworks, to choose not to stay in a prefigured curriculum. This requires both considerable resources and considerable courage...' (1989: 12). He advocates the need to develop collaboration rather than competition among individuals:

> The notion of co-operation and collectivism extends to teachers as well as to children, involving whole staff decision making on policies which affect the whole school. It extends also to team planning and team teaching...enabling children and teachers to experience variety in social relationships and organisations. Co-operation and collectivism reaches further into the school with the suggestion of mixed age classes or older children working with younger children for part of their time in school. The keynote perhaps is flexibility of learning arrangements. (1989: 13)

Morrison also argues that the school community should be drawn on as a concrete curriculum resource; that an integrated curriculum should be fostered; and finally, that the school 'needs to keep together the individual and a broadly socially derived curriculum' (1989: 14). Richmond Road's educational approach clearly demonstrates these characteristics in its pursuit of an emancipatory conception of multicultural education—initially under Laughton, and now without him. The individual and socially derived curriculum apparent within the school also provides a model by which we can move beyond the seeming impasse reached in the structure/agency debated discussed in Chapter 2. It is possible after all, it seems, to successfully implement a view of educational knowledge that recognises both cultural distinctiveness (including distinctions in cultural knowledge bases) and academic rigour.

A view of learning and the learner's role—and the location of learning

Along with a critically conceived view of the role of educational knowledge at Richmond Road comes a diversified view of learning and teaching. All participants in the educational process—children, teachers, non-teaching staff, and parents—are seen as learners in given situations. Likewise, all those involved in the school have the ability *and opportunity* to teach where appropriate. The location of learning and teaching at Richmond Road can be anywhere. Laughton's promotion of the notion of provisional authority was to establish and facilitate the depth and variety of learning and teaching now undertaken at the school. Traditional hierarchies in school organisation—between administrators and teachers, teachers and pupils, and the school and its community—have been reconstituted in the process; creating another moment of contradiction. As Cazden observes, in her study of the school, the result is that while 'Richmond Road is first and foremost a school for children, it's also—and more remarkably—a learning community for adults... The adult learning is about teaching, about other cultures, and about oneself' (1989: 146). One might add, of course, that these aspects constitute the children's learning at the school as well. The participatory, reciprocal and non-hierarchical relationships set in place at Richmond Road *facilitate* the learning of all those involved within them. As Lionel Pedersen states, 'I suppose...what people started realising is that *everybody* can learn. All you differ at is the rate that you work at—kids *and* teachers—and it's always a two way progression. The more the kids learn the more we learn and vice versa' (Interview, 26 February, 1990).

The reciprocity apparent in the learning arrangements adopted at Richmond Road derived from Laughton's concern to link knowledge with responsibility. For both children and teachers this has involved exercising responsibility for knowledge already held by contributing expertise and skills to the group as a whole. In the case of teachers, this has also involved knowing when *not* to contribute in order to allow for the contribution of others. The tuakana-teina relationships established within the school—for children within family groups, and for teachers through the staff development process—provide the principal means by which these reciprocal learning processes occur.

A view of resources appropriate for learning—and of assessment that learning has taken place

Another principal tenet in Richmond Road's approach to learning, particularly in relation to children's learning, is the emphasis given to the *process* rather than the *product*. While not uninterested in the educational product (given the emphasis on 'access to power'; see above) the school advocates a generative model of learning in preference to a goal-oriented approach. Laughton came to the view that if children are to achieve control over their own learning and to derive enjoyment from it, the learning model adopted needs to be both child-centred and resource-based. Stenhouse's curriculum process approach provided such a model, and the key element within it of resourcing children's learning has subsequently become a central feature of Richmond Road's pedagogical approach. The way resources are planned, prepared and utilised at Richmond Road illustrates the school's attempt to integrate rather than isolate curriculum areas: 'This gives concepts and activities an inter-connectedness. A holistic view of the world is promoted and options and choices for both teachers and children are increased' (Richmond Road School, 1986: 5). Resources at the school are differentiated—'this means they can be completed in a variety of ways, allowing for different learner abilities and results... [they are] open enough to allow for alternative means and modes of learning' (Richmond Road School, 1985: 4). Resources are also problem-posing—'they should be concerned with genuine questions not with providing answers' (Richmond Road School, 1985: 4). Accordingly, resources developed by teachers at the school allow children to experience a wide range of independent and collaborative learning experiences and a variety of learning contexts at levels appropriate to their varying stages of development. In addition, they are able to incorporate a recognition of cultural differences not readily available in school texts.

Resource development and use is also underpinned by the close monitoring of children's individual learning in order to achieve the accurate matching of children to resources. Testing is eschewed because of its traditional association with academic (and cultural) prescription and the consequent disadvantaging of minority children. The result is a high degree of literacy among children at Richmond Road because they '[keep] on having learning chances and learning experiences' (Margaret Leaming: Interview, 28 May, 1991). The cohort study in Chapter 8 clearly attests to the success of this monitoring process.

A view of language and its educational use

At Richmond Road the learning processes and opportunities outlined above are conducted within an awareness of the centrality of language and its legitimising role in the educational process. Richmond Road endorses Bourdieu's suggestion that 'language is not only an instrument of communication or even of knowledge, but also an instrument of power' (1977; cited in Thompson, 1984: 46). In this, again, is a moment of contradiction since the school recognises the processes of exclusion and domination which result for minority children through the uncritical acceptance of majority language use in most schools. In contrast, Richmond Road actively tries to redress these processes by the incorporation of other languages (and their attendant cultures) in and through the curriculum. Language is not seen as an end in itself—it is not divorced from culture—but neither is its centrality to cultural maintenance minimised, as it is so often in 'benevolent' approaches to multicultural education. As we saw in Chapter 7, this fostering of a diversity of languages and cultures, and its formal recognition in the bilingual curricula operating within the school, arose from Jim Laughton's extensive background in language issues and his recognition—against the prevailing deficit view of the time—of the cultural and intellectual advantages of bilingualism. Laughton was specifically concerned to empower minority children by recognising and giving status to the languages they brought to the school, and by recognising and encouraging their development for the benefit of the whole school and wider community. This may also explain the subsequent academic achievements of Richmond Road's students since, as Cummins has argued, 'the extent to which [minority] students' language and culture are incorporated into the school programme constitutes a significant predictor of [their] academic success' (1986: 25).

The incorporation of language(s) in the curriculum and the integration of language activities across the curriculum[3] are also significant factors in the educational development of the ethnic minority children at Richmond Road. In this regard, the integrative approach adopted by the school is strongly reminiscent of Cummins's (1986) 'reciprocal interaction' model of pedagogy. Cummins discusses this model within the context of bilingual education and the possibilities, therein, of fostering success for minority students:

> A central tenet of the reciprocal interaction model is that 'talking and writing are means to learning'... The use of this model in teaching requires a genuine dialogue between student and teacher in both oral and written modalities, guidance and facilitation rather than control of student learning by the teacher, and the encouragement of student/student talk in a collaborative learning context. This model emphasizes...meaningful language use by students rather than the correction of surface forms. Language use and development are consciously integrated with all curricular content...and tasks are presented to students in ways that generate intrinsic rather than extrinsic motivation. In short, pedagogical approaches that empower students encourage them to assume greater control over setting their own learning goals and to collaborate actively with each other in achieving these goals. The development of a sense of efficacy and inner direction in the classroom is especially important for students from dominated groups whose experiences so often orient them in the opposite direction. (1986: 28–29)

Such an approach stands in sharp contrast to the ERO team's noticeable concern in their initial report on Richmond Road for more didactic teaching and subject demarcation, particularly in language areas (see Chapter 9). As the school's rejoinder at the time clearly states, these are the very practices which have marginalised minority children in the educational process in the first place. The integrative pedagogical approach which Richmond Road has adopted—and the clear ascription to the status of language(s) and culture(s) within that approach—is seen as one aspect, albeit a key one, of achieving change for minority students. In advocating such a position, the school continues to contest alternative educational paradigms which militate against its educational intentions. The signalling of 'new social or institutional forces', or 'the beginnings of new organisational forms' (Angus, 1986b) are, after all, only achieved through conflict.

À view of the organisation of learning situations

In Chapter 6, we saw that Laughton's attempts to establish new organisational forms at Richmond Road, particularly through the establishment of vertical rōpū (family groupings), were gradual and carefully managed.

Laughton's success in establishing these organisational systems within the school was due to his ability to instil and cultivate in others an enthusiasm for the project, and his willingness to allow people the necessary time to change. He drew in senior teachers who were willing to model the initial developments and he implemented the structural changes required by family grouping across the entire school over a period of 8–9 years.

This process of organisational change, in itself, is of considerable interest. In the field of educational administration, for example, while much has been written on the role of the principal, very little research has been devoted to the characteristics associated with successful innovators. Even less research has been conducted on the strategies adopted by principals to achieve change (Ramsay et al., 1991). Moreover, and again in relation to research in educational administration, very little work as yet has been attempted on providing accounts of minority schooling that recognise the processes of reproduction to which minority groups are subject within education. While a critical conception of the nature of school organisation is beginning to develop (see, for example, Ball, 1987; 1989; Bates, 1986; Connell, 1985; Connell et al., 1982), the dominance of technicist models of schooling[4] has led to an essentially conservative and rampantly monocultural conception of school organisation in educational administration research.[5] It is hoped that this account of Richmond Road, and Jim Laughton's role within it, may be a start in a new direction. Certainly, the model of family grouping—with its emphasis on inclusiveness and mutual support, and its development of extended relationships—provides us with an example of what can be achieved for minority children through organisational change at the school level. Family grouping at Richmond Road is able to facilitate the recognition of cultural differences while also according responsibility for cultural interaction. It has redefined the teaching and learning process for both teachers and children. And it is, as such, the basis on which the participatory, non-hierarchical, non-competitive and interactive learning and teaching arrangements established within the school can function. As I argued in Chapter 3, without this kind of structural reorganisation an *effective* approach to multicultural education which actually makes a difference for minority children *cannot* be achieved. Any attempt which excludes institutional change must remain extrinsic and additional to existing organisational structures that act to disadvantage minority children. That this reorganisation at Richmond Road was given such priority by Laughton, and that it forms the basis upon which his other educational initiatives can stand, attest to his recognition of this fact.

A view of racial integration

Family grouping has also been central to providing the means by which *cultural recognition*—the valuing of cultural differences—can be tied in with an emphasis on *cultural interaction*—the responsibility to make intercultural relationships work. As Laughton has argued, 'this school's educational provisions arise [from] the perceived need to recognise and celebrate difference and to try and weave from the many cultural threads a fabric, a unity that retains the colour and texture of each' (Principal's Report, 9 February, 1988). In Bourdieu's terminology (see Chapter 2), *all* cultures are valued for their cultural capital at Richmond Road and there is no privileging of one particular *habitus* over another.

Richmond Road's approach recognises and acknowledges the validity of cultural difference but also emphasises the notion of unity (although at no point does it confuse the latter concept with uniformity; see Chapter 6). This cultivation of a respect for difference, along with the reciprocal responsibilities required of all school participants to make intercultural relationships work, perhaps explains why racism is not apparent at Richmond Road. The school, given its recognition of power relations, is certainly not unaware of the broader processes of racism at work in society. However, the nature of the relationships established at Richmond Road would appear to largely preclude (or at least certainly minimise) their effects within the school. These relationships—and the responsibilities which inhere in them—are modelled by staff and children in the organisational structures of the school, are supported by the reciprocal learning and teaching arrangements, and are reinforced by curriculum content. The results affect all Richmond Road's participants; children, parents and teachers. The family atmosphere of the school, for example, was consistently highlighted by both pupils and ex-pupils. Folole Asaua, a Samoan student who is now completing secondary school, recalls her experience of Richmond Road in this regard:

> It was really strange in primary [school], everyone just got on with everyone. It wasn't like one [ethnic] group would be here and a bunch of groups over there. We all just mixed in, even with the palangi [Europeans] which was really good. There was no such thing [as racism], we didn't think of racism as a problem. Everyone was just like one big family... Somehow we just had this atmosphere that we would get on with everyone. I don't know how it happened but it was just the way we were. If there were newcomers we'd just go up and get on with them and start making friends from there— bring them into the family. I guess we were open, we welcomed anybody, that's how we were at primary [school]. (Interview: 21 November, 1992)

As we saw in Chapter 6, parents also accord with this conception of the school: 'It's like a big family, a happy family—a big whānau. To me it's like an extended family' (Steve Williams: Interview, 17 November, 1992). And it is a theme which is echoed at a personal level by Tuloto Mareko, the senior teacher in the Samoan bilingual unit:

>When I first came to this school I said 'we brown people, everybody's going
>to look down to us'... So everywhere I go it was (pause) I will just sit back
>and listen and watch, just observing the people and the way they react. When
>I came to this school it seems that they're not putting the brown people
>down—especially, I talk about me—but they're lifting them up. And from
>there I learnt how to respect other people too, other people's culture, their
>way of life... I always talk about cultural maintenance here. I always talk
>about that—how they promote the other cultures in the school and the
>different ways of promoting, maintaining the cultures in the school. To me
>the key thing in this school is everybody's working together—the teachers,
>the children, everybody is working together. (Interview, 29 May, 1991)

Personal recollections such as these could be said to tend towards idealism.
Nevertheless, the inclusive and egalitarian nature of school relationships is a
theme which is consistently emphasised by both school participants and
observers. My own observations, also, can only reiterate this consensus. Put
simply, people get on well with each other at Richmond Road. This does not
preclude conflict situations arising—as we saw in Chapter 6—but it does
provide a supportive and reciprocal framework in which differences can be
effectively addressed and resolved (see also Corson, 1993, Chap. 7). The
strength of family relationships is one of Richmond Road's defining characteristics.

A view of aims, objectives and outcomes

As in all schools, there are limitations in Richmond Road's educational
approach. I also recognise and acknowledge from my own theoretical position
that multicultural education is only one dimension of a societal response to
cultural and democratic pluralism and that both it and the school are limited
in their ability to achieve social change (Lynch, 1986). Despite these caveats,
however, the school's approach to multicultural education demonstrates a
remarkable consistency between educational intention and practice. This interrelatedness between theory and practice—of 'understand[ing] the processes
and mechanisms by which macro forces are mediated at the [micro] level...'
(Angus, 1987: 31)—has formed the basis for contesting reproductive processes via the structural changes undertaken at the school.

The success of this change process must rest, as Laughton argues, 'on the
individual teacher's belief in the veracity of the ideas and their translation into
practice' (Principal's Report, 4 October, 1988). This veracity of belief was
initially modelled and cultivated by Laughton among his staff but it is also
clear that those currently involved with the school, which no longer has
Laughton to lead it, have taken over this role for themselves. There is
something infectious about Richmond Road's educational agenda. Possibly

more than any other feature, what is most apparent at the school is the belief in what *can* be achieved for minority children *combined with* a realistic and informed appraisal of what it is that they are up against. Those involved at Richmond Road are realistic about the limits of schooling in changing broader processes of social and cultural reproduction but this recognition does not deter them from trying to accomplish as much as possible within those limits—more, perhaps, than many might have imagined possible. Richmond Road recognises that it can do little for minority children upon their leaving the school, since it is aware (much more than most schools are) of the variety of societal factors which might subsequently impinge on these children's life chances. However, in response to the question inevitably asked of the school concerning the success of its educational 'products', it argues that if the *process* of cultural maintenance and access to power has been properly attended to within the school, the 'products' should at least be able to take care of themselves. By equipping minority children with both cultural recognition *and* academic skills, something usually denied them by schooling, the opportunity for such children to succeed in a society which invariably undermines them is much greater than it might otherwise have been. As Pedersen observes, concerning the present economic and social difficulties evident in New Zealand society: 'If the Richmond Road model has any significance, the children who've been through here will be coping all right' (Interview, 12 August, 1991). Laughton argues, along similar lines:

> We should aim to have children leave our institutions able, if not eager to face the burgeoning prospect of life—clients who can handle the prospect of unemployment or of employment. And that's a tall order. They need to be self reliant, to be independent in ways that we never were. And on the other hand, they need to be committed to community in the wider sense, across society, in ways that we seldom are... (Richmond Road School, 1983: 29–30)

High ideals, certainly, but imbued with a deep sense of realism concerning the enormity of the task at hand, a deep understanding of traditional education's complicity in the obstruction of these aims, and a deep commitment to realising a new educational approach which might be successful, against the odds, in promoting them. The continued effectiveness of Richmond Road's educational approach lies in its grasp of educational theory, in its ability to successfully relate that theory to educational practice, in its interrelatedness and internal consistency, and in its ability to involve and gain the support of teachers, parents and children in and for the process of change.

Notes to Chapter 10

1. In minority education, for example, the assimilationist/pluralist dichotomy is rendered almost meaningless by the range of ideologies of cultural pluralism apparent in the multicultural debate (see Chapter 3).
2. While the components of Brown's framework are adopted here they are not necessarily followed in the order she outlines. This is in keeping with her analysis since she goes on to suggest that the model 'provides a vertical or in depth perspective... [and] consists of a list of features to be identified which are not necessarily hierarchical, although they may be connected with one another' (1988: 56).
3. See the discussion of 'language experience' in Chapter 7.
4. As seen in rational organisation theory, or systems theory: see Gorton, 1980; Hanson, 1979; Hoy & Miskel, 1982; Orlosky et al., 1984.
5. For a more extensive discussion of this topic, see May (1992b).

11 The Practice of Theory

> If a school is in any way an institute of learning, it must be able
> to change the perception of things... (Lionel Pedersen: Interview,
> 25 February, 1991)

The radical theorist and antiracist education advocate, Cameron McCarthy
(1990), elaborates on three broad models adopted by multiculturalists in his
critique of multicultural education. These are the cultural understanding,
cultural competence, and cultural emancipation models of multicultural education (see also Gibson, 1976; 1984; Grant & Sleeter, 1989; Sleeter & Grant,
1987). The cultural understanding model approaches multicultural education
via cultural relativism. It aims for racial harmony by emphasising reciprocity
and consensus and places enormous influence on changing the attitudes of
students and teachers. The cultural competence model, however, argues that
attitudinal change is not a sufficient basis for contesting the marginalisation
of ethnic minority students. Along with developing ethnic identity and knowledge about other ethnic groups, proponents of this model advocate a competence in the 'public culture' for minority students. This familiarity with
mainstream culture should not be at the expense though of the minority
student's own ethnic heritage. Finally, the cultural emancipation model argues
that minority students' educational achievement (and thus their position(s) in
society) will be improved by restructuring the curriculum. In this view, the
scope of current school knowledge will be enlarged and diversified by incorporating the knowledge(s), histories and experiences of marginalised ethnic
groups within the curriculum.

McCarthy offers compelling critiques of each of these approaches to multicultural education. Cultural understanding, he suggests, emphasises the individual at the expense of the social. Cultural competence has a hard (if not
impossible) task of balancing ethnic identity against the Anglo-centric
demands of mainstream culture. And cultural emancipation has an unwar-
ranted optimism about the impact of the multicultural curriculum on the social
and economic futures of minority students. McCarthy concludes that in all of
these approaches to multicultural education schools 'are not conceptualized as
sites of power and contestation in which differential interests, resources and
capacities determine the maneuverability of competing racial groups and the
possibility and pace of change' (1990: 56).

As I have argued in previous chapters, the nature of these criticisms of multicultural education is largely valid. Popular conceptions of multicultural education have tended to undertheorise the structural constraints which operate within schooling and attribute too much to attitudinal and even curriculum change. To some degree, this is also a reflection of the difficulties experienced more broadly in the sociology of education (see Chapter 2). The macro/micro divide in educational research reveals a clear pattern here. Conflict theorists have tended to operate at a level of abstraction which denies the possibility of human agency. Liberal theorists have tended to operate at the micro-level within 'common-sense' conceptions of schooling which do little, if anything, to contest broader structural constraints. Attempts to bridge this divide, notably by resistance theorists, have also struck difficulty. While recognising the need to combine both critical theory and practice, the means by which this can be outworked has remained too vague for effective implementation in schools. Barry Troyna has recently argued, in specific relation to antiracist education, for the need to directly address this theory/practice impasse: '[Critical] theory and practice cannot be founded upon mere articles of faith: both must be reflexive and subject to rigorous empirical scrutiny if their transformative potential is to be realized. This will only be achieved when the present division between theory and practice is eliminated' (1993: 116).

It is my contention that, in the field of multicultural and antiracist education[1] at least, Richmond Road provides us with a way forward. Returning to McCarthy's analysis above, it is interesting to see that Richmond Road belies both his typology and critique of multicultural education. Elements of all three models of multicultural education outlined by McCarthy can be seen in Richmond Road's approach. For example, the school does emphasise the importance of attitudes and attitudinal change emphasised in the cultural understanding model. However, it does so only within a broadly conceived and critical conception of social and cultural relations. Attitudes of cultural pluralism have their place (and a positive one at that) but that is all; they are not asked to do more than they are able.

Richmond Road is also centrally concerned with the cultural competence model's emphasis on both fostering ethnic identity and providing access to mainstream culture. The notions of 'cultural maintenance' and 'access to power' clearly attest to this dual concern. However, the apparent contradiction that McCarthy outlines between these two aims can be effectively addressed; as it has been by the school. Richmond Road has shown that through structural change at the school level in all facets of school organisation, curriculum, pedagogy and assessment, the delivery of necessary school knowledge—the 'cultural necessary'—need not necessarily be tied to a single 'cultural arbitrary', that of the dominant group.[2] Structural alternatives can be employed for delivering necessary school knowledge which are not only inclusive of the values and practices of both minority and majority cultures but are non-hier-archically construed.

As Bourdieu has argued, the valorisation of the dominant (ethnic) group's cultural capital is not significantly threatened while we still have a curriculum organised around the knowledge code of the dominant group. The alternative which Richmond Road demonstrates is a genuine multicultural system 'in which different value systems and lifestyles are accorded equal status and prestige, and *with full institutional alternatives*' (Harker, 1990a: 42; my emphasis). Such a system not only has various knowledge codes in operation but also has 'a variety of ways of transmitting these knowledge codes using culturally appropriate pedagogical methods, and with a variety of options available to evaluate when successful transmission has taken place' (Harker, 1990a: 39–40). Richmond Road's delivery of knowledge(s) stands in sharp contrast to the European-type collection code (Bernstein, 1971; 1990) which dominates in most schools (see Chapter 3). The attributes of this collection code are worth revisiting here, if only to show how the school has been able to effectively reconstitute them:

(1) Knowledge is seen as private property with its own power structure and market situation...

(2) Subject loyalty is developed in students...

(3) Students learn within a given frame...they accept the authority of the teachers.

(4) The evaluative system places emphasis upon attaining states of knowledge rather than ways of knowing—how much do you know rather than how do you know it and how does it relate to other things that you know.

(5) The pedagogical relationship tends to be hierarchical and ritualised.

(6) The pupil is seen as ignorant with little status and few rights—being initiated into successively higher levels within a subject by those who already 'know'.

(7) Educational knowledge (high status) is kept separate from common sense knowledge (low status)—except for the less able children whom the system has given up educating (Harker, 1990a: 38).

Richmond Road's distinctly different conception of educational know-ledge(s) also answers the criticisms directed at resistance theory for its inability to incorporate a conception of 'necessary' knowledge within an emancipatory educational approach (see Chapter 2). These criticisms suggested that foster-ing a 'relevant' curriculum as a critique of the social construction of know-ledge is all very well, but denying children access to the core skills required in mainstream society will simply result in the further marginalising of the already marginalised. The difficulties associated with this position have been clearly illustrated in Britain, for example, by the opposition of African-Caribbean parents to community education initiatives for Black children (see Burtonwood, 1986; Nixon, 1984; Stone, 1981). Community education's preoccupation with affirming social and cultural *identity* led to their programmes stressing affective goals (self expression, self fulfilment etc.) rather than core competencies (such as reading and writing) and did little to change the position of Black children in British society. In response to both the continuing educational failure and the resulting high levels of unemployment faced by their children, African-Caribbean parents withdrew their support from community education and established supplementary schools which concentrated on traditional skills. As Maureen Stone argued in her influential book, *The Education of the Black Child in Britain* (1981), pluralism devoid of academic rigour is no substitute for equality (see also Burtonwood, 1986).[3]

Richmond Road recognises this point clearly. It is as concerned with core competencies as it is with cultural pluralism. However, in addressing the issue of academic achievement, the school has not made the mistake of endorsing a return to the traditional monocultural curriculum which the criticisms of the 'relevant' curriculum necessarily imply. The cultural arbitrary of the dominant group can be separated, it seems, from the cultural necessary in a pluralistic and critically conceived educational approach. In fact, as we have seen at Richmond Road, where children feel secure within a school which reflects the distinctive elements of their class or ethnic cultural arbitrary, their capacity to assimilate the cultural necessary of the school is enhanced.

Returning to McCarthy's analysis, we can see that Richmond Road also demonstrates, in its approach, elements of the cultural emancipation thesis. The school has reconstituted the curriculum with the knowledge(s), histories and experiences of *all* its students. More than this though, Richmond Road has recognised the need to extend this conception beyond merely the curriculum to include all school structures. Cultural pluralism at the school is combined with structural pluralism—the reform of the school's organisational structures. An approach such as this critically reconceives the nature of cultural knowledge and practices as represented in school structures; namely, curriculum, pedagogy, assessment and school organisation. The result at Richmond Road has been cultural *incorporation* and *organic* change rather than merely cultural *inclusion* and *incrementalism* (Hulmes, 1989; see also Chapter 3).

Despite the significant advance that Richmond Road's approach offers to the debate on multicultural education, the school continues to be aware of what it is up against. It is not *overly* optimistic about the role of the school in contesting wider societal inequalities. However, it is acutely aware of just how much *can* be achieved within these constraints. As James Banks has argued:

The radical critique of schooling is useful because it helps us to see the limitations of formal schooling. However, the radical paradigm is limited because it gives us few concrete guidelines about what can be done after we have acknowledged that schools are limited in their ability to bring about equality for...minority students. When designing educational reform strategies, we must be keenly sensitive to the limitations of formal schooling. However, we must be tenacious in our faith that the school can play a limited but cogent role in bringing about equal educational opportunities for... minority students and helping all students to develop cross-cultural understandings and competencies. In order [for this to occur]... *[an] holistic paradigm, which conceptualizes the school as an interrelated whole, is needed to guide educational reform...* Conceptualizing the school as a social system suggests that we formulate and initiate a change strategy that reforms the total school environment in order to implement multicultural education successfully. (1986b: 22; emphasis in original)

Enormous difficulties remain in achieving an emancipatory educational approach which makes a difference for minority children, of that there is no doubt. Richmond Road shows us, however, that it is, nevertheless, possible. The school demonstrates how an informed conflict theory of education can be effectively combined with a 'formal critical practice' (Gilbert, 1987; see Chapter 2) where the interests of minority children *as a group* 'are sought, defined and promoted, both hypothetically, in critique and reflection, and actually, in classroom and school social relations' (Gilbert, 1987: 52). In so doing, the school is—and is seen to be—very much a site of power and contestation. At Richmond Road, dominant power relations as expressed in schooling are actively resisted and, where possible, reconstituted in its approach to multicultural education.

Educational Effectiveness: The Benchmark for Multicultural Education

In a recent North American report on 'effective schools', Bryk & Driscoll provide a detailed study of the positive effects on students of schools which demonstrate 'communal school organization'. In their executive summary, they argue:

Based on a review of recent research on effective schools and more general theoretical literature on the structure and function of communities, we argue that three core concepts comprise a communal school organization: (1) *a system of shared values* among the members of the organization, reflected primarily in beliefs about the purposes of the institution, about what students should learn, about how adults and students should behave, and about what kinds of people students are capable of becoming; (2) *a common agenda of activities* designed to foster meaningful social interactions among school members and link them to the school's traditions; and (3) *a distinctive pattern of social relations,* embodying an ethos of caring that is visibly manifest in collegial relations among the adults of the institution and in an extended teacher role. Further, we posit that all three of these features are essential. *When they occur simultaneously, their influence is reinforcing,* and in combination they create a coherent organizational life that has powerful effects on teachers and students alike (1988: 1; my emphasis)

Richmond Road, as we have seen, clearly demonstrates the organisational characteristics outlined by Bryk & Driscoll. In discussing this particular report also, Courtney Cazden reaches a similar conclusion:

These features [outlined by Bryk & Driscoll] were derived from a study of 357 US Catholic and public high schools. But they seemed, from my many previous visits to the school, to fit Richmond Road amazingly well, and gave me an additional (and more international) reason to try and write about the school. (1989: 144)

Like Cazden, I wish to suggest that a key strength of Richmond Road as a possible model for multicultural education lies in its educational effectiveness. In Chapter 3, I outlined Sonia Nieto's (1992) conception of a critically conceived approach to multicultural education. In conclusion, I want to briefly revisit her argument in light of Richmond Road's example. Nieto argues that multicultural education needs to be critically reconceived as broad-based school reform. The resulting model of multicultural education she suggests includes the following characteristics:

Multicultural education is antiracist education

A critically conceived approach to education must begin with a recognition of unequal power relations in schools and in the wider society. Being antiracist and anti-discriminatory also means paying attention to all areas in which some students may be favoured over others. Richmond Road clearly locates unequal power relations at the centre of its educational endeavours. It also directly addresses and reconstitutes school structures that have traditionally disadvantaged minority children. The school answers radical criticisms of multicultural education because it is aware of broader structural constraints and is active in contesting them.

Multicultural education is basic education

Richmond Road does not consign itself to the educational irrelevance of a 'relevant' curriculum. Its emphasis on access to power effectively addresses the need to teach the common or core curriculum and to promote academic excellence. However, the affiliated notion of cultural maintenance sees the school promote both a plurality of educational knowledge(s) within the school and a plurality in the delivery of such knowledge(s). By this, the core curriculum is reconstituted to include a broader conception of the role and legitimacy of culture(s) and language(s) other than that of the dominant group. As Ellen Swartz has argued, 'multicultural education is a restatement of sound educational pedagogy and practice that requires the representation of all cultures and groups as significant to the production of knowledge' (1992: 34–35; see Chapter 3). The result is a conception of literacy which incorporates the notion of multicultural literacy.

Multicultural education is important for all students

Perhaps the most effective criticism levelled against multicultural education is its preoccupation with ethnic minority students. Multicultural education needs to be more expansive. While it should be concerned with the educational inequalities faced by minority students it should not be confined to these concerns lest it return to the pathological conceptions held of minority students in the past. There are two points to be made here in relation to Richmond Road's educational approach. First, given the nature of unequal power relations, the cumulative educational disadvantage of minority students needs to be acknowledged and addressed as a crucial starting point. As McCarthy has argued, drawing on Bob Connell's work, 'a "new" critical curriculum should privilege the human interests of the least advantaged' (1990: 132). Much of Richmond Road's endeavours can be said to begin from this perspective. However, the school is also intensely interested in and committed to all its students. This can be seen in the emphasis on intercultural relationships and, more centrally perhaps, in the efficacy of the school's educational approach for *all* its pupils. As Nieto argues, 'a broadly conceptualized multicultural education focusing on school reform represents a substantive way of changing the curriculum, the environment, the structure of schools, and the instructional strategies so that all students can benefit' (1992: 215).

Multicultural education is pervasive

Relatedly, Nieto argues that multicultural education should permeate the whole school environment; the physical classroom environment, the curriculum, the staffing composition of the school, the instructional strategies adopted, and the relationships among teachers and students and community. In such an approach, the curriculum would be completely overhauled, parents and community people would be more visible and active in the school, and 'teachers, parents and students would have the opportunity to work together to design motivating and culturally appropriate curricula... The complexion of the school, both literally and figuratively, would change' (1992: 216).

Again, this process of structural change is clearly evident at Richmond Road. It has occurred over a period of twenty years and has resulted in a school whose curriculum, pedagogy, organisation and outreach are all consistent with a broadly conceptualised multicultural philosophy.

Multicultural education is education for social justice

All good education should connect theory with reflection and action—what Freire has termed 'praxis'. However, as I have consistently argued, there are considerable difficulties in achieving this critical theory/practice combination. Perhaps the crucial element in Richmond Road's success here is the democratic and reciprocal nature of its school and school–community relationships. Allied with this has been the direct engagement of teachers (and parents) in the curriculum decision-making process. The strength of Richmond Road's staff development process—arising from Laughton's fostering of direct teacher participation and leadership in curriculum matters—is certainly pivotal to the subsequent effectiveness of the school's policy and practice. Richmond Road could almost be said to be a place of continual action research since its teachers actively, critically and reflectively engage in educational research and practice on a regular basis. The importance of this kind of direct engagement with theory—what I would term the practice of theory—is highlighted all the more by the opposing trends elsewhere towards the deskilling of teachers (see Apple, 1986). Such trends marginalise and disempower teachers and serve to reinforce the status quo within education. Teachers, and school communities more generally, cannot hope to change existing social and cultural arrangements in schooling until they first have the knowledge and vocabulary to be able to mount a credible opposition. Richmond Road shows just what such a high degree of theoretical literacy can achieve.

Multicultural education is a process

The emphasis on content in many multicultural education initiatives often sees process receive only peripheral attention; changing the process is too hard for most schools. However, for multicultural education to have any effect process must underline and direct content, not the other way around. Richmond Road demonstrates that while attending to the process is complex, problematic, controversial, and time-consuming, real and substantive change can result. As Lionel Pedersen comments: 'The praxis of Richmond [Road] School is inherently based on understandings, commitment to these, and structures that support the implementation of its espoused pedagogy. As the process is the product, so is the theory the practice. What we say and do is who we are'. (Principal's Report, 13 March, 1990)

Multicultural education is critical pedagogy

Drawing on Cummins (1989), Nieto argues that 'transmission' models of education exclude and deny students' experiences and therefore cannot be multicultural. In contrast, critical pedagogy is multicultural by definition because it is based on the experiences and viewpoints of students rather than on an imposed culture. Critical pedagogy is not limited to students' experiences, however, and this allows for critical and reflexive engagement—among both pupils and staff—with the nature of social and cultural relations and the differential positioning(s) which result from these relations. Richmond Road actively fosters this kind of critical engagement by promoting a pedagogy which 'move[s] beyond theorizing about our practice along the lines of "this works for me"...to ask questions instead about why we act as we do, and whose interests are served by continuing in this manner' (Smyth, 1989: 57).

Given all of the above, Nieto's concludes that a critically conceived approach to multicultural education is simply good pedagogy. Cazden makes exactly the same point when she compares the characteristics of Richmond Road with those highlighted by Bryk & Driscoll's analysis of effective schools. Cazden also suggests, as do I, that Richmond Road provides us with a working model, applicable internationally, of just what can be achieved in implementing an effective approach to multicultural education. Through the structural reform of the total school environment, Richmond Road demonstrates how the vague and seemingly ubiquitous notion of 'cultural pluralism' (see Chapter 3) can be rehabilitated into a recognisable, realistic and achievable form. By critically reconstituting multicultural education, the notion of cultural pluralism comes to be situated within a *realist* conception of society. Processes of social and cultural reproduction are taken into account in such an approach and are also contested, where possible, at the level of the school. As Olneck has argued:

> If pluralism is to have any distinctive meaning or to be authentically realized, it must...recognize in some serious manner, the identities and claims of groups *as groups* and must facilitate, or at least symbolically represent and legitimate, collective identity. It must enhance the salience of group membership as a basis for participation in society and ensure that pedagogy, curriculum, and modes of assessment are congruent with valued cultural differences. (1990: 148; emphasis in original)

Moreover, in exploring Richmond Road's educational endeavours via critical ethnography, this study has also aimed to account for the persistent criticism levelled at educational critical theory which, as Anderson identified in Chapter 4, is 'its tendency toward social critique without developing a theory of action...' (1989: 257). The theory of action at Richmond Road and the new organisational forms which have arisen from it are clearly apparent.

The demands on schools (organisationally, pedagogically and relationally) of implementing a similar approach would be great, but Richmond Road shows that it can be done—that multicultural education can be made to work.

It seems fitting then to end this account of Richmond Road with an assessment of the school from an ex-pupil. After all, whatever I or others might say, the school's educational endeavours largely stand or fall on the experiences of its students. Folole Asaua provides us with this perspective. When I interviewed her in 1992 she was in the 6th Form (16 yrs) at secondary school. She wished to complete her secondary schooling and go on to study law at university 'because basically I'm really interested in helping younger people in our generation, helping people in my [Samoan] culture... I want to encourage them to go on and do academic studies because there are a lot of us [Pacific] Islanders that aren't doing very well in school'. In discussing her current educational perceptions and ambitions, Folole clearly and repeatedly acknowledged the influence of Richmond Road, both academically and culturally. Her closing comment highlights her ongoing appreciation of and commitment to Richmond Road some 5 years on: 'Now I guess I'm real proud that I went to that school. I learnt a lot from that school. It's where I found my identity, my culture... That school is one of the best' (Interview, 21 November, 1992).

Schools—even schools like Richmond Road—can only do so much. Both Richmond Road itself and this particular account of it clearly recognise the limits of schooling here. However, as Folole Asaua attests, the educational initiative and innovation apparent at Richmond Road augur well for the possibilities of change. Multicultural education may be able to make a difference after all.

Notes to Chapter 11

1. I have argued in Chapter 3 that a critically conceived approach to multicultural education is also fundamentally antiracist.
2. For a discussion of these terms see the section on Bourdieu in Chapter 2; see also, Chapter 5.
3. This is a position we also saw Senese (1991) outline in Chapter 2.

Bibliography

ALTHUSSER, L. (1971) Ideology and ideological state apparatuses. In B. BREWSTER (Tr.) *Lenin and Philosophy and Other Essays*. New York: Monthly Review Press, 127–186.

ANDERSON, G. (1989) Critical ethnography in education: Origins, current status, and new directions. *Review of Educational Research* 59, 249–270.

ANGUS, L. (1986a) Developments in ethnographic research in education: From interpretive to critical ethnography. *Journal of Research and Development in Education* 20, 59–67.

— (1986b) Research traditions, ideology and critical ethnography. *Discourse* 7, 61–77.

— (1987) A critical ethnography of continuity and change in a Catholic school. In R. MACPHERSON (ed.) *Ways and Meanings of Research in Educational Administration*. Armidale: University of New England Press, pp. 25–52.

— (1988) *Continuity and Change in Catholic Schooling: An Ethnography of a Christian Brothers College in Australian Society*. Lewes: Falmer Press.

APPEL, R. and MUYSKEN, P. (1987) *Language Contact and Bilingualism*. London: Edward Arnold.

APPLE, M. (1979) *Ideology and Curriculum*. London: Routledge and Kegan Paul.

— (1986) *Teachers and Texts: A Political Economy of Class and Gender Relations in Education*. New York: Routledge and Kegan Paul.

— (1992) Education, culture and class power: Basil Bernstein and the neo-marxist sociology of education. *Educational Theory* 42, 127–145.

APPLE, M. and TAXEL, J. (1982) Ideology and the curriculum. In A. HARTNETT (ed.) *Educational Studies and Social Science*. London: Heinemann, pp. 166–178.

ATKINSON, P. (1985) *Language, Structure and Reproduction: An Introduction to the Sociology of Basil Bernstein*. London: Methuen.

BAGLEY, C. (1992) In-service provision and teacher resistance to whole-school change. In D. GILL, B. MAYOR and M. BLAIR (eds) *Racism and Education: Structures and Strategies*. London: Sage, pp. 226–250.

BAKER, C. (1988) *Key Issues in Bilingualism and Bilingual Education*. Clevedon: Multilingual Matters.

— (1993) *Introduction to Bilingualism and Bilingual Education*. Clevedon: Multilingual Matters.

BALL, S. (1987) *The Micro-politics of the School*. London: Methuen.

— (1989) Micro-politics versus management: Towards a sociology of school organisation. In S. WALKER and L. BARTON (eds) *Politics and the Processes of Schooling*. Milton Keynes: Open University Press, pp. 218–241.

BANKS, J. (1986a) Multicultural education and its critics: Britain and the United States. In S. MODGIL, G. VERMA, K. MALLICK and C. MODGIL (eds) *Multicultural Education: The Interminable Debate*. Lewes: Falmer Press, pp. 221–231.

— (1986b) Multicultural education: Development, paradigms and goals. In J. BANKS and J. LYNCH (eds) *Multicultural Education in Western Societies*. Eastbourne: Holt, Rinehart and Winston Ltd, pp. 2–28.

— (1988) *Multiethnic Education: Theory and Practice* (2nd edn). Newton, MA: Allyn and Bacon.

BANKS, J. and LYNCH, J. (eds) (1986) *Multicultural Education in Western Societies.* Eastbourne: Holt, Rinehart and Winston Ltd.

BATES, R. (1986) *The Management of Culture and Knowledge.* Victoria: Deakin University.

BEE, B. (1980) The politics of literacy. In R. MACKIE (ed.) *Literacy and Revolution: The Pedagogy of Paulo Freire.* London: Pluto Press, pp. 39–56.

BERNSTEIN, B. (1971) On the classification and framing of educational knowledge. In M. YOUNG (ed.) *Knowledge and Control: New Directions for the Sociology of Education.* London: Collier-Macmillan, pp. 47–69.

— (1990) *The Structuring of Pedagogic Discourse: Class, Codes and Control* Vol. 4. London: Routledge and Kegan Paul.

BOGUSLAW, R. (1971) The power of systems and systems of power. In R. PORRUCCI and M. PILISUK (eds) *The Revolution Emerging: Social Problems in Depth.* Little, Brown and Boston.

BOURDIEU, P. (1974) The school as a conservative force: Scholastic and cultural inequalities. In J. EGGLESTON (ed.) *Contemporary Research in the Sociology of Education.* London: Methuen, pp. 32–46.

— (1984) *Distinction: A Social Critique of the Judgement of Taste.* Cambridge, MA: Harvard University Press.

— (1990a) *In Other Words: Essays Towards a Reflexive Sociology.* Cambridge: Polity Press.

— (1990b) *The Logic of Practice.* Cambridge: Polity Press.

BOURDIEU, P. and PASSERON, J. (1977) *Reproduction in Education, Society and Culture.* London: Sage Publications.

— (1990) *Reproduction in Education, Society and Culture* (2nd edn). London: Sage Publications.

BOURDIEU, P. and WACQUANT, L. (1992) *An Invitation to Reflexive Sociology.* Chicago: Chicago University Press.

BOWLES, S. and GINTIS, H. (1976) *Schooling in Capitalist America.* New York: Basic Books.

— (1980) Contradiction and reproduction in educational theory. In L. BARTON, R. MEIGHAN and S. WALKER (eds) *Schooling, Ideology and the Curriculum.* Lewes: Falmer Press, pp. 51–65.

BRANDT, G. (1986) *The Realisation of Anti-racist Teaching.* Lewes: Falmer Press.

BREEN, M., CANDLIN, C. and WATERS, A. (1979) Communicative materials design: Some basic principles. *RELC Journal* 10 (2) 1–13.

BROWN, C. (1988) Curriculum responses to ethnic minority groups: A framework for analysis. *Educational Review* 40, 51–68.

BRYK, A. and DRISCOLL, M. (1988) *The High School as Community: Contextual Influences and Consequences for Students and Teachers.* Madison, WI: National Center on Effective Schools.

BULLIVANT, B. (1981) *The Pluralist Dilemma in Education: Six Case Studies.* Sydney: Allen and Unwin.

— (1986) Towards radical multiculturalism: Resolving tensions in curriculum and educational planning. In S. MODGIL, G. VERMA, K. MALLICK and C. MODGIL (eds) *Multicultural Education: The Interminable Debate.* Lewes: Falmer Press, pp. 33–47.

BURTONWOOD, N. (1986) *The Culture Concept in Educational Studies.* Windsor: NFER-Nelson.

CALHOUN, C., LIPUMA, E. and POSTONE, M. (eds) (1993) *Bourdieu: Critical Perspectives*. Cambridge: Polity Press.

CARR, W. and KEMMIS, S. (1983) *Becoming Critical: Knowing Through Action Research*. Victoria: Deakin University Press.

CARRINGTON, B. and SHORT, G. (1989) *'Race' and the Primary School: Theory into Practice*. Windsor: NFER-Nelson.

CARTER, B. and WILLIAMS, J. (1987) Attacking racism in education. In B. TROYNA (ed.) *Racial Inequality in Education*. London: Tavistock, pp. 170–183.

CAZDEN, C. (1989) Richmond Road: A multilingual/multicultural primary school in Auckland, New Zealand. *Language and Education: An International Journal* 3, 143–166.

CENTRE FOR CONTEMPORARY CULTURAL STUDIES, UNIVERSITY OF BIR-MINGHAM (CCCS). (1981) *Unpopular Education: Schooling and Social Democracy in England Since 1944*. London: Hutchinson.

CHILCOTT, J. (1987) Where are you coming from and where are you going? The reporting of ethnographic research. *American Educational Research Journal* 24, 199–218.

CHURCHWARD, F. (1991) He ara hou: 'The family model'. Unpublished master's thesis, University of Auckland, Auckland.

CLARK, R., FAIRCLOUGH, N., IVANIC, R. and MARTIN-JONES, M. (1990) Critical language awareness, Part I: A critical review of three current approaches to language awareness. *Language and Education: An International Journal* 4, 249–260.

— (1991) Critical language awareness, Part II: Towards critical alternatives. *Language and Education: An International Journal* 5, 41–54.

CLAY, M. (1979) *The Early Detection of Reading Difficulties: A Diagnostic Survey with Recovery Procedures*. Auckland: Heinemann.

— (1985) *The Early Detection of Reading Difficulties* (3rd edn). Auckland: Heinemann.

CODD, J. and GORDON, L. (1991) School charters: The contractualist state and education policy. *New Zealand Journal of Educational Studies* 26, 21–34.

CODD, J., HARKER, R. and NASH, R. (eds) (1990) *Political Issues in New Zealand Education* (2nd edn). Palmerston North, Dunmore Press.

COLE, M. (1986) Teaching and learning about racism: A critique of multicultural education in Britain. In S. MODGIL, G. VERMA, K. MALLICK and C. MODGIL (eds) *Multicultural Education: The Interminable Debate*. Lewes: Falmer Press, pp. 123–147.

COLLINS, R. (1977) Functional and conflict theories of educational stratification. In J. KARABEL and A. HALSEY (eds) *Power and Ideology in Education*. New York: Oxford University Press, pp. 118–136.

CONNELL, R. (1985) *Teacher's Work*. Sydney: Allen and Unwin.

CONNELL, R., ASHENDEN, D., KESSLER, S. and DOWSETT, L. (1982) *Making the Difference*. Sydney: Allen and Unwin.

CORSON, D. (1990) *Language Policy Across the Curriculum*. Clevedon: Multilingual Matters.

— (1993) *Language, Minority Education and Gender: Linking Social Justice and Power*. Clevedon: Multilingual Matters.

CROZIER, G. (1989) Multi-cultural education: Some unintended consequences. In S. WALKER and L. BARTON (eds) *Politics and the Processes of Schooling*. Milton Keynes: Open University Press, pp. 59–81.

CUMMINS, J. (1983) *Heritage Language Foundation. A Literature Review*. Ontario: Ministry of Education.

— (1986) Empowering minority students: A framework for intervention. *Harvard Educational Review* 56, 18–36.

— (1989) The sanitized curriculum: Educational disempowerment in a nation at risk. In D. JOHNSON and D. ROEN (eds) *Richness in Writing: Empowering ESL Students*. New York: Longman.

CUMMINS, J. and SWAIN, M. (1986) *Bilingualism in Education*. Harlow: Longman.

DES (DEPARTMENT OF EDUCATION AND SCIENCE). (1985) *Education for All: Report of the Committee of Inquiry into the Education of Children from Ethnic Minority Groups* (The Swann Report). London: HMSO.

DURKHEIM, E. (1956) *Education and Sociology*. New York: The Free Press.

EDUCATION REVIEW OFFICE. (1991) (March) *Richmond Road School*. Waitematā, Auckland.

— (1993) (March) *Assurance Audit Report: Richmond Road School*. Waitematā, Auckland.

EDWARDS, A. (1987) Language codes and classroom practice. *Oxford Review of Education* 13, 237–247.

ELLEY, W. (1992) *How in the World do Students Read? IEA Study of Reading Literacy*. The Hague, Netherlands: The International Association for the Evaluation of Educational Achievement.

ELLEY, W. and MANGUBHAI, F. (1983) The impact of reading on second language learning. *Reading Research Quarterly* 19, 53–67.

ERICKSON, F. (1979) Mere ethnography: Some problems in its use in educational practice. *Anthropology and Education Quarterly* 10, 182–188.

FAIRCLOUGH, N. (1989) *Language and Power*. London: Longman.

FENTON, S. (1982) Multi-something education. *New Community* 10, 432–434.

— (1984) *Durkheim and Modern Sociology*. Cambridge: Cambridge University Press.

FERGUSSON, D., LLOYD, M. and HORWOOD, L. (1991) Family, ethnicity, social background and scholastic achievement. *New Zealand Journal of Educational Studies* 26, 49–63.

FIGUEROA, P. (1991) *Education and the Social Construction of 'Race'*. London: Routledge.

FILLION, B. (1983) Let me see you learn. *Language Arts* 60, 702–710.

FITZ-GIBBON, C. (1983) Peer-tutoring: A possible method for multi-ethnic education. *New Community* 11, 160–166.

FOSTER, P. (1990) *Policy and Practice in Multicultural and Anti-racist Education: A Case study of a Multi-ethnic Comprehensive School*. London: Routledge.

GEE, J. (1990) *Social Linguistics and Literacies: Ideology in Discourses*. London: Falmer Press.

GEERTZ, C. (1973) *The Interpretation of Cultures*. New York: Basic Books.

GIBSON, M. (1976) Five conceptual approaches to multicultural education. *Anthropology and Education Quarterly* 7 (4) 7–18.

— (1984) Approaches to multicultural education in the United States: Some concepts and assumptions. *Anthropology and Education Quarterly* 15, 94–119.

GIBSON, M. and OGBU, J. (eds) (1991) *Minority Status and Schooling: A Comparative Study of Immigrant and Involuntary Minorities*. New York: Garland Publishing.

GIDDENS, A. (1979) *Central Problems in Social Theory: Action, Structure and Contradiction in Social Analysis*. London: Macmillan.

— (1981) *A Contemporary Critique of Historical Materialism*. London: Macmillan.

GILBERT, R. (1987) The concept of social practice and modes of ideology critique in schools. *Discourse* 7, 37–54.

GINSBURG, H. (1986) The myth of the deprived child: New thoughts on poor children. In U. NEISSER (ed.) *The School Achievement of Minority Children: New Perspectives*. Hillsdale, NJ: Erlbaum.

GIROUX, H. (1981) *Ideology, Culture and the Process of Schooling*. Philadelphia: Temple University Press.

— (1983a) *Theory and Resistance in Education: A Pedagogy for the Opposition*. South Hadley: Bergin and Garvey.

— (1983b) Theories of reproduction and resistance in the new sociology of education: A critical analysis. *Harvard Educational Review* 53, 257–293.

— (1984) The paradox of power in educational theory and practice. *Language Arts* 61, 462–465.

GORDON, B. (1992) The marginalized discourse of minority educational thought in traditional writings on teaching. In C. GRANT (ed.) *Research and Multicultural Education: From the Margins to the Mainstream*. Bristol, PA: Falmer Press, pp. 19–31.

GORDON, L. (1993) (September) Who controls New Zealand schools? Decentralised management and the problem of agency. Paper presented to the British Educational Research Association (BERA) Annual Conference, Liverpool.

GORTON, R. (1980) *School Administration and Supervision*. Dubuque: W.C. Brown.

GRAMSCI, A. (1971) *Selections from Prison Notebooks* (Q. HOARE and G. NOWELL SMITH (eds)) London: Lawrence and Wishart.

GRANT, C. (ed.) (1992) *Research and Multicultural Education: From the Margins to the Mainstream*. Bristol, PA: Falmer Press.

GRANT, C. and MILLAR, S. (1992) Research and multicultural education: Barriers, needs and boundaries. In C. GRANT (ed.) *Research and Multicultural Education: From the Margins to the Mainstream*. Bristol, PA: Falmer Press, pp. 7–18.

GRANT, C. and SLEETER, C. (1989) *Turning on Learning: Five Approaches for Multicultural Teaching Plans for Race, Class, Gender and Disability*. Columbus: Merrill.

HAKUTA, K. (1986) *Mirror of Language: The Debate on Bilingualism*. New York: Basic Books.

HAMMERSLEY, M. (1992) *What's Wrong with Ethnography?: Methodological Explorations*. London: Routledge.

HANSON, E. (1979) *Educational Administrative and Organizational Behaviour*. Boston: Allyn and Bacon.

HARKER, R. (1984) On reproduction, habitus and education. *British Journal of Sociology of Education* 5, 117–127.

— (1990a) Schooling and cultural reproduction. In J. CODD, R. HARKER and R. NASH (eds) *Political Issues in New Zealand Education* (2nd edn). Palmerston North: Dunmore Press, pp. 25–42.

— (1990b) Bourdieu: education and reproduction. In R. HARKER, C. MAHAR and C. WILKES (eds) *An Introduction to the Work of Pierre Bourdieu*. London: Macmillan, pp. 86–108.

HARKER, R., MAHAR, C. and WILKES, C. (eds) (1990) *An Introduction to the Work of Pierre Bourdieu*. London: Macmillan.

HARKER, R. and MAY, S. (1993) Code and habitus: Comparing the accounts of Bernstein and Bourdieu. *British Journal of Sociology of Education* 14, 169–178.

HATCHER, R. (1987) Race and education: Two perspectives for change. In B. TROYNA (ed.) *Racial Inequality in Education*. London: Tavistock, pp. 184–200.

HINGANGAROA SMITH, G. (1986) Taha Māori: A Pākehā privilege. *Delta* 37, 11–23.

— (1990) Taha Māori: Pākehā capture. In J. CODD, R. HARKER and R. NASH (eds) *Political Issues in New Zealand Education* (2nd edn). Palmerston North: Dunmore Press, pp. 183–197.

HIRSH, W. (1990) *A Report of Issues and Factors relating to Māori Achievement in the Education System.* Auckland: Ministry of Education.

HODSON, D. (1986) *Towards a model for school-based curriculum development. Delta* 38, 29–35.

HOLDAWAY, D. (1984) Introduction. In H. VILLERS, F. CHURCHWARD, M. FITZGERALD, J. GLASSON and T. MCFAYDEN (eds) *Richmond Road School: 1884–1984.* Auckland: Richmond Road School Publications, pp. 3–5.

HOLMES, J. (1984) *Bilingual Education (Occasional Publication 11).* Wellington: Victoria University English Language Institute.

HOLMES, M. and WYNNE, E. (1989) *Making the School an Effective Community: Belief, Practice and Theory in School Administration.* Lewes: Falmer Press.

HOY, W. and MISKEL, C. (1982) *Educational Administration: Theory, Research and Practice* (2nd edn). New York: Random House.

HUCKER, B. (1984) A changing community. In H. VILLERS, F. CHURCHWARD, M. FITZGERALD, J. GLASSON and T. MCFAYDEN (eds) *Richmond Road School: 1884–1984.* Auckland: Richmond Road School Publications, pp. 12–14.

HUGHES, J. (1980) *The Philosophy of Social Research.* London: Longman.

HULMES, E. (1989) *Education and Cultural Diversity.* London: Longman.

HUNN, J. (1961) *Report on the Department of Māori Affairs.* Wellington: Government Printer

IRWIN, K. (1988) Racism and education. In W. HIRSH and R. SCOTT (eds) *Getting it Right: Aspects of Ethnicity and Equity in New Zealand Education.* Auckland: Office of the Race Relations Conciliator, pp. 49–60.

— (1989) Multicultural education: The New Zealand response. *New Zealand Journal of Educational Studies* 24, 3–18.

JEFFCOATE, R. (1984) Ideologies and multicultural education. In M. CRAFT (ed.) *Education and Cultural Pluralism.* Lewes: Falmer Press.

JENKINS, R. (1992) *Pierre Bourdieu.* London: Routledge.

JENSEN, A. (1981) *Straight Talk about Mental Tests.* New York: Free Press.

KA'AI, T. (1990) A history of New Zealand education from a Māori perspective. Unpublished master's thesis, University of Auckland, Auckland.

KARABEL, J. and HALSEY, A. (eds) (1977) *Power and Ideology in Education.* New York: Oxford University Press.

KEMMIS, S. (1983) *Orientations to Curriculum and Transition: Towards the Socially-critical School.* Melbourne: Victoria Institute of Secondary Education.

KEMMIS, S. and MCTAGGART, R. (eds) (1988) *The Action Research Planner* (3rd edn). Geelong: Deakin University.

KING, R. (1980) Weberian perspectives and the study of education. *British Journal of Sociology of Education* 1, 7–23.

KOCH, R. (1982) Syllogisms and superstitions: The current state of responding to writing. *Language Arts* 59, 464–471.

LANGE, D. (1988) *Tomorrow's Schools.* Wellington: Government Printer.

LATHER, P. (1986a) Research as praxis. *Harvard Educational Review* 56, 257–277.

— (1986b) Issues of validity in openly ideological research: Between a rock and a soft place. *Interchange* 17, 63–84.

LAUDER, H. and WYLIE, C. (eds) (1990) *Towards Successful Schooling.* London: Falmer Press.

LAUGHTON, J. (1984) And the last word. In H. VILLERS, F. CHURCHWARD, M.
FITZGERALD, J. GLASSON and T. MCFAYDEN (eds) *Richmond Road School:
1884–1984*. Auckland: Richmond Road School Publications, pp. 37–40.
— (1985a) Māori bilingual option. Richmond Road School Working Paper.
— (1985b) Assessment. Richmond Road School Working Paper.
LEGAT, N. (1991) (February) Shopping for schools: The liberals' dilemma and white
flight. *Metro* 61–70.
LISTON, D. (1988) Faith and evidence: Examining marxist explanations of schooling.
American Journal of Education 96, 323–350.
LUKES, S. (1973) *Emile Durkheim. His Life and Work: A Historical and Critical Study*.
Harmondsworth: Penguin.
LUTZ, F. (1984) Ethnography: The holistic approach to understanding schooling. In R.
BURGESS (ed.) *Field Methods in the Study of Education*. Lewes: Falmer Press, pp.
107–119.
LYNCH, J. (1986) Multicultural education: Agenda for change. In J. BANKS and J.
LYNCH (eds) *Multicultural Education in Western Societies*. Eastbourne: Holt, Rine-
hart and Winston Ltd, pp. 178–195.
— (1987) *Prejudice Reduction and the Schools*. London: Cassell.
MALLEA, J. (1989) *Schooling in Plural Canada*. Clevedon: Multilingual Matters.
MANATŪ MĀORI. (1991) *E Tipu e Rea. Māori Education: Current Status*. Wellington:
Ministry of Māori Affairs.
MASEMANN, V. (1982) Critical ethnography in the study of comparative education.
Comparative Education Review 26, 1–15.
MAY, S. (1991) Making the difference for minority children: The development of an
holistic language policy at Richmond Road School, Auckland, New Zealand. *Language, Culture and Curriculum* 4, 201–217.
— (1992a) The relational school: Fostering pluralism and empowerment through a
'language policy across the curriculum'. New Zealand Journal of Educational Studies
27, 35–51.
— (1992b) Establishing multicultural education at the school level: The need for structural change. *Journal of Educational Administration and Foundations* 7, 11–29.
— (1993) Redeeming multicultural education. *Language Arts* 70, 364–372.
— (1994) School–based language policy reform: A New Zealand example. In A.
BLACKLEDGE (ed.) *Teaching Bilingual Children*. London: Trentham Press.
MAYBIN, J. (1985) Working towards a school language policy. In *Every Child's
Language: An In-service Pack for Primary Teachers*. Clevedon: The Open University
and Multilingual Matters, pp. 95–108.
MCCARTHY, C. (1990) *Race and Curriculum: Social Inequality and the Theory and
Politics of Difference in Contemporary Research on Schooling*. Basingstoke: Falmer
Press.
MEHAN, H. (1992) Understanding inequality in schools: The contribution of interpretive
studies. *Sociology of Education* 65, 1–20.
MEIGHAN, R. (1981) *A Sociology of Educating*. London: Holt, Rinehart and Winston.
MEIGHAN, R. and BROWN, C. (1980) Locations of learning and ideologies of educa-
tion. In L. BARTON, R. MEIGHAN and S. WALKER (eds) *Schooling, Ideology and
the Curriculum*. Lewes: Falmer Press, pp. 131–151.
MEIGHAN, R. and ROBERTS, M. (1979) Autonomous study and educational ideolo-
gies. *Journal of Curriculum Studies* 11, 53–67.
METGE, J. (1986) *He tikanga Māori: Teaching and Learning*. Wellington: Government
Printer.

— (1990) *Te Kō hao o te Ngira: Culture and Learning.* Wellington: Learning Media, Ministry of Education.

MIDDLETON, S., CODD, J. and JONES, A. (eds) (1990) *New Zealand Education Policy Today.* Wellington: Allen and Unwin.

MODGIL, S., VERMA, G., MALLICK, K. and MODGIL, C. (eds) (1986) *Multicultural Education: The Interminable Debate.* Lewes: Falmer Press.

MORRISON, K. (1989) Bringing progressivism into a critical theory of education. *British Journal of Sociology of Education* 10, 3–18.

MULLARD, C. (1982) Multiracial education in Britain: From assimilation to cultural pluralism. In J. TIERNEY (ed.) *Race, Migration and Schooling.* London: Holt.

NASH, R. (1986) Educational and social inequality; The theories of Bourdieu and Boudon with reference to class and ethnic differences in New Zealand. *New Zealand Sociology* 1, 121–137.

— (1990a) Bourdieu on education and social and cultural reproduction. *British Journal of Sociology of Education* 11, 431–447.

— (1990b) In defence of a common curriculum and a universal pedagogy. In J. MORSS and T. LINZEY (eds) *Growing Up: The Politics of Human Learning.* Auckland: Longman Paul.

NASH, R. and HARKER, R. (1988) Massive differences in educational attainment within the Pākehā middle class: A crisis for theory and policy. Paper presented to the New Zealand Council for Educational Research (NZCER) Policy Conference, Wellington.

NIETO, S. (1992) *Affirming Diversity: The Sociopolitical Context of Multicultural Education.* New York: Longman.

NIXON, J. (1984) Multicultural education as a curriculum category. *New Community* 12, 22–30.

OGBU, J. (1987) Variability in minority school performance: A problem in search of an explanation. *Anthropology and Education Quarterly* 18, 312–334.

OLNECK, M. (1990) The recurring dream: Symbolism and ideology in intercultural and multicultural education. *American Journal of Education* 98, 147–183.

ORANGE, C. (1987) *The Treaty of Waitangi.* Wellington: Allen and Unwin.

ORLOSKY, D., MCLEARY, L., SHAPIRO, A. and WEBB, L. (1984) *Educational Administration Today.* Columbus: Merrill.

PAREKH, B. (1986) The concept of multi-cultural education. In S. MODGIL, G. VERMA, K. MALLICK and C. MODGIL (eds) *Multicultural Education: The Interminable Debate.* Lewes: Falmer Press, pp. 19–31.

PARSONS, T. (1961) The school class as a social system: Some of its functions in American society. In A. HALSEY, J. FLOUD and C. ANDERSON (eds) *Education, Economy and Society.* New York: The Free Press.

— (1970) Some considerations on the comparative sociology. In J. FISCHER (ed.) *The Social Sciences and the Comparative Study of Educational Systems.* Scranton, PA: Intern Textbook Co.

PEARCE, F. (1989) *The Radical Durkheim.* London: Unwin Hyman.

PETERS, R. (ed.) (1973) *The Philosophy of Education.* London: Oxford University Press.

PORTER, J. (1975) Ethnic pluralism in Canadian perspective. In N. GLAZER and D. MOYNIHAN (eds) *Ethnicity: Theory and Experience.* Cambridge, MA.: Harvard University Press.

RAMSAY, P., HAWK, K., MARRIOT, R., POSKITT., J. and HAROLD, B. (1991) (July) Creating conditions for shared decision making: The role of the principal. Paper presented to the first New Zealand Conference on Research in Educational Administration, Auckland.

RICHMOND ROAD SCHOOL (1983) Learning and teaching in multi-cultural settings. Seminar given at Auckland Teachers' College by Principal and Staff.
— (1985) Resource preparation perspectives. Richmond Road School Working Paper.
— (1986) Cultural diversity: Challenge and response. Richmond Road School Working Paper.
— (1991) Richmond Road School Board of Trustees' response to the Education Review Office Waitematā draft report. Richmond Road School Working Paper.
— (1992) Application for equity grant, 1993. Richmond Road School Working Paper.
— (n. d.) Richmond Road School mathematics. Richmond Road School Working Paper.
ROBBINS, D. (1991) *The Work of Pierre Bourdieu: Recognizing Society*. Milton Keynes: Open University Press.
ROMAINE, S. (1989) *Bilingualism*. Oxford: Basil Blackwell.
RYAN, P. (1989) *The Revised Dictionary of Modern Māori* (3rd edn). Auckland: Heinemann.
SARUP, M. (1986) *The Politics of Multiracial Education*. London: Routledge and Kegan Paul.
SENESE, G. (1991) Warnings on resistance and the language of possibility: Gramsci and a pedagogy from the surreal. *Educational Theory* 41, 13–22.
SHARP, R. and GREEN, A. (1975) *Education and Social Control: A Study in Progressive Primary Education*. London: Routledge and Kegan Paul.
SIMON, J. (1986) *Ideology in the Schooling of Māori Children* (Delta Monograph, 7). Palmerston North: Department of Education, Massey University.
SIMON, R. (1982) *Gramsci's Political Thought: An Introduction*. London: Lawrence and Wishart.
SKILBECK, M. (1984) *School-based Curriculum Development*. London, Harper and Row.
SLAVIN, R. (1983) *Co-operative Learning*. London: Methuen.
SLEETER, C. and GRANT, C. (1987) An analysis of multicultural education in the United States. *Harvard Educational Review* 57, 421–444.
SMITH, L. and KEITH, P. (1971) *Anatomy of Educational Innovation*. New York: Wiley.
SMITH, L., PRUNTY, J., DWYER, D. and KLEINE, P. (1987) *The Fate of an Innovative School: The History and Present Status of the Kensington School*. New York: Falmer Press.
SMYTH, W. (1989) A critical pedagogy of classroom practice: Education reform at the chalkface. *Delta* 41, 53–64.
SPOLSKY, B. (1989) Māori bilingual education and language revitalisation. *Journal of Multilingual and Multicultural Development* 10, 89–106.
STENHOUSE, L. (1975) *An Introduction to Curriculum Research and Development*. London: Heinemann.
STONE, M. (1981) *The Education of the Black Child in Britain: The Myth of Multiracial Education*. Glasgow: Fontana.
SWARTZ, E. (1992) Multicultural education: From a compensatory to a scholarly foundation. In C. GRANT (ed.) *Research and Multicultural Education: From the Margins to the Mainstream*. Bristol, PA: Falmer Press, pp. 32–43.
TAIT, E. (1988) A critical appraisal of multicultural education. In W. HIRSH and R. SCOTT (eds) *Getting it Right: Aspects of Ethnicity and Equity in New Zealand Education*. Auckland: Office of the Race Relations Conciliator, pp. 74–78.
THARP, R. (1989) Psychocultural variables and constants: Effects on teaching and learning in schools. *American Psychologist* 44, 349–359.
THOMPSON, J. (1984) *Studies in the Theory of Ideology*. Cambridge: Polity Press.
TROYNA, B. (ed.) (1987) *Racial Inequality in Education*. London: Tavistock.

— (1993) *Racism and Education*. Buckingham: Open University Press.

TROYNA, B. and WILLIAMS, J. (1986) *Racism, Education and the State: The Racialization of Educational Policy*. Beckenham: Croom Helm.

VERMA, G. (ed.) (1989) *Education for All: A Landmark in Pluralism*. London: Falmer Press.

VILLERS, H., CHURCHWARD, F., FITZGERALD, M., GLASSON, J. and MCFAYDEN, T. (eds) (1984) *Richmond Road School: 1884–1984*. Auckland: Richmond Road School Publications.

WALKER, R. (1990) *Ka Whawhai tonu matou: Struggle Without End*. Auckland: Penguin.

WALLER, W. (1965) *The Sociology of Teaching*. New York: John Wiley.

WEBER, M. (1978) Classes, status groups and parties. In W. RUNCIMAN (ed.) *Selections in Translation*. Cambridge: Cambridge University Press, pp. 43–56.

WEXLER, P. (1983) Movement, class and education. In L. BARTON and S. WALKER (eds) *Race, Class and Education*. London: Croom Helm.

WILCOX, K. (1982) Ethnography as a methodology and its application to the study of schooling. In G. SPINDLER (ed.) *Doing the Ethnography of Schooling: Educational Anthropology in Action*. New York: Holt Rinehart and Wilson.

WILLIAMS, R. (1976) Base and superstructure in marxist cultural theory. In R. DALE, G. ESLAND and M. MACDONALD (eds) *Schooling and Capitalism: A Sociological Reader*. London: Routledge and Kegan Paul, pp. 202–210.

— (1981) *Culture*. Glasgow: Fontana.

WILLIS, P. (1977) *Learning to Labour*. Farnborough: Saxon House.

— (1983) Cultural production and theories of reproduction. In L. BARTON and S. WALKER (eds) *Race, Class and Education*. London: Croom Helm.

WRIGHT MILLS, C. (1959) *The Sociological Imagination*. Oxford: Oxford University Press.

YEOMANS, A. (1983) Collaborative group work in primary and secondary schools: Britain and USA. *Durham and Newcastle Research Review* 10, 95–105.

YOUNG, M. (ed.) (1971) *Knowledge and Control: New Directions for the Sociology of Education*. London: Collier-Macmillan.

YOUNG, R. (1992) *Critical Theory and Classroom Talk*. Clevedon. Multilingual Matters.

Index

220 MAKING MULTICULTURAL EDUCATION WORK

— student participation 107, 111-112
— teacher participation 81, 99, 107-108, 166, 197
participatory relationships 95, 182, 185
Passeron, J. 2, 24, 31
paternalism 127, 128
Pearce, E. 13
pedagogy 6, 8, 19, 22-23, 24, 29, 40, 42, 43-46, 62, 72, 77, 98-126, 135, 150, 170, 171, 175, 178, 184, 191, 193, 196-198
— critical pedagogy 6, 19, 45, 175, 178, 198
— culturally appropriate pedagogy 42, 77, 167, 192
— invisible pedagogies 22, 23
— pedagogical change 98, 125-126
— visible pedagogies 22, 23
peer tutoring 43, 76, 104-108, 125, 169, 170
— tuakana-teina 104-108, 119, 122, 152, 167, 169, 182
Peters, R. 68, 98, 100, 110, 167, 169, 180
philosophy 6, 12, 14, 26, 38, 43, 45, 51, 60, 62, 65, 67-69, 79, 85, 94, 106, 152, 153, 155, 157, 162, 169, 175, 180, 197
pluralism
— cultural pluralism 4-6, 8, 34-35, 37, 38, 40, 41, 42, 46-47, 61, 71, 94, 138, 160, 161, 162, 180, 187, 189, 191, 193, 198
— democratic pluralism 187
— language pluralism 161
— structural pluralism 5, 41, 42, 61, 160, 193
policies 4, 5, 8, 26, 33, 34, 44, 62, 71, 82, 114, 155, 159-162, 174, 181
— antiracist policy 99, 160
— educational policy 82, 83, 176
— language policy 26, 71, 126, 161, 169-170
— language policy across the curriculum (LPAC) 126, 161, 169-170
— minority education policy 4-7, 8, 32-46, 62
— monitoring policy 149
— open door policy 58
— policy on assessment 171-172
— policy on community involvement 165-166
— policy on curriculum delivery 166-168

— policy on equity 172-174
— policy on policy development 161-162
— policy on school organisation 163-164
— school policies 8, 53, 55, 58, 62, 82, 155, 156, 159, 160-174, 197
policy development 53, 71, 82, 99, 126, 160, 161-162
political-economy model 16
Ponsonby 56, 58, 59
Porter, J. 33, 46
positivism 54
power (see also access to power) vii, viii, 15-17, 19, 21, 22, 24-25, 26, 29, 38, 39, 41, 42, 52, 61, 71, 76, 82-84, 92, 94, 101, 106, 108, 112, 113, 131, 135, 138, 140, 167, 179-180, 182, 183, 188, 190-192, 194-196
power relations 6, 8, 15, 21, 22, 25, 32, 38, 41, 44, 45, 50, 54, 61, 77, 82, 85, 86, 127, 180, 186, 194-196
— dominant power relations 127, 180, 194
— unequal power relations 44, 61, 82, 195, 196
practice of theory 197
praxis 6, 45, 197
pre-schools 57, 60, 73, 86, 89-90, 96, 114, 154, 164-166, 174
principal
— as catalyst 99, 151
— as facilitator 67, 72, 79, 82, 100, 103, 129, 151, 181-182
— as innovator 60, 64, 68, 71, 150-151, 175, 185
— as visionary 64, 99, 150-151
process
— process approach 110, 162, 163, 169, 180, 182
— process model 110, 111, 114, 129, 135, 136, 157, 171, 172
— process of change 46, 53, 71, 73, 78, 92, 153, 188
provisional authority 88, 98-110, 112, 158, 160, 167, 180, 181
punishment 91-92

qualitative research 51, 53, 54-55
quantitative research 54-55

racial groups 190